Behind the Throne
The Siblings of Monarchs Past & Present

Roger Povey

To Tom
Hope you enjoy this
book.

Copyright © Roger Povey 2014 All rights reserved. No part of this publication may be reproduced, stored in a retrieval system, or transmitted in any means, electronic, mechanical, photocopying, recording or otherwise, without the prior written permission of the publisher.

ISBN 978-1-499-60440-5

Introduction

Much of history is full of the exploits of Kings and Queens, but what of their siblings and near relations? While a dull-as-dishwater monarch lorded it on the throne, their brother, sister, uncle, aunt, cousin, nephew, niece or even an in-law, may well have been creating all sorts of turmoil or wonders.

In this volume, I have included rulers of British and other current kingdoms that are still extant and those of former kingdoms.

Perhaps this book will go someway to throw a spotlight of some of the more interesting of them.

I have not included too much about the reigning monarch or delved into the countries history as that is well documented.

I have also not included siblings that died early or succeeded their siblings and have mentioned issue only of those that did go on to add a little to history or knock a pompous crown sideways, or off entirely. Enjoy.

Roger Povey
Hastings May 2014

Royal Siblings of Current Monarchies

Kings & Queens of England & Scotland

House of Wessex

The first King in English History to be acknowledged as King of England or King of the English was **King Athelstan of Wessex (893-939)**. He managed, through either diplomacy or strength of arms, to bring nearly all the ruling monarchs of England under his suzerainty. He reigned from 924 until 939. He did not marry and left no issue. He was the son of King Edward the Elder of Wessex and his first wife Ecgwynn. He was a grandson of King Alfred the Great. William of Malmesbury, a twelfth century historian, mentions that Athelstan would never tire of telling his court that as a child he had been embraced by his grandfather and made a knight at an unusual early age. Alfred had given him a scarlet cloak, a diamond studded belt and a Saxon sword with a golden scabbard. His throne was passed to his brother Edmund.

His sister, **Eadgifu (902-955)** was the daughter of Edward the Elder and his second wife Elfflaed. In 919, she married King Charles II of France and was the mother of King Louis IV of France. Three years after her marriage, Charles was deposed and held prisoner by Herbert III, Count of Vermandois. Eadgifu decided to take her son Louis and return to England and the protection of her brother's court. They stayed in England until 936 when 16-year-old Louis was recalled to France to be crowned King. Eadgifu retired to a convent with her job seemingly done. She had protected her son until his accession to the throne. In 951, she left the convent to marry Herbert 'the Old' Count of Meaux probably for diplomatic reasons, as he was the son of her husband's deposer, Herbert III, Count of Vermandois. His sister, **Eadgyth (910-946)** was the daughter of Edward the Elder and his second wife Elfflaed. Not much is known of her early life until she married

Otto I, Holy Roman Emperor for diplomatic reasons, sisters and daughters of ruling monarchs have very rarely married for love.. She had two children, Luitgarde who married Conrad, Duke of Lorraine and her son Luidorf, who became Duke of Swabia after his marriage to Ida, daughter of Herman I, Duke of Swabia. They had two children, Otto, later Duke of Bavaria and Swabia and Mathilde who became the Abbess of a monastery in Essen. Luidorf also founded the city of Stuttgart in southern Germany.

His sister, **Eadhild(911-938)** was the daughter of Edward the Elder and his second wife Elfflaed. She married Hugh the Great, Duke of the Franks and Count of Paris. She died without any issue. His sister, **Aelfgifu** married Boleslaus II, Duke of Bohemia. The dates of her birth and death are not known. Their son, Boleslaus III succeeded him.

He was called *'the worst of all men who have ever sat on the Bohemian throne'*. He was ousted and exiled by two of his brothers. He returned with armed support from Poland and regained the throne. Soon he was back to his old ways ordering the massacre of many of his Bohemian nobles in revenge. It is said he slashed his son-in-law to death with his own sword. He was lured to a castle in Krakow Poland on the pretext of a visit and was trapped, blinded and imprisoned. It is believed he died in captivity there in 1037.

His brother, **Edmund of Wessex (922-946)** became Edmund I, King of the English upon the death of his brother Athelstan and reigned from 939 until 946. He was murdered by Leofa, an exiled thief, while attending a St Augustine's Day Mass in Pucklechurch. When Edmund's courtiers rushed in, they took hold of the assassin and tore him limb from limb. Edmund married Elfgifu of Shaftesbury. They had two sons who would reign as Kings of England, **Eadwig** and **Edgar**. (see below) His brother, **Eadred of Wessex (923-955)** He succeeded his brother Edmund I. He reigned as King of England from 946 until his death and spent his reign consolidating the northern part of his kingdom. He did not marry or have issue. Eadred was succeeded by his nephew, **King Eadwig of Wessex (941-959)**, he reigned as King of England from 955 until his death. He did not marry or have issue and was succeeded by Edmund I's second son **King Edgar of Wessex (943-975)**. He reigned as King of England from 959 until his death. He was known as 'The Peaceful'. He married Aethelflaed, then Wulthryth and finally Aelfthryth, and had issue. Two of his children also reigned as Kings of England. His first child to reign was **Edward, known as 'The Martyr'(962-978)**. He was assassinated in the courtyard of Corfe Castle probably on the order of his step-mother, Aelfthryth. He was unmarried and without issue. Edgar's second son, **Ethelred, known as the 'Unready'(968-1016)** ascended the throne. He lost the throne in 1014 to **King Sweyn Forkbeard** who reigned until his death when Ethelred claimed back the throne. His soubriquet did not mean he was unprepared, it means he had bad counsel or never took advice. Ethelred means 'noble counsel' and Unraed mean 'bad counsel'. Ethelred married Aelfgifu of York and she gave birth to **Edmund II Ironside King of England (989-1016)**. He reigned in 1016 for only 6 months, it is mentioned by Henry of Huntingdon, another twelfth century historian, states that Edmund was murdered by a son of an ealdorman, Edric and probably with the contrivance of his father, by secreting himself in a toilet pit. When Edmund came to relieve himself he was stabbed in the bowels. The assassin left the knife embedded and made his escape. Edric then went to court, saluted Canute, and told him what had happened and that he, Canute, was now undisputed King of England. Canute, fuming at the death of a king, told Edric he would exalt him and place him higher than all the other nobles for this deed and he was as good as his word. He had Edric beheaded and his head was place on a tall pole that did place him high above all the others. Canute was not stupid, if his knights and barons would kill one king, what would stop them from killing another, he let them know the consequences of the action from the start. After Aelfgifu's death, Ethelred married Emma of Normandy. She was the daughter of Richard I 'The Fearless' Duke of Normandy. Her marriage to Ethelred produced **King Edward the Confessor**.

Emma also gave birth to Godgifu**(1003-1047)**. She married in the first place, Drogo of Mantos, Count of the Vexin. She and Drogo had issue. Their son, Ralph the Timid was made Earl of Hereford, he died in 1057 Emma married secondly, Eustace II, Count of Boulogne but had no issue. His sister, **Saint Edburga of Winchester (d.960).** She became a nun and was possibly Abbess of Nunnaminster in Winchester where her tomb is located. After her canonization in 972, some of her remains were transferred to Penrose Abbey in Worcestershire in 972. She died unmarried and without issue.

House of Denmark

Canute (Cnut) I, King of England, Denmark, Norway and parts of Sweden (990-1035) He was the son of Sweyn Forkbeard, who was a disputed King of England for less than a year and his Polish Princess wife. He invaded England and won most of the country but made a Treaty with King Edmund Ironsides that he would leave Wessex in peace but after Edmund's murder, he took over the whole kingdom. He married twice, his first wife was Aelfgifu of Northampton, daughter of Aelfhelm, an ealdorman of Southern Northumbria. They had three children, Sweyn, a future King of Norway and Harald Harefoot, a future King of England. His second wife was Emma of Normandy, daughter of Robert I, 'the Fearless, Duke of Normandy, ex-wife of Ethelred the Unready and mother of Edward the Confessor and great aunt of William the Conqueror. They had two children including Harthacnut a future King of Denmark and England.

Ask anyone to tell you something about King Canute and they will invariably mention how he tried to stop the waves and for years it was supposed he tried to do it to show how powerful he was. He did command the waves to go back, but this was to show to his sycophantic courtiers who insisted he was the most powerful man, that he was as powerless as they were, compared to God.

His brother, **Harald II King of Denmark(d.1018)**, his date of birth is not known. He acted as regent in Denmark for his father King Sweyn I when he was campaigning in England. His brother Canute succeeded him. His sister, **Estrid Svensdatter (990-1057)**. She is believed to have married twice with her first husband probably being Vsevolod, Prince of Vladimir-Volynsk son the Russian Grand Duke Vladimir I, the Great. Her second husband was Ulf Jarl and they had one son Sweyn who would become King of Denmark.

Harold Harefoot, King of England (1015-1040) was the son of King Canute and Aelfgifu of Northampton. He is believed to have married Elfgifu and had a son Elfwine who became a monk on the continent. Harold died from what was said to be *'unknown causes'* and was buried at Westminster Abbey but was exhumed, beheaded and thrown into the fens near the Thames when Harthacnut took the throne. His remains were eventually found and reburied in the aptly named St Clement Danes Church. His brother, **Sweyn Knutsson, King of Norway (1016-1035)** He reigned as King of Norway from 1030 until his death. There is no record of any marriage or issue. His sister, **Gunhilda of Denmark (1020-1038)** She was the daughter of King Canute and his second wife Emma of Normandy. She married Henry III, King of Germany, son and heir to Conrad, Holy Roman Emperor. They had one daughter Beatrice, who would become an Abbess. His brother, **Harthacnut, King of Denmark, King of England (1018-1042)**. He reigned as King of England from 1040 until 1042. He desecrated his half-brother's grave at the instigation of Elfric, archbishop of York (see above) and exacted an intolerable tax on the people of England to pay off his mercenaries. He never married or had issue and died at a wedding while drinking the health of the bride, probably of a stroke. He was succeeded by his half-brother Edward the Confessor.

House of Wessex

Edward, known as 'the Confessor', King of England (1004-1066). He reigned as King from 1042 until his death. He was the son of Ethelred the Unready and Emma of Normandy and was elected to the throne following the death of Harthacnut with the support of the mighty Godwine family headed by the formidable Godwine, Earl of Wessex[1]. Godwine suggested that Edward should marry his daughter Edith because of the help he received and this was agreed as he was under some obligation for his throne to the Godwine's. The Godwine's began to prove dangerous so he banished them. It seems that Edward a rather pious individual had taken a vow of celibacy and the marriage was never consummated and this above all created the strife and concern that culminated on the field of battle just outside Hastings in 1066.

Many historians cite that this celibacy vow meant that Edward had already intended for Duke William of Normandy to be his heir and in William's mind, Harold Godwine swearing fealty to him in Normandy confirmed this. In the end Harold was elected, which was the way to make kings at that time and ruled for less than a year. His brothers and sisters are mentioned above.

King Harold II of England (1020-1066) was the last of the Anglo-Saxon Kings. He was the son of Earl Godwine of Wessex and Gytha Thorkelsdottir, a sister-in-law if King Canute. He was married by common law, which although not recognized

---

[1] Godwine died suddenly at a royal banquet in Winchester on 15 April 1053 after he choked on a piece of bread after declaring himself ever loyal to king Edward. Some say it was divine intervention.

by the Church made the children legitimate, to Edith of Mercia and Edith Swan-Neck (the Fair). He had eight children of which information about five of them is known, the others may have died at birth or when young or disappeared abroad after Hastings. His daughter Gytha of Wessex married Vladimir Monomakh, Grand Duke of Kievan Rus and had five children. Isabella of France, the Queen of King Edward II of England, is directly descended from King Harold through Gytha.

King William freed his son Ulf of Wessex in 1087 when he (William) was on his deathbed. Ulf later joined forces with Robert Curthose, eldest son of the Conqueror, in his attempts to secure the English crown. He was knighted by Curthose and then disappears from history. Two of his sons, Godwine of Wessex and Edmund of Wessex, invaded England in 1068 and again in 1069 with the help of the King of Leinster, High King of Ireland. This failed, they invaded Cornwall in 1082, but this was another failure. Their later years were spent in piracy harassing English ships until they died in obscurity in Ireland. His daughter, Gunhild of Wessex after inheriting her mother's estates became a rich woman. She was abducted and married by Alan Rufus (the Red) Earl of Richmond. After his death, she married his nephew, Alan, earl of Cornwall and earl of Richmond. There was no issue from either marriage. His sister, **Edith of Wessex (1025-1075)** married King Edward the Confessor and is mentioned above. His brother **Sweyn Earl of Mercia (1020-1052)** He was exiled from the kingdom and died upon returning from a bare-foot pilgrimage to the Holy Land.

His brother, **Tostig, Earl of Northumbria (1024-1066)** was married Judith, the daughter of Count Baldwin IV of Flanders who was the aunt of Matilda of Flanders who married William Duke of Normandy and eventually King of England. They had two children, Ketil Tostisson and Skuli Tostisson. They married and had issue but details are not extant. Tostig because of all his machinations was exiled and stripped of his earldom. He sided with King Harald III Hardrada and died along side him at the Battle of Stamford Bridge in 1066. His brother, **Gyrth, Earl of East Anglia (1032-1066)** died beside his brother Harold at the Battle of Hastings. It is asserted by Orderic Vitalis and William of Malmesbury that Gyrth tried to dissuade Harold from meeting William in battle and to let him lead the army so as not to break the oath Harold made to William. His brother **Leowine, Earl of Kent** also died alongside Harold at the Battle of Hastings. This was the end of the reign of the Anglos Saxons

Kingdom of England - House of Normandy

The first Norman King of England was **King William I, Duke of Normandy (1027-1087)**. He was the illegitimate son of Robert I, Duke of Normandy and Herleva, the daughter of a local Falaise artisan. He became Duke of Normandy following the death of his father who was on a pilgrimage to Jerusalem. William's early years were fraught with anarchy and rebellion. His protectors had a job on their hands looking after him. He soon reached maturity as was able to put down a lot himself. He married Matilda of Flanders, the daughter of Baldwin V, Count of Flanders. Despite Matilda's many refusals and William's rather rough way of courting her, she eventually agreed. It not only provided a powerful ally, but it also seemed to be a love-match. He considered himself heir to the childless King Edward the Confessor of England on three main bases.

Firstly, he was Edward's cousin, secondly, he stated that Edward had promised the kingdom to him when he visited England and thirdly, he had received the promise from the most powerful Earl in the country, Harold Godwinson, Earl of Wessex. Harold had sworn on a casket of sacred relics to help him to the throne. It was these three reasons, together with the, in William's opinion, usurpation of the crown by Harold, that William decided to invade England. The story of the Battle of Hastings is well documented and I will leave William the

Conqueror here and we will look at his siblings.

His sister, **Adelaide (1030-1089)**. She was the illegitimate daughter of Robert, Duke of Normandy. She married three times, her first husband was Enquerrand II, Count of Ponthieu and they had a daughter, Adelaide, Countess of Aumale who married William de Breteuil. He was the son of William FitzOsbern, 1st Earl of Hereford. There was no issue from this marriage. Adelaide married, secondly, Lambert II Count of Lens he was the son of Eustace I, Count of Boulogne. They had a daughter, Judith of Lens who married Waltheof, Earl of Huntingdon. This marriage produced three children. Two are known about. Maud married King David I of Scotland and her sister, Adelaide married Raoul III of Conches. Adelaide of Normandy finally married Odo of Champagne and their son was Stephen, Count of Aumale who married Hawise de Mortimer and had four children. His brother, **Odo, Bishop of Bayeux, Earl of Kent (1032-1097)** was the son of William's mother Herleva and Herluin de Conteville, the man she married after William's birth. Odo became a close and trusted companion of William and helped him amass ship for the Conquest. He fought at the Battle of Hastings, although an ordained Christian Cleric and Bishop of Bayeux. He is depicted on the Bayeux Tapestry (which incidentally isn't a tapestry it's an embroidery) with club or mace in hand, as it did not seem right for a bishop to wield a sword. It seemed to be wrong to draw blood with a sword but alright to crush a skull with a mace.

After the battle, Odo, who had been created Earl of Kent, was essentially second man in the kingdom and acted as Regent during William's absences on the Continent. He is also accredited with ordering the production of the Bayeux Tapestry. As they say, power corrupts and in 1076, he was tried for defrauding the Crown and the Diocese of Canterbury and was forced to hand over most of his vast wealth. In 1082, he was disgraced and imprisoned for organizing an expedition to Italy with, it was believed, the intention of making himself Pope. He decided to atone for his sins, or make more money, by joining the First Crusade and died outside Palermo in 1097. His brother, **Robert, Count de Mortain (1031-1090)** was the younger son of Herleva and Herluin de Conteville and the younger brother of Odo of Bayeau. He was created Count of Mortain in 1049. Robert was a great supporter of William and provided 120 ships for the Conquest and after the battle was given vast estates. In 1088, he sided with his brother Odo of Bayeux in a revolt against William II, which failed. He was pardoned and spent the rest of his life in Normandy, dying there in 1090.

Robert married Matilda, daughter of Roger de Montgomery, 1st Earl of Shrewsbury. They had issue, a son, William, Count of Mortain, an extremely arrogant and angry man. He demanded all of his fathers titles and lands from his cousin King Henry I of England. Granted some not all, he argued intently and sided with Henry's older brother Robert Curthose who was striving for the English crown as the oldest son of William I. He was caught with Robert Curthose at the Battle of Tinchbrai as they attacked Henry's possessions in Normandy. He was stripped of all remaining honours and became a Cluniac monk at Bermondsey Abbey.

King William II Rufus (1058-1100) ascended the throne in 1087 upon the death of his father King William 'the Conqueror'. For reasons known only to the Conqueror, he appointed William Rufus to the throne of England and gave the Duchy of Normandy to his elder son, Robert Curthose. Most of William Rufus' reign was reacting to the constant attacks made by his brother Robert in his attempt to usurp the English throne. William Rufus did not marry or have any issue, legal or not. He spent most of his time with his male favourites, which gave rise to suggestions of homosexuality on his part. Known for his love of hunting, he spent the 2nd of August 1100 in the New Forest.

In the late afternoon sun, a bolt or arrow was loosed in his direction, shot, it is believed, by one of his entourage Walter Tyrel, and struck him. He expired on the spot and the courtiers with him fled to their own estates including his younger brother Henry who raced to Winchester to secure the treasury and then on to London where he was crowned King a few days later.

His older brother, **Robert Curthose, Duke of Normandy (1053-1134)** was the eldest son of William the Conqueror but was overlooked for the crown of England and had to settle with being the Duke of Normandy. This rankled with him and rebelled against King William Rufus and afterwards his younger brother King Henry I. When William Rufus died without an heir, he saw his chance to take the crown as eldest son of the Conqueror, unfortunately Henry had already secured the crown of England. He ended up with very little as he had mortgaged the Dukedom of Normandy to William Rufus to pay for his crusading. His lifetime was spent feuding with his father and brothers and ended his life imprisoned in Cardiff Castle. He died there in 1134. He married Sybillia of Conservano and had issue. His son William Clito was born in 1102 and died in 1128. His soubriquet, Clito meant 'Prince' or 'Man of Royal Blood'. He married Sybylla of Anjou. There was no issue from this marriage. He later married Joanna of Montferrat and again, this marriage was childless. His brother, **King Henry I of England (1068-1135)** was born possibly in Selby Yorkshire. He married Matilda of Scotland the daughter of King Malcolm III of Scotland and his wife St Margaret. He had two known legitimate children. Henry's daughter, **Matilda, Empress of the Holy Roman Empire, Queen of the Romans (1102-1167),** married in the first instance, Henry V Holy Roman Emperor and King of Germany, there were no children from this union. Her second husband was Geoffrey V, Count of Anjou. Her son Henry would eventually become King Henry II of England. Matilda had been nominated by her father as heir to the throne following his son's death and called herself Lady of the English. Her arrogance and attitude to the nobility was a block to getting their support. So Stephen of Blois, a grandson of the Conqueror, reigned until his death and then the crown was passed to Henry II. (see below) Henry I's son, William, heir to the throne, was born in 1103. He married Matilda of Anjou but drowned without issue in 'The White Ship' tragedy in 1120. His wife eventually became a nun and later Abbess of Fontrevault.

His sister, **Cecilia of Normandy (1056-1126)** never married and had no issue. She became a nun and eventually Abbess of Holy Trinity. His sister **Constance of Normandy (1058-1190)** married Alan IV, Duke of Brittany. There was no issue from this marriage. His sister, **Adela of Normandy (1065-1137)** married Stephen II Count of Blois. It was her son who became King Stephen I of England.

House of Blois

King Stephen of England (1092-1154) was the son of Count Stephen-Henry of Blois and Adele of Normandy, daughter of William the Conqueror. He married Matilda of Boulogne. She was the daughter of Eustace IV, Count of Boulogne and Mary, daughter of King Malcolm III of Scotland and his wife St Margaret. He had five legitimate and two illegitimate children.

When King Henry I died in 1135, Stephen quickly hurried to England and claimed the throne. He believed he had a better chance of preserving order in the realm rather than leaving it to the haughty and petulant ex-Empress Matilda, Henry's daughter and heir. It was Matilda's indifference to the barons coupled with her utter dislike of London and its citizens, a mutual feeling, that slowly allowed Stephen to sit more securely on the throne. Stephen and Matilda were both prisoners of each other at one time. This period in history was called 'The Anarchy[2]'. It has been said that during this time that *'Christ and his Angels slept'*. It was finally decided that Stephen would rule England until his death and then the crown would go to Matilda's son Henry Plantagenet, who would reign as King Henry II.

His brother, **William, Count of Sully (1085-1150)** was older than Stephen and had a more direct claim, was overlooked as a possible King of England due to mental instability, hence his sobriquet 'William the Simple'. He married Agnes, heiress to the Lordship of Sully-sur-Loire. They had a daughter, Margaret de Sully who was born in 1105 and died in 1145. She married Henry, Count of Eu, Lord of Hastings. Their son, Henry de Sully who died in 1189 became Abbot of Fécamp. His brother **Theobald II, Count of Champagne (1190-1152)**, administered his mother's estates during her lifetime and he gave refuge to Pierre Abelard, lover of Heloise. He married Matilda, daughter of Engelbert, Duke of Carinthia. They had four children, their two sons married daughters of Louis VII and Queen Eleanor of Aquitaine. Henry I of Champagne married Marie of France and eventually became King of Jerusalem after the Second Crusade and Theobald V Count of Blois married Alix of France. His sister, **Lucia-Mahaut of Blois** married Richard d'Avranches, 2nd Earl of Chester. They both drowned with Henry I of England's heir William in the 'White Ship' on 25 November 1120. His sister **Agnes of Blois,** no dates known, married Hugh III of Le Puiset and had issue. Information is scant. His sister **Eleanor of Blois** married Raoul I, Count of Vermandois. They had one son, Hugh II Count of Vermandois. He gave up his titles in 1160, became a monk, and was canonized in 1177. His sister, **Alix of Blois (1100-1145),** married Renaud III of Joigni and had issue. His sister **Adelaide of Blois** married Milo II, Viscount of Troyes. There was no issue from this marriage. His brother

---

[2] Anarchy means - No Government

Henry of Blois was Abbot of Glastonbury Abbey and Bishop of Winchester.

House of Plantagenet

King Henry II of England (1133-1189) was the son of the Empress Matilda, daughter of King Henry I and Geoffrey V, Count of Anjou. He came to the throne as Stephen's heir and reigned from 1154 until 1189. He married the ex-Queen of France, Eleanor of Aquitaine. He had 10 children and two of them, Richard and John reigned as Kings of England. He spent most of his reign battling with his sons who were aided and abetted by their mother. He died in 1189. His brother, **Geoffrey, Count of Nantes (1134-1158)**, was a continual thorn in his brother Henry's side. He attempted to abduct Eleanor of Aquitaine after her divorce from King Louis VII of France with a view to marrying her and taking over the vastly wealthy Duchy of Aquitaine. He then joined forces with King Louis to attack Normandy after Eleanor's marriage to Henry II, which had been a surprise to Louis. Eventually Henry suggested him for the vacant county of Nantes, which he accepted and died there in 1158 unmarried and without issue. His brother, **William X, Count of Poitou (1136-1164)** was a faithful follower of Henry, fighting by his side. Henry gave him vast lands in both England and Normandy. He fell in love with Isabel de Warrene, 4th Countess of Surrey. As she was a cousin of William de Blois, a son of King Stephen, there was a case of possible consanguinity, a closeness of blood ties, forbidding the marriage. This was not always a problem as you could request a dispensation from the Pope.

Unfortunately, the rift between Henry II and Thomas Becket, Archbishop of Canterbury was beginning and Becket refused to support the request and because of that, it was refused. It is said that William died of a broken heart a little later and Henry blamed Becket for his brother's death and probably brought their dispute to a head.

King Richard I the Lionheart (1157-1199). He reigned from 1189 until his death in 1199. He was the son of King Henry II and Eleanor of Aquitaine. He was also Duke of Normandy, Duke of Aquitaine, Duke of Gascony, Lord of Cyprus, Count of Maine and Overlord of Brittany. He married Berengaria of Navarre the daughter of King Sancho VI of Navarre and Sancha of Castile. They married in Cyprus when Richard was on his way to the Holy Land on crusade. There was no issue from this marriage. From an early age, Richard was a soldier and spent a lot of his youth helping put down rebellions against his father. He was King for 10 years but visited his realm rarely and then only to raise revenue for his crusading. He once said that he would sell London if a buyer were available. While Richard was out of the country his brother, Prince John, acted as regent and did his best to undermine the barons and cause trouble for Richard.

Richard was captured on his way back from the Crusade by Leopold V, Duke of Austria and handed over to Henry VI, the Holy Roman Emperor. A ransom of 150,000 marks or 65,000 pounds of silver was demanded for his release. Despite the machinations of his brother Prince John, the money was paid and Richard returned home. He forgave his scheming brother and named him his heir in place of his brother Geoffrey's son Arthur of Brittany who was legally next in line to the throne. Richard spent the latter years of his life trying to reclaim parts of Normandy lost during England's dispute with the King of France. While he was besieging a castle in Chalus in Normandy in 1199, he was hit by a crossbow bolt fired by the young son of the custodian of the castle. The wound turned gangrenous and on his deathbed, he called for the boy who had fired the bolt and forgave and pardoned him. After his death, the boy was killed and flayed by Richard's courtiers in revenge.

His brother, **Henry, the Young King (1155-1183)** was

heir to his father Henry II following the death of his older brother, William IX, Count of Poitiers who died aged three years. He was crowned King Henry in 1170 whilst King Henry II was still alive as this was an old French custom. He was known as 'The Young King'. He married Margaret of France, the daughter of King Louis VII of France. They had just one child, William of England who died in infancy. Henry died of dysentery in the summer of 1183 while campaigning against his father and brother Richard in the Limousin. His brother, **Geoffrey II, Duke of Brittany (1158-1186)** married Constance of Brittany, daughter and heiress of Conan, Duke of Brittany. This was a diplomatic marriage instigated by King Henry that would stop Henry attacking Brittany. Geoffrey and Constance had two surviving children, their first child was Eleanor, Fair Maid of Brittany, she was born in 1184. As a potential threat to King John's throne, Eleanor was imprisoned in various locations following her father's death.

After John's death, his son Henry III kept her imprisoned for the same reason. She was still a Royal Princess and treated as such. In her later years, she became a nun dying at Bristol in 1241. Their second child was Arthur of Brittany who was born in 1187. Arthur was the son and heir of Geoffrey, Duke of Brittany and would be heir to King Richard the Lionheart if the king had no issue.

When Richard was on his deathbed, he decided that the twelve year old Arthur was too young for the English crown and nominated John as his successor. John did not want Arthur around to become a centre for opposition to his reign had him imprisoned in the Chateau de Falaise under the guardianship of Huburt de Burgh. John had ordered De Burgh to mutilate and blind Arthur, but he refused. John then had Arthur transferred to Rouen under the guardianship of William De Braose. He was never really seen again and is believed to have been murdered by either William De Braose or John himself in a drunken fit of anger and thrown into the Seine. His sister,

Matilda of England, Duchess of Saxony (1156-1189) was the eldest daughter of King Henry II and Queen Eleanor of Aquitaine. She married Henry the Lion, Duke of Saxony & Bavaria and had four surviving children. She married, in the first instance, Geoffrey III, Count of Perche and then secondly, Enguerrand III, Lord of Coucy. There was no issue from these marriages. Her eldest son was Henry V, Count Palatinate of the Rhine. He married twice, his first wife was Agnes of Hohenstaufen and had issue. His second wife was Agnes of Landsberg. There was no issue from this marriage.

After the death of his cousin Arthur I, Duke of Brittany in April 1203, Henry effectively became the heir of his uncle John Lackland to the English throne, this ended though when John's son (the future Henry III) was born in October 1207. His son, Otto IV, Holy Roman Emperor & Duke of Swabia was born in 1175 and died in 1218. He married twice, his first wife was Beatrice, daughter of King Philip of the Germans and his second wife was Marie of Brabant. There was no issue from these marriages.

Their youngest son was William, Duke of Landsberg he was born in 1184 and died in 1213. He married Helena, daughter of King Valdemar I of Denmark. Their only child was Otto who went on to inherit all his fathers titles and property and eventually became the first Duke of Brunswick-Lüneburg.

His sister, **Eleanor of England, Queen of Castile (1162-1214)** married King Alfonso VIII of Castile. There were ten surviving children including Berengaria who became Queen of Leon and Castile, Urraca, Queen of Portugal, Blanche, Queen of France, Eleanor, Queen of Aragon and Henry who succeeded his father as King of Castile. His sister, **Joan of England (1165-1199)** married twice, in the first instance William II King of Sicily. There is was no surviving issue of this marriage. Her second husband was Raymond VI, Count of Toulouse. They had one son Raymond VII, Count of Toulouse He married twice but there was no issue from either marriages. His brother, **John,** later **King John of England (1166-1216)** had a life and reign that is well documented and I do not intend to go into it here. He married twice, his first wife was Isabel, Countess of Gloucester. There was no issue from this marriage. His second wife was Isabella of Angoulême. For details of issue from this marriage, see Henry III below.

King Henry III (1207-1272) ascended the throne in 1216 aged 9 years old. His reign was a collection of wars and rebellions He married Eleanor of Provence and had several children including Edward I, King of England. He died in 1272. He reigned for 56 years a phenomenal achievement in those times.

His brother, **Richard, 1st Earl of Cornwall, Count of Poitou and King of the Romans (1209-1272).** married three times, his first wife was Isabel Marshal of Pembroke, granddaughter of William Marshal, 1st Earl of Pembroke perhaps the greatest knight in the history of this country. They had four children. Three of these children died as infants and the one surviving child, Henry of Cornwall, born in 1235 was murdered by his cousins Guy and Simon De Montfort in 1271 in revenge for the beheading of their father at the Battle of Evesham. His second wife was Sanchia of Provence, they had two sons, the eldest died in infancy and the second Edmund, succeeded his father to his title. His sister, **Joan of England Queen Consort of Scots (1210-1238)** married Alexander II King of Scots. There were no issue from this marriage. His sister **Isabella, Holy Roman Empress (1214-1241)** married Frederick II, Holy Roman Emperor, King of Germany and Sicily. They had a daughter. His sister, **Eleanor, Countess of Pembroke (1215-1275)** married twice, firstly William Marshal, 2nd Earl of Pembroke. There was no issue in this marriage. Secondly, she married Simon De Montfort, 6th Earl of Leicester. They had three children who died unmarried and without issue.

King Edward I (1239-1307). He was the first son of King Henry

III of England and his wife Eleanor of Provence. Edward was called Longshanks due to him being just over 6ft. tall. He acquired his other soubriquet, Hammer of the Scots, following his battles with the Scots. His reign was spent fighting the Welsh as well as the Scots. He married twice. His first wife was Eleanor of Castile, they had 16 children of which six survived including Edward the future King Edward II of England. Eleanor died in 1290 and the grief-stricken Edward, for this marriage was a love match, had a cross of stone erected at each place the cortège rested for the night to be used as a cenotaph for prayer for the Queen's soul.

Twelve crosses were erected from Lincoln to London, the most famous one being Charing Cross. Only three of the crosses now exist and not in their entirety, at Geddington and Hardingstone and at Waltham Cross. His second marriage was to Margaret of France, the daughter of King Philip III of France and Maria of Brabant. This marriage produced three children. The reign of King Edward I is well documented so I will leave it there to concentrate on his siblings.

His sister, **Margaret of England (1240-1275)** married when she was 11 years old, the 10-year-old Alexander III, King of Scots. Following their maturity, they had three children. Margaret, Princess of Scotland born in 1261 and died 1283 married Eirik II King of Norway. They were the parents of Margaret, Maid of Norway who was heir to the Scottish throne following Alexander III's death. She died on her way from Norway to France and this led to King Edward I's involvement in the choosing of the next King of Scotland. They had two other children who died young. His sister, **Beatrice of England (1242-1275)** married John II, Duke of Brittany and they had six children. His brother, **Edmund Crouchback 1st Earl of Leicester & Lancaster** was born in 1245 and died in 1296. Edmund's soubriquet, Crouchback or Crossback had nothing to do with a physical deformity, It meant that as he had attended the Ninth Crusade, he was entitled to wear a crusaders cross on the back of his garments. He married twice. His first wife was Lady Aveline de Forz. She died four years after the marriage aged 15. The marriage had no issue. His second wife was Blanche of Artois and they had three children.

King Edward II (1284-1327). He was the son of King Edward I and his first wife Eleanor of Castile. He married Isabella of France, the She-Wolf, daughter of King Philip IV of France and Joan I of Navarre. They had four children including the future King Edward III of England. His reign is also well documented and only a brief mention is warranted here. He continually promoted his favourites, Piers Gaveston and the Despensers so much so that he was believed to be homosexual. He was deposed by his wife Queen Isabella and her lover Roger Mortimer and was forced to abdicate in favour of his 14 year old son and was eventually murdered in Berkeley Castle by having his entrails burnt out.

Isabella and Mortimer acted as Regents for the young Edward III until his maturity. Mortimer annoyed Edward with his arrogance and attitude towards him. He acted more like King than Regent. Edward reached maturity and then took action, he had Mortimer arrested and executed and his mother imprisoned for the rest of her life, albeit in abject luxury.

His sister, **Eleanor, Princess of England (1269-1298)** married Henry III, Count of Bar. They had three children. His sister, **Joan of Acre, Princess of England (1272-1307** was called Joan of Acre because she was born in Acre in the Holy Land while her parents were on Crusade. She married twice, firstly, Gilbert De Clare, Earl of Hereford and Gloucester. They had four children. Her second marriage was to Sir Ralph de Monthermer. This marriage also produced four children. His sister, **Margaret, Princess of England (1275-1333)** married John II, Duke of Brabant. They had one son, John who succeeded to his father's dukedom. His sister, **Mary, Princess of England (1279-1332)** did not marry and became a Benedictine nun at

Amesbury Wiltshire. His sister, **Elizabeth, Princess of England (1282-1316)** married twice, her first husband was, John I, Count of Holland. There was no issue from this marriage. Her second marriage was to Humphrey de Bohun, Earl of Hereford. There were seven children of this marriage. His brother, **Thomas of Brotherton, 1st Earl of Norfolk (1300-1338)** married twice, his first wife was Alice Hales. They had three children. His second wife was Mary Brewes. There was no issue in this marriage. His brother, **Edmund of Woodstock, Earl of Kent (1301-1330)** married Margaret Wake, 3rd Baroness Wake of Liddell. There were four children from this marriage including, Joan of Kent, known as the Fair Maid of Kent. She went on to marry Prince Edward, the Black Prince the son of King Edward III.

King Edward III (1312-1377) was King of England from 1327-1377. Edward was the founder of the Order of The Knights of the Garter. He married Philippa of Hainault, daughter of William III, Count of Holland and Hainault and Joan of Valois daughter of King Philip III of France. He fought the French at the Battle of Crecy being successful mainly due to his use of longbow men. After the battle, Edward laid siege to Calais. King Philip VI of France was unable to free or support them so they asked for surrender. Edward agreed, providing they turn over six of their most prominent citizens to be executed as an example. His heavily pregnant wife is believed to have begged him to be lenient and he relented.

He had ten children but none of his children ascended to the throne. His son, Edward, the Black Prince, Prince of Wales died before his father and it was the Prince of Wales' son Richard who became king after Edward III and reigned as King Richard II of England.

His brother, **John of Eltham, Earl of Cornwall (1316-1336)** never married and had no issue. His sister, **Eleanor of Woodstock (1318-1355)** married Reginald II, the Black, Duke of Guelders. They had two sons. Reginald tired of Eleanor and banished her from court stating that she had leprosy. She returned to court at a later date and stripped to show she was not a leper. This forced her husband to take her back. His sister, **Joan of the Tower 1321-1362)** was called Joan of the Tower because she was born in the Tower of London. She married David II, King of Scotland. There was no issue from this marriage.

Edward, the Black Prince, Prince of Wales (1330-1376) died, probably of a dropsy type illness or cancer. He was the son of King Edward III and Queen Philippa of Hainault. He never succeeded to the throne as he died before his father. Again, his life is well documented, and we will leave it there. His son Richard succeeded to throne following his father's death.

King Richard II (1367-1399) He reigned from 1377 until his death in, probably of starvation, in 1399. He was one of the first kings to believe that the throne was a God-given honour. He was also the first monarch to insist he be called Highness and Majesty. King Richard was forced to abdicate by Henry Bolingbroke, son of John of Gaunt, a grandson of King Edward III. Henry usurped the throne as King Henry IV. His sister, **Isabella, Princess of England (1332-1379)** married Enguerrand VII of Coucy, 1st Earl of Bedford. They had two daughters, Marie de Coucy, later Countess of Soissons who was born in 1366 and died 1404. She married Henry of Bar, a nephew of King Charles V of France and had two sons. Their daughter Philippa de Coucy was born in 1367 and died in 1411. She married Robert de Vere, Earl of Oxford, this marriage was childless. His brother, **Lionel of Antwerp, 1st Duke of Clarence** was born in 1338 and died in 1368. He married twice, his first wife was Elizabeth de Burgh, 4th Countess of Ulster. They had a daughter, Philippa Countess of Ulster. Lionel of Antwerp's second wife was Violante Visconti. There was no issue from this marriage. His brother, **John of Gaunt (1340-**

1399) was the third surviving son of King Edward III and Philippa of Hainault. He was called John of Gaunt because he was born in Ghent and this was voiced as Gaunt in England. He married three times, his first wife was Blanche of Lancaster the daughter of Henry of Grosmont, Duke of Lancaster, England's richest and most powerful peer. Henry inherited the Lancaster titles following the death of Blanche's father and old sister. They had issue including the future King Henry IV of England. (see below).

His second wife was the Infanta[3] Constance of Castile, They had two children, John who died in infancy and Catherine of Lancaster who was born in 1373 and died in 1418. She married King Henry III of Castile. His third wife was Katherine Swynford. She had formerly been his mistress. They had issue that were legitimized by this marriage.

His brother, **Edmund of Langley, 1st Duke of York (1341-1402)** married twice, his first wife was Infanta Isabella of Castile the daughter of King Peter of Castile and Maria de Padilla. She was also the sister of his brother John of Gaunt's second wife. They had two sons, Edward of Norwich 2nd Duke of York born in 1373 and died in 1415 during the Battle of Agincourt.

Their second son was Richard of Conisburgh, 3rd Earl of Cambridge. He was born in 1385 and executed in 1415 for his part in a plot against King Henry V. Edmund's second wife was Joan Holland. There was no issue from this marriage.

His sister, **Mary of Waltham (1344-1362)** married John V, Duke of Brittany. She died young and there was no issue from this marriage. His sister, **Margaret of Windsor (1346-1361)** married John Hastings, 2nd Earl of Pembroke. She died after two years of marriage aged just 15. His brother, **Thomas of Woodstock, 1st Duke of Gloucester (1355-1397)**. It is believed that he was murdered by a group of men under the leadership

---

[3]Infanta translates to Princess and Infante to Prince in Spanish and Portuguese kingdoms

of Thomas Mowbray, Duke of Norfolk. It is also believed that it was on the orders of King Richard II because of Thomas' part in the Lords Appellant rebellion to oust him from the throne. He married Eleanor de Bohun. They had issue.

House of Lancaster

King Henry IV (1367-1413) reigned from 1399 until 1413. He was the son of John of Gaunt and Blanche of Lancaster and a grandson of King Edward III.

He was called Henry Bolingbroke after his birth in Bolingbroke Castle in Lincolnshire. Following an altercation with Thomas de Mowbray, the Duke of Norfolk he was banished from the realm for ten years. His father, John of Gaunt died in 1399 and when Bolingbroke tried to inherit the Lancaster land and titles, Richard refused this and took them for himself. The land and titles of the Duke of Lancaster are still vested in the English crown to this day. He extended Bolingbroke's banishment to life and went off to campaign in Ireland. Bolingbroke took this opportunity to return to England and rally support for his attempt on the throne. He caught and imprisoned Richard, as mentioned above, and assumed the crown.

His sister, **Philippa of Lancaster (1360-1415)** married King John of Portugal. There was issue from this marriage including Henry the Navigator. His sister, **Elizabeth of Lancaster (1364-1426)** married three times, her first husband was John Hastings, 3rd Earl of Pembroke. There was no issue from this marriage. Her second husband was John Holland, 1st Duke of Exeter. There was issue from this marriage. Her third husband was Sir John Cornwall, Baron Fanhope & Milbroke. There was issue from this marriage. All the Beaufort issue were the children of John of Gaunt and Katherine Swynford.

His **sister Catherine of Lancaster (1372-1418)** was the daughter of John of Gaunt and Constance of Castile She married King Henry III of Castile and had issue including Marie who was born in 1401 and died in 1458. Marie married King Alfonso of Aragon and was never in good health and probably suffered from Epilepsy. Because of gynecological problems the marriage was not consummated until she was sixteen, there was no issue and Marie spent the rest of her life in a loveless marriage

His brother, **John Beaufort 1st Earl of Somerset 1373-1410)** married Margaret Holland. They had six children including John who was born in 1403 and died in 1444 who became the first Duke of Somerset. This John married Margaret Beauchamp and they had one daughter, Lady Margaret Beaufort who would become the mother of the future King Henry VII of England. Another daughter, Joan, who was born in 1404 and died in 1445 married King James I of Scotland and was the mother of King James II of Scotland.

His brother, **Henry Beaufort, Bishop of Winchester (1375-1447)** was the unusual combination of a Cardinal-Bishop and a member of the Royal House of Plantagenet.

His brother, **Thomas Beaufort, Duke of Exeter (1377-1427)** married Margaret Neville there was no issue from this marriage. His sister, **Joan Beaumont (1379-1440)** married Robert Ferrers, Baron Boteher of Wen. They had issue.

King Henry V (1386-1422) reigned from 1413 until 1422. He was the son of King Henry IV and his 16 year old wife Mary de Bohun. He was the grandson of John of Gaunt and the great grandson of King Edward III. He was the second English monarch from the House of Lancaster. He was supposed to have had a *'riotous'* youth but this was probably just Shakespearean poetic license as for the most of his early years was spent fighting Owain Glyndwr during the Welsh revolt and then, as his father's health deteriorated, he took a wider share of politics. After succeeding to the crown he began to assert his right to the throne of France, His most famous conflict was the Battle of Agincourt where Henry's longbow men won the day.

He married the daughter of King Charles VI of France, Catherine de Valois, and received the promise that the throne of France was his following Charles death. They had one son, the future King Henry VI of England. Henry died of dysentery while campaigning in France. His widow, a little later, married Owen Tudor and were the great grandparents of Henry Tudor, the future King Henry VII.

His brother, **Thomas of Lancaster, Duke of Clarence (1388-1421)** married Lady Margaret Holland. There was no issue from this marriage. His brother, **John of Lancaster, Duke of Bedford (1389-1435)** married twice, his first wife was Anne of Burgundy. She was the daughter of John 'the Fearless', Duke of Burgundy. It was a happy but childless marriage. Anne died of the plague in Paris in 1432. His second wife was Jacquetta of Luxembourg. There was no issue from this marriage. His brother, **Humphrey of Lancaster, Duke of Gloucester (1390-1447)** married in 1422, his first wife Jacqueline, Countess of Hainault & Holland. There were no surviving children from this marriage, it was annulled in 1428, and Jacqueline died, disinherited in 1436. His second wife whom he married in 1441 was Eleanor Cobham. They had two children. Eleanor consulted astrologers to try to divine the future with a view to enhance the prospects of her husband. Two of her astrologers predicting that King Henry VI would suffer a life-threatening illness which worried the King, his advisors also consulted astrologers and stated, of course, that they could predict no such thing. Eleanor was accused of trying to predict the King's death and was eventually exiled and imprisoned for life for practicing witchcraft against the King. His sister, **Blanche of England (1392-1409)** married Louis III Elector Palatine. They had one son, Ruprecht who did in early adulthood. His **sister Philippa of England** was born in 1394 and died in 1430. She married Eric of Pomerania, King of Denmark, Norway &

Sweden. There was no issue from this marriage.

King Henry VI (1421-1471) was the only child of King Henry V and his wife Catherine of Valois. He died or was possibly murdered in 1471 in the Tower of London after he was overthrown. He ascended the throne aged 9 months and the country was ruled by a succession of royal uncles until he came of age. He came to maturity in 1437 and took the reins of government. He allowed himself to be ruled by a few noble favourites and by his heir the Duke of York. Henry married Margaret of Anjou in an aim to ease the problems with France, which according to the Treaty of Troyes that his father made with his grandfather, Charles VI the Mad of France, Henry now ruled. The story of Charles' actual son, the Dauphin is well known and the assistance given by Joan of Arc to gain him the throne of France.

Henry began a slow descent into insanity, it seems he inherited a little of his grandfather Charles insanity. Charles believed that he was made of glass and would shatter if anyone should touch him. Soon factions were calling on Edward, Duke of York to come back from Ireland and take the throne. Henry aided and abetted by The Earl of Warwick, the King Maker as he was called, fought against this.

Edward succeeded and ascended the throne in 1461 only to lose it in 1470 to Henry VI's forces. Edward finally succeeded to the throne, Henry was imprisoned in the Tower of London where he died. Edward, Duke of York became until his death, King Edward IV of England.

King Edward IV (1442-1483) was the first king of the House of York He reigned from 1461 until 1470 and then from 1471 until 1483. He married Elizabeth Woodville and two of their children were destined to become *'The Princes in the Tower'*.

His sister, **Anne of York (1439-1476)** was the daughter of Richard Plantagenet, 3rd Duke of York and his wife the Lady

Cecily Neville. She married twice, her first husband was Henry Holland, 3rd Duke of Exeter. There was a daughter from this marriage, the Lady Anne Holland who married Thomas Grey, 1st Marquess of Dorset. Her second husband was Thomas St Leger, there was also a daughter of this marriage, Anne St Leger who married George Manners, 11th Baron de Ros.

His brother, **Edmund, Earl of Rutland (1443-1460)** was killed at the age of 17 at the Battle of Wakefield in Yorkshire during the War of the Roses. He died unmarried and without issue.

His sister, **Elizabeth of York (1444-1503)** married John de la Pole 2nd Duke of Suffolk. There was issue from this marriage including Edmund who as 3rd Duke of Suffolk was beheaded by King Henry VIII as a Yorkist pretender.

His sister, **Margaret of York (1446-1503)** married Charles the Bold, Duke of Burgundy. There was no issue from this marriage.

His brother, **George Plantagenet, Duke of Clarence (1449-1478)** married Isabella Neville the eldest daughter of Richard Neville, 16th Earl of Warwick. They had two children, their daughter Margaret married Sir Richard Pole, through her father she was the 8th Countess of Shrewsbury. She was to live through many problems caused by her brothers and son. It reached a point where King Henry VIII had her imprisoned in the Tower of London. As Henry was unable to wreak revenge on the others of the Pole family as they had fled abroad, he decided to execute Margaret. She was taken to the scaffold protesting her innocence and caused a rumpus by evading the clutches of the inexperience executioner until she was caught and held down and suffered the ten separate blows of the axe it took to dispatch her. She was later considered a Catholic Martyr and beatified by Pope Leo XIII.

George himself was executed on the orders of his brother King Edward IV on the grounds of Treason. He was, by his own choice, drowned in a butt of Malmsey Wine, or maybe in his bath as baths during that time were cut down wine butts.

His brother, **King Richard III (1452-1485)** married Anne Neville. They had one son, Edward of Middleham, Prince of Wales. He died in 1484 aged ten years old. Again, Richard's life is well documented but a brief précis is probably needed. Richard, following the death of his older brother Edward IV, acted as regent for Edward's son, Edward V and his brother Richard, Duke of York. Richard then had Edward IV's children declared bastards and took the throne himself as King Richard III. He died at the Battle of Bosworth Field whilst fighting Henry Tudor soon to be King Henry VII. A skeleton was exhumed in a Leicester car park that has been identified as Richard's. There is now discussion as were to rest his bones.

House of Tudor

King Henry VII (1491-1547) reigned from 1485 until 1509. He ascended the throne after routing King Richard III at the Battle of Bosworth Field. He was the son of Edmund Tudor, 1st Earl of Richmond and the Lady Margaret Beaufort. Edmund was the son of Owen Tudor and Catherine de Valois, widow of King Henry V of England. Margaret was the daughter of John Beaufort, 1st Duke of Somerset and Margaret Beauchamp of Bledsoe. Her father was a great, grandson of King Edward III. He had no siblings.

King Henry VIII (1497-1547). Henry's and his life and reign are greatly documented as are his three children Edward, son of Jane Seymour, Mary, daughter of Catherine of Aragon and Elizabeth, daughter of Anne Boleyn. So let us look at his siblings.
    His brother, **Arthur Tudor, Prince of Wales (1486-1502)** To strengthen his claim to the throne, as Henry VII, like King Henry IV, was a usurper of the throne, had genealogists trace

his line. They traced Henry's ancestors back to the early Welsh and English Kings including 'King' Arthur, well they would, wouldn't they. He decided to name his first son the name Arthur after his 'illustrious forefather'. Arthur married the Infanta Catherine of Aragon. They married in 1501 and moved to Ludlow Castle on the Welsh Border. Arthur died suddenly on 2 April 1502 of was is believed to be consumption. Catherine went on to marry King Henry VIII. His sister, **Margaret Tudor (1489-1541)** married three times, her first husband was King James IV of Scotland. Their children were James who would become James V of Scotland and prepared the ground for the eventual Stuart dynasty that ruled England. Her next husband was Archibald Douglas, 6th Earl of Angus. From this marriage Margaret became the grandmother of Henry Stuart, Lord Darnley who married Mary, Queen of Scots. Her third husband was Henry Stewart, 1st Baron Methven. There was no surviving issue from this marriage.

His sister, **Mary Tudor (1496-1533)** married twice, her first husband was Louis XII, King of France. They were no issue from this marriage, as Louis died three months into the marriage. Her second husband was Charles Brandon, 1st Duke of Suffolk. Although Henry was aware of the feelings between Brandon and his sister, he sent Brandon to France to bring back Mary after the death of Louis XII. Henry had specifically got a promise from Brandon that he would not propose to Mary during this trip. As always, love conquerors all and Brandon and Mary married secretly in France in 1515. This was technically treason as Brandon had married a Royal Princess without the King's permission. Calls were made for Brandon's imprisonment and execution but because of Henry's love for Mary and affection for Brandon, he permitted the marriage after they paid a hefty fine. They had issue. Their daughter, Lady Frances Brandon married Henry Grey, 3rd Marquess of Dorset and became the mother of Lady Jane Grey, the tragic Nine Day Queen of England. She was also a great granddaughter of King Henry VII, which authorized her claim to the throne.

King Edward VI (1537-1553) died unmarried and without issue. He was persuaded on his deathbed to ignore his father's instructions as to the line of accession, which would have been Mary then Elizabeth Queen if Edward had no heir. He was asked to make his heir Lady Jane Grey, as she was a Protestant and Mary an avid Catholic.

His sister, **Mary, Princess of England (1516-1558)** ascended the throne as Queen Mary I of England, after defeating Queen Jane Grey and reigned from 1553-1558. She married King Philip II of Spain with a hope to bring Catholicism back to England as the state religion. She had no issue apart from what may have been a phantom pregnancy or illness, historians are divided. His brother, **Henry Fitzroy Duke of Richmond (1519-1536)** was the illegitimate son of King Henry VIII and his teenage mistress, Elizabeth Blount. He married Mary Howard, daughter of Thomas, 3rd Duke of Norfolk. There was no issue. Henry Fitzroy, due the lack of male heirs was seriously considered by King Henry as a possible heir to the throne. He died in 1536 and a son Edward was born a year later. His sister, **Elizabeth, Princess of England (1533-1603)** ascended the throne as Queen Elizabeth I of England in 1558 and reigned until 1603. The fact that she never married was a bone of contention in the country. She reigned during an enlightening time including the Spanish Armada and Shakespeare. She was succeeded by her cousin, King James VI of Scotland.

Queen Jane Grey (1537-1554) reigned as Queen for only nine days. She was the daughter of Henry Grey, 1st Duke of Suffolk and lady Frances Brandon. She was the great granddaughter of King Henry VII of England, a great niece of King Henry VIII and a first cousin once removed of King Edward VI so she was no interloper. When Edward was on his deathbed, his advisors, not wanting the Catholic Mary to succeeded to the throne, suggested to Edward, who was an avid Protestant, to revoke his father's Third Succession Act which named his sisters as heir and make his cousin Lady Jane Grey as his direct heir as she was also a Protestant.

The main protagonists for this were her father and John Dudley, Duke of Northumberland who had instigated the marriage of Jane to his younger son Lord Guildford Dudley which would give him great power in England if Jane were Queen and there was also the possibility of a Dudley King of England. Unfortunately, aristocratic and public support was going over to Mary and eventually she was swept to the throne and Jane was imprisoned. Her father, husband and father-in-law were eventually executed as was she on 12 February 1554

Her sister, **Lady Catherine Grey (1540-1568)** had the same royal connections as her sister Jane and younger sister Mary. After Jane's execution she was a potential successor to her cousin Queen Elizabeth I if she did not produce heirs. She married twice, first the Henry Herbert, this was before the Queen Jane debacle, he acceded to the title Earl of Pembroke. When the trouble with Jane Grey began, Herbert wanted to distance himself from it as he new heads would roll.

He arranged for his marriage to Catherine to me annulled on the basis that it was not consummated, Catherine was 14 years old at the time.

She married again in 1560 much to the anger of Queen Elizabeth as she had not asked permission. She married the Queen's cousin, Edward Seymour and thoughts of usurpation ran through Elizabeth's mind. The Queen had Catherine imprisoned and Edward was sent abroad and upon his return imprisoned him with Catherine. They had two sons while incarcerated, Edward Seymour who would become an ancestor of Queen Elizabeth the Queen Mother and Thomas who had no issue. Following the birth of their second child, Queen Elizabeth had them permanently separated and Catherine died of consummation aged just 27.

Her sister, **Lady Mary Grey (1545-1578)** married Thomas Keyes, a serjeant porter and was found out by the Queen and they were separated. She died during a plaque epidemic and never did see her husband again.

House of Stuart

King James I & IV of Scotland (1566-1625) reigned as King of England from 1603 until 1625. He was the son of Mary, Queen of Scots and her second husband Henry Stewart, Lord Darnley.

Both Mary and Darnley were great, grandchildren of King Henry VII. James inherited a kingdom bankrupt from Irish and Spanish wars and Catholic intolerance. This culminated in 1605 with the Gunpowder Plot. He had no siblings. His son Charles became King

King Charles I of England (1600-1649) He reigned from 1625 until his execution in 1649. His reign is also well documented. His son became **King Charles II.**

His brother, **Henry Frederick, Prince of Wales** died of Typhoid Fever aged 18 in 1612. His younger brother Charles became King after James. His sister **Elizabeth Stuart, Princess of England (1596-1662)** married Frederick V Elector Palatine and they had thirteen children. When her husband accepted the throne of Bohemia, she became Queen of Bohemia. Her husband's reign being rather short, she acquired the soubriquet 'The Winter Queen'. Her son, Prince Rupert, fought along side King Charles during the English Civil War. Her daughter, Sophia of Hanover married Ernest Augustus, Elector of Brunswick-Lüneburg and their son George became King George I of England.

King Charles II (1630-1685) was the son of King Charles I and his wife Henrietta Marie of France. He reigned from 1660 until

1685. He was brought back after the death of Oliver Cromwell and the ineffectual rule of Cromwell's son Richard. His accession was called the Reformation. He married Catherine of Braganza but there was no children from this marriage. He was succeeded to the throne by his brother James, who reigned as King James II

His sister, **Mary, Princess Royal (1631-1660)** married William II, Prince of Orange. Their son, William II of Orange, later became King William III of England. His brother, **Henry, Duke of Gloucester (1640-1660)** did not marry and died of smallpox aged 20. His sister, **Henrietta, Princess of England (1644-1670)** Philippe of France, Duke of Orléans. There were four children of this marriage. Their daughter Marie married King Charles II of Spain, and their daughter Anne married Victor Amadeus II, Duke of Savoy, the future King of Sardinia. Henrietta was the ancestor of King Louis XVI who was beheaded with his wife Marie Antoinette during the French Revolution.

King James II of England & VII of Scotland (1633-1701) reigned from 1685 until the Glorious revolution in 1688. He married Anne Hyde. They had issue, Princess Mary who reigned jointly with her husband **King William III of England**. Princess Anne who married Prince George of Denmark and reigned as **Queen Anne of England**. As Anne had no surviving issue, despite many pregnancies, the line of succession passed to the offspring of Sophia of the Rhineland Palatinate, Duchess of Brunswick-Lüneburg, and a granddaughter of King James I of England.

James' second marriage was to Mary of Modena. They had issue from this marriage. Their son James became the 'Old Pretender' after James II was disposed during the 'Glorious Revolution' that brought his daughter and her husband to the English Throne as William and Mary. James, the Old Pretender was the father of Charles, the Young Pretender also known as

'Bonnie Prince Charlie'.

Kingdom of Great Britain - House of Hanover

King George I (1660-1727) reigned as King of England from 1714 until 1727. He was the son of Ernest Augustus, Elector of Hanover and his with Sophia, Countess of Simmerin. Sophia was a granddaughter of King James I, which made her issue legitimate Protestant heirs as it had been decreed that no Catholics could rule England. He married Sophia Dorothea of Celle and they had two children including the future King George II of England.

George, before ascending the English throne, had his wife imprisoned for having an affair with Philip, Count von Konigsmarck. Although George was very blatant with his mistresses, he took a dim view of Sophia doing the same. Sophia was imprisoned in Arlhen House in her native Celle for the rest of her life and never actually became a 'de facto' Queen of England. Von Konigsmarck, it is believed, was murdered on George's orders.

His brother, **Friedrich Augustus (1661-1690)** died at the Battle of St Georgen without marrying or having any issue. His brother, **Maximilian Wilhelm (1666-1726)** had a fine military career achieving the rank of Marshal. He commanded the Hanoverian troops in the Spanish War of Succession and was in command of the cavalry under Prince Eugene of Savoy during the Battle of Blenheim. He died unmarried and without issue. His sister, **Sophia Charlotte of Hanover (1668-1705)** married Frederick I King of Prussia. They had one son, Frederick William who succeeded his father as King of Prussia. His brother, **Karl Philipp of Hanover (1669-1690)** died at the Battle of Pristina unmarried and with no issue. His brother, **Christian Heinrich of Hanover (1974-1702)** and died at the Battle of Munderkingen when he drowned in the Danube. His brother, **Ernest Augustus (1674-1728)** served with Leopold I, the Holy Roman Emperor during the War of the Spanish Succession. He later became Prince-Bishop of Osnabruck. He died unmarried and without issue.

King George II (1683-1760) reigned as King of England from 1727 until 1760. He was the son of King George I, King of England and his imprisoned wife, Sophia Dorothea of Celle.

When he was Prince of Wales, there existed between the King and him a state of what seemed to be utter hatred. A symptom of Georgian monarchy that prevailed. I suppose that when one is waiting for the other to die before he can succeed, animosity is the least of the feelings. As King, George II was the last British monarch to lead his troops to war as he did at the Battle of Dettingen in 1743. He also had to endure a Jacobite uprising lead by the 'Young Pretender' Bonnie Price Charlie. This was finally ended at the Battle of Culloden in 1745 and is mainly remembered for the brutality of George's second son, William, Duke of Cumberland. His atrocious acts after the battle gave him the well-deserved soubriquet of 'Butcher' Cumberland.

George II married Caroline of Ansbach they had eight children including Frederick, Prince of Wales, the father of the future King George III. When Caroline was on her deathbed, she begged her husband to remarry. George thinking I am sure to make her feel a little better told her that he wouldn't remarry but just have mistresses. I really wish I could have seen her face at that moment. His sister, **Sophia Dorothea of Hanover (1687-1757)** married Frederick William I King of Prussia. They had ten children.

Frederick, Prince of Wales (1707-1751) died before he could succeed to the throne, his son George reigned as King George III. He married Princess Augusta of Saxe-Gotha. She was the daughter of Frederick II, Duke of Saxe-Gotha-Altenburg and Magdalena Augusta of Anhalt-Zerbst. They had nine children including George William Frederick, the future King George III of England. There was the usual animosity between father and son. Frederick is believed to have died from a burst abscess in his lung.

His sister, **Princess Anne of Great Britain, Princess Royal (1709-1759)** married William IV, Prince of Orange. There were three children of this marriage.

His sister, **Princess Amelia of Great Britain (1711-1786)** never married and spent the majority of her time with charitable organizations. It has been said that she was the mother of composer Samuel Arnold after she had an affair with a commoner, Thomas Arnold. This has never been proven. His sister, **Princess Caroline of Great Britain (1713-1757)** never married and died childless. His brother, **Prince William, Duke of Cumberland (1721-1765)** known as 'Butcher' Cumberland following the Battle of Culloden during the Jacobite Uprising of 1745. He killed soldiers and non-combatants alike. He died unmarried and childless.

His sister, **Princess Mary of Great Britain (1723-1772)** married Frederick II, Landgrave of Hesse-Kassel. There was issue from this marriage.

His sister, **Princess Louisa of Great Britain (1724-1751)** married Frederick V, King of Denmark & Norway. The couple had four children. Louisa died following complications due to a miscarriage.

King George III of Great Britain & King of Hanover from 1814(1738-1820) reigned as King of England from 1760 until his death. It was one of the longest reigns of a British Monarch. He was the son of Frederick, Prince of Wales and the Princess Augusta. He married Charlotte of Mecklenburg-Strelitz and they had fifteen children. Two of his sons, George and William would become Kings of England. His madness and loss of the American Colonies is well known. Let us look at his siblings.

His sister, **Princess Augusta of Wales (1737-1813)** married Charles William Ferdinand, Duke of Brunswick. They had three children. Her daughter Caroline would become the consort of King George IV of England. His brother, **Prince Edward, Duke of York (1739-1767)** was a close companion to his brother George and was his brother's heir until the birth of George III's first son. He died unmarried and without children. His sister, **Princess Elizabeth of Wales (1741-1759)** did not marry or have issue. She died of inflammation of the bowels aged 18 years. His brother, **Prince William, Duke of Gloucester (1743-1805)** married Maria Walpole, Countess Waldegrave. They had three children, Princess Sophia of Gloucester was born in 1773 and died in 1844. She never married or had children, Princess Caroline of Gloucester was born in 1774 and died in 1775 aged 8 months. Their son, Prince William Frederick, Duke of Gloucester born in 1776 and died in 1834. He married Princess Mary of Great Britain, his cousin, they had no issue. His brother, **Prince Henry, Duke of Cumberland (1745-1790)** married Anne Luttrell. She had been married before and was a commoner as was her first husband. Henry married her and although George III disliked the idea of Henry marrying a previously married commoner, he permitted the marriage but then he brought in the Royal Marriages Act 1772 which forbade descendants of George II, male or female marrying without the Monarch's consent. Henry and Anne had no issue. His sister, **Princess Louisa (1749-1768)**. In delicate health all her life, she died unmarried and without issue aged 19 years. His brother, **Prince Frederick (1750-1765)** died unmarried and without issue. His sister, **Princess Caroline Matilda (1751-1775)** married Christian VII, King of Denmark & Norway. They had two children.

King George IV (1742-1830) was Regent from 1811 until 1820 and reigned as King of England from 1820 until 1830. He was the son of King George III of England and his wife Charlotte of Mecklenburg-Strelitz. He married, purely to have his debts paid of, Caroline of Brunswick. Caroline was the daughter of

George III's elder sister. Both George and Caroline detested the sight of each other and remained together only to consummate the married which also produced an heir to the throne Charlotte. Charlotte married Prince Leopold of Saxe-Saalfeld but died giving birth to a stillborn son. She was 21 years old.

His brother, **Frederick, Duke of York (1763-1827).** For most of his career he was a soldier. He was not the greatest of Generals, promoted purely because of his Royal rank. He is believed to have been the Grand Old Duke of York mentioned in the Nursery Rhyme. He married Princess Frederica of Prussia the daughter of King Frederick William II of Prussia and his first wife and cousin, Elisabeth Christine of Brunswick-Lüneburg.

Frederick and Frederica were actually double first cousins, which meant that they both shared both sets of grandparents. Look it up, it's very interesting. Perhaps this double degree of consanguinity was the reason that there was no issue from this marriage. His brother, **William, Duke of Clarence (1765-1837)** spent most of his early life in the Royal Navy eventually becoming Lord High Admiral. He spent his early life living with a Mrs Jordan, an actress and having 10 illegitimate children with her. When King George IV lost his daughter and heir, it fell upon the surviving brothers to forsake their mistresses and marry to produce legal heirs to the throne.

When George died in 1830, he was the next in line and succeeded to the throne as **King William IV**. He married Princess Adelaide of Saxe-Meiningen. They were no issue from this marriage. His sister, **Princess Charlotte, Princess Royal (1766-1828)** married Frederick, King of Württemberg. There was no issue from this marriage. His brother, **Edward, Duke of Kent (1767-1820)** was a soldier all his life he was Commander-in-Chief of British Forces in North America and after achieving the rank of Field Marshal was appointed Governor of Gibraltar. He married Princess Victoria of Saxe-Coburg-Saalfeld. They had one child, a daughter Princess Alexandrina Victoria of

Kent. She was born in 1819 and died in 1901. She ascended the throne as **Queen Victoria** in 1837. His sister, **Princess Augusta Sophia (1768-1840)** spent most of her life with her parents and died unmarried and without issue aged 71. There is no obvious reason as to why she never married, as she was believed to be the 'prettiest of the princesses'. It seems that King George III was loathe to lose his daughters to marriage. He wanted them around him. His sister, **Princess Elizabeth (1770-1840)** married Frederick, Landgrave of Hesse-Homburg. There was no issue from this marriage. His brother, **Prince Ernest Augustus (1771-1851)** was a soldier for most of his life until 1837 when Victoria ascended the throne. Because of Salic Law, which prevented a female ruling in Hanover, Ernest became King of Hanover ending 120 years of British & Hanoverian joint history. He married Princess Frederica of Mecklenburg-Strelitz. They had one child, a son, George, who succeeded his father as King George V of Hanover.

His brother, **Prince Augustus Frederick, Duke of Sussex (1773-1843)** married Lady Augusta Murray, the daughter of the 4th Earl of Dunmore. This marriage was eventually annulled because it contravened the Royal Marriages Act of 1772. There were two children from this marriage and were put solely in the charge of their mother who received a £4000 a year pension. The children were, a son, Augustus Frederick d'Este born in 1794 and died in 1848. He is the earliest reported person for whom a definite diagnosis of Multiple Sclerosis was made. He died unmarried and without issue, and a daughter, Augusta Emma d'Este she was born in 1801 and died in 1866. She married Thomas Wilde, Baron Truro. There was no issue from this marriage. Prince Augustus married again without permission and in contravention of the Royal Marriages Act 1772, glutton for punishment wasn't he.

This time he married Lady Cecilia Buggin the daughter of the 2nd Earl of Arran. She was never titled or recognized as Her Royal Highness Duchess of Sussex. Queen Victoria created her Duchess of Inverness in her own right in 1840. There was no issue from this marriage.

His brother, **Prince Adolphus, Duke of Cambridge (1774-1850)** married Princess Augusta of Hesse-Cassel. They had three children. Their son George, Duke of Cambridge was born in 1819 and died in 1904. He married Sarah Louise Fairbrother and had issue because the marriage contravened the Royal Marriage Act it was not recognized in Law. They had two daughters, Princess Augusta of Cambridge was born in 1822 and died in 1916. She married Fredrich Wilhelm, Grand Duke of Mecklenburg and had issue and Princess Mary Adelaide of Cambridge she was born in 1833 and died in 1897. She married Francis, Duke of Teck. Their daughter Princess Mary of Teck born in 1867 and died in 1953 was first betrothed to Prince Albert Victor, first son of Edward, Prince of Wales and his wife, Princess Alexandra. Albert Victor died and then Mary was betrothed to and married Prince George of England who would in turn become King George V of Great Britain and grandparents of our present Queen Elizabeth II. His sister, **Princess Mary (1776-1857)** married her cousin Prince William, Duke of Gloucester. There was no issue from this marriage. His sister, **Princess Sophia(1777-1848)** died unmarried and without issue aged 70. His sister, **Princess Amelia (1783-1810)** died unmarried and without issue after an illness aged 27.

House of Saxe-Coburg-Gotha

King Edward VII (1841-1910) reigned as King from 1901 until 1910. He was the son of Queen Victoria and her husband Prince Albert, the Prince Consort. He married Princess Alexandra of Denmark. They had six children including the future King George V of England.

His sister, **Princess Victoria, Princess Royal (1840-1901)** married Frederick III, German Emperor & King of Prussia. Their son, Wilhelm II German Emperor born in 1859 and died in 1941. He married Princess Auguste Viktoria of Schleswig-Holstein. Wilhelm II led Germany into the First World War. His sister, **Princess Alice (1843-1878)** married Louis IV, Grand Duke of Hesse and by the Rhine. Their daughter, Princess Victoria who was born in 1863 and died in 1950 married Prince Louis of Battenburg. She was the grandmother of Prince Philip Consort to Queen Elizabeth II. Their second daughter, Princess Alix of Hesse who was born in 1872 and died in 1918. She married Tsar Nicholas II of Russia and died with her husband and children during the Russian Revolution. His brother, **Prince Alfred, Duke of Edinburgh (1844-1900)** married Grand Duchess Maria Alexandrovna of Russia. They had five children. His sister, **Princess Helena** was born in 1846 and died in 1920. She married Prince Christian of Schleswig-Holstein-Sonderburg. They had issue. His sister, **Princess Louise (1848-1939)** married John Douglas Campbell 9th Duke of Argyll. They was no issue from this marriage. His brother, **Prince Arthur, Duke of Connaught (1850-1942)** served as Governor General of Canada. He married Princess Louise Margaret of Prussia. There was issue from this marriage. His brother, **Prince Leopold, Duke of Albany (1853-1884)** married Princess Helene of Waldeck & Pyrmont. They had two children, a daughter, Princess Alice, Countess of Athlone and a son Charles Edward Duke of Saxe-Coburg and Gotha. Leopold never saw his son as he was a haemophiliac and had fallen and injured his knee earlier. He died a few days later. He had inherited the disease from his mother, Queen Victoria. His sister, **Princess Beatrice (1857-1944)** married Prince Henry of Battenburg. There was issue from this marriage.

House of Saxe-Coburg-Gotha / House of Windsor

King George V (1865-1936) reigned as King of England from 1910 until 1936. He was the second son of Edward, Prince of Wales, later King Edward VII of England and the Princess

Alexandra of Denmark, later Queen Alexandra. During the First World War, it was thought prudent to discard the dynasty's German titles and the Royal Family became the House of Windsor. He married Princess Mary of Teck who was originally destined to become the wife of George's older brother, Prince Albert Victor. They had six children including the future King Edward VIII and King George VI.

His brother, **Prince Albert Victor, Duke of Clarence (1864-1892).** Prince Eddy, as he was affectionately known, was heir to the throne after his father Edward, Prince of Wales (Edward VII). He spent time in both the Navy and the Army. During his short life he was the subject of many a rumour, It was alleged that he fathered a child on a civil servant's wife while on tour in India, the next, that he attended a Homosexual Brothel at Cleveland Street in London and also that he was 'Jack the Ripper'. These, of course, have been strenuously denied and as for being the 'Ripper' The Prince was not in London during that fateful autumn in 1888. He was due to marry Princess Mary of Teck but fell ill during the influenza pandemic of 1889-92, contracted pneumonia. He died at Sandringham House on 14 January 1892. His affianced Mary of Teck went on to marry Prince Eddy's younger brother who went on to be King George V. His sister, **Princess Louise, Princess Royal (1867-1931)** married Alexander Duff, 1st Duke of Fife They had three children. His sister, **Princess Maud (1869-1938)** married King Haakon VII of Norway. They had a son, Olaf who succeeded his father as King of Norway.

King George VI (1895-1952) reigned as King from 1936 until 1952. He was the second son of King George V and Queen Mary. He married Lady Elizabeth Bowes-Lyon the daughter of Claude Bowes-Lyon, Lord Glamis, later 14th Earl of Strathmore and Cecilia Cavendish-Bentinck. They had two children, Princess Elizabeth (Queen Elizabeth II) and Princess Margaret Rose

His brother, **Edward, Prince of Wales (1894-1972)** succeeded his father King George V as **King Edward VIII**.

As Prince of Wales, despite honest feeling for the British people and their welfare, he had a series of romantic attachments that culminated with an American divorcee, Wallis Simpson. He was determined to marry her and the government was just as determined that he would not. It all came to a head when Edward abdicated the throne in favour of his brother the Duke of York. Edward was created His Royal Highness the Duke of Windsor and left the country never to return until his death. He married Wallis Simpson in France. There was no issue in this marriage. The Duke of York reluctantly ascended the throne as King George VI. Together with his wife, as Queen Elizabeth, he steered Great Britain through the Second World War and proved to be one of the better monarchs of this country.

He died in 1952 when his elder daughter, Princess Elizabeth was in Africa with her husband, the Duke of Edinburgh. She returned to England as **Queen Elizabeth II**. They were four children of this marriage including Charles, the present Prince of Wales. Her sister, Princess Mary Rose married Tony Armstrong Jones, Lord Snowdon and had issue. His sister, **Princess Mary, Princess Royal (1897-1965)** married Henry Lascelles, 6th Earl of Harewood and had issue. His brother, **Prince Henry, Duke of Gloucester (1900-1974)** married Lady Alice Montagu Douglas Scott, the daughter of John Montagu Douglas Scott, 7th Duke of Buccleuch They had two sons, Prince William of Gloucester who was born in 1941 and died in 1972. William, heir to the Dukedom, died in an aeroplane accident. He was unmarried and had no issue. Their second son, Prince Richard of Gloucester, now Duke of Gloucester was born in 1944 and he married Birgitte Van Deurs. They had three children. His brother, **Prince George, Duke of Kent (1902-1942)** was supposed to have had a string of lovers, both male and female and to have taken drugs. He died in 1942 while flying to Iceland on a RAF Short Sunderland Flying Boat on official business as Senior Welfare Officer. He married Princess Marina of Greece and Denmark. They had issue. His brother, **Prince John (1905-1919)** was continually ill and suffered epileptic fits all of his young life. He lived apart from the rest of the Royal Family and had his own household. He died aged 13 years.

Kingdom of Scotland

The title King of the Scots was not really established until perhaps Robert the Bruce, but previous kings were either King of the Picts, of the Scots or of Alba. We begin with King Malcolm II, a descendant of the great Kenneth MacAlpin.

House of Alpin

Malcolm II, King of the Scots (990-1034) reigned as King from 1005 until his death. He had three children probably with concubines as no wives are recorded. His brother, **Boite (992?-1058)** was the father of Gruoch the future wife of Macbeth whom he married to enable him to assume the crown of Scotland.

House of Dunkeld

Duncan I, King of the Scots (1001-1040) reigned as King from 1034 until his death. He was the son of Bethóc, eldest daughter of Malcolm II and Crinán, Lay Abbot of Dunkeld. He married Suthen and they had three children including Malcolm and Duncan future Kings of Scotland. He died in 1040 during a battle in Moray, the domain of Macbeth, and Macbeth took the crown.

His brother, **Maldred of Allerdale, Lord of Cumbria (dates unsure)**. No dates are known or details of marriage or issue.

Macbeth I, Mormaer[4] **of Moray later King of the Scots (1005?-1057)** was the son of Findláech mac Ruidrí Mormaer of Moray, his mother was believed to be a daughter of Malcolm II. His father was killed in 1020 by his own people and Macbeth's quest for the throne was started by revenge. Many of his father's murderers were hunted down and slain including Gille Coemgáin who widow Gruoch was taken as a wife by Macbeth and Macbeth adopted Lulach, her son by Gille as heir. He was killed by Duncan II, son of Malcolm III and was succeeded by his adopted son Lulach. There is no record of brothers or sisters.

Lulach, known as 'the Unfortunate' or 'the Simple-Minded' (1033-1058) was the son of Macbeth's wife Gruoch and a stepson of Macbeth. He was crowned in Scone on August 1057 and was assassinated by his successor Malcolm III in March 1058. He had a son by an unnamed wife or concubine named Máel Snechtai of Moray. He had no siblings.

Malcolm III, known as 'Canmore' ("Big Head"), King of the Scots (1040-1093) was the son of Duncan I and he married twice, his first wife was Ingebjorg Finnsdottir, the daughter of Earl Finn Arnesson and they had one son Duncan, a future King of the Scots. His second wife was Margaret of Wessex, later known as St Margaret of Scotland. She was the daughter of Edward the Exile and English Prince who was the grandson of Edmund Ironside, King of England. They had eight children including three sons who would be future Kings of the Scots and a daughter who would become a Queen Consort of England. His brother, **Mael Muire (pre 1040-1134?)** became Mormaer of Atholl, later changed to Earl of Atholl. He has no record of any marriages or issue.

Donald III, King of the Scots (pre 1040-1099) brother of

---

[4] Mormaer translates as Lordship.

Malcolm III was born before 1040 and died in 1099. He had one daughter, Bethoc by an unnamed wife or concubine.

Duncan II, Kings of the Scots (1060-1094) was the son of Malcolm III and Ingebjorg Finnsdottir. He reigned for just a year being killed in battle. He married Ethelreda, daughter of the Earl of Northumbria and they had one son named William fitzDuncan. His brother Edgar revolted and succeeded him

Edgar I, King of the Scots (1074-1107) he reigned as King from 1097 until his death. Despite the fight to obtain the crown, enlisting the support of King William Rufus of England at one time, his reign was quite uneventful. He remained unmarried and without issue. He died after naming his brother Alexander as his heir.

Alexander I, King of the Scots (1078-1124) was the son of Malcolm III and was King from 1107 until his death. He married Sybilla de Normandie, the illegitimate daughter of King Henry I of England. His only issue was the illegitimate son, Malcolm. His brother David succeeded him.

David I, King of the Scots, Prince of the Cumbrians, Earl of Northampton and Huntingdon (1084-1153) reigned as King from 1124 until his death. He was the youngest son of Malcolm III and Margaret of Wessex. He married Maud, 2nd Countess of Huntingdon and they had one son named Henry. He married Ada de Warrene, daughter of William de Warrene 2nd Earl of Surrey and they had seven children including Malcolm and William future Scottish kings.

Malcolm IV, King of Scotland (1141-1165) reigned from 1153 until his death. He was the eldest son of Henry, Earl of Huntingdon and Ada de Warrene, daughter of William de Warrene, 2nd earl of Surrey and was a grandson of David I. He suffered poor health and died unmarried and without issue aged 24 and was succeeded by his brother William. His sister, **Ada of Huntingdon (1139-1216)** married Floris III, Count of Holland and they had ten children including Floris who would become a bishop of Glasgow. His sister, **Margaret of Huntingdon, later Duchess of Brittany (1145-1201)** married three times, her first husband was Conan IV, Duke of Brittany and Earl of Richmond. They had one daughter Constance, she married Geoffrey Plantagenet, son of King Henry II of England and his wife Eleanor of Aquitaine. They had a son, Arthur who following the death of King Richard I Lionheart of England should have had the crown of England as his father Geoffrey was older than John, but Richard thought it best to put it in the hands of an adult and named his brother John as his heir.

John eventually had Arthur murdered or, as some legends have it, murdered him himself, to remove the threat to his crown. After Geoffrey's death Constance married Humphrey de Bohun, Hereditary Constable of England and had a daughter, Margaret. Her third husband was Sir William Fitzpatrick Hertburn and they had one son.

His brother, **David of Scotland, Earl of Huntingdon (1144-1219)** married Matilda, daughter of Hugh, 3rd Earl of Chester and they had seven children. His sister, **Marjorie of Scotland** whose birth and death dates are not recorded, married Gilla Crist, Earl of Angus and they had one daughter Beatrix, who married Walter Stewart, 3rd High Steward of Scotland. There was also a son Alexander who succeeded his father as High Steward. This marriage began the line that would culminate in the crown of Scotland when King Robert III ascended the throne in 1390. (See below)

William I, 'the Lion', King of the Scots (1143-1214) reigned as King from 1165 until his death aged 71. He was much more of a warrior king than his pious and weak brother Malcolm and spent a lot of his reign trying to gain control of Northumbria to no avail. Had he done so he would have been able to add the sobriquet, 'the Great' to his name. He married Ermengarde de Beaumont and they had four children including a son who would succeed his father as Alexander II of Scotland.

Alexander II, King of the Scots (1198-1249) reigned as King from 1214 until his death. He spent a lot of his reign fighting against his future father-in-law King John of England alongside the English barons who wanted to put Prince Louis of France on the English throne. Alexander even made it south as far as Dover, well you cannot go much further south in England, to pay homage to Louis for the English lands he held.

However, John died and the barons decided that John's infant son would be a better king and more compliant so Alexander returned to Scotland slightly abashed and Louis returned to France slightly richer after being paid off by the barons. He married Joan, the 11 year old daughter of King John but there was no issue from this marriage. His second wife was Marie de Courcy, a descendant of King Louis VI of France and they had one son, Alexander, who would succeed his father.

His sister, **Margaret of Scotland, later Countess of Kent (1193-1259)** married Hubert de Burgh, 1st Earl of Kent who had been involved with the abduction of Arthur of Brittany but had refused to blind him as ordered by King John. They had one child. His sister, **Isabella of Scotland, later Countess of Norfolk (1195-1253).** Together with her sister Margaret, she had been held as hostage by King John at Corfe Castle to quell her father's invasions of England. She was then forced to marry Roger Bigod, 4th Earl of Norfolk, the marriage was childless.

His sister, **Marjorie of Scotland, later countess of Pembroke (1200-1244)** married Gilbert Marshal, 4th Earl of Pembroke, there marriage was childless.

Alexander III, King of the Scots (1241-1286) reigned from 1249 until his death. He ascended the throne upon the death of his father at the age of seven and the country was controlled by the Earl of Menteith and Alan Durward, Justicar of Scotia who spent most of Alexander's minority arguing. He married Margaret of England, the eleven years daughter of King Henry III of England and they had two children including Margaret who would become a Queen Consort of Norway. All of Alexander's children predeceased him and he was in dire need of an heir. He married Yolande de Dreux and whilst leaving Edinburgh on a dark and stormy night, anxious to visit the warm bed of his 22 year-old Queen, he ignored the entreaties of his courtiers and rode off into the night only to stumble off a cliff edge and fall to his death.

Yolande was believed to be pregnant but gave birth to a stillborn child. As there was no heir, Scotland was thrown into a succession crisis as Margaret, the Maid of Norway the seven year old recognized heir had died in Orkney.

After six years of interregnum and the Scottish barons vying for the crown or supporting those who were, agreed that King Edward I of England should choose the next King. He chose John Balliol.

House of Balliol

John de Balliol, King of the Scots (1249-1314) was known as Empty Cloak because of his ineffectiveness was born in 1249 and died in 1314. He reigned as King from 1292 until 1296. He was soon removed, he abdicated, and Robert I, the Bruce, took the throne. He married Isabella de Warenne, daughter of the 6th Earl of Surrey and they had one son Edward who following his father's death attempted to claim the crown but it came to nothing. He had at least seven siblings but not a lot is known about them. What is known is listed below.

His brother, **Sir Hugh de Balliol (?-1271** married Agnes de Valance, daughter of William de Valance, 1st Earl of Pembroke, the marriage was childless. His brother, **Alan de**

Balliol died unmarried and without issue. His brother, **Sir Alexander de Balliol** married Eleanor de Genoure. The marriage was without issue. His sister, **Margaret de Balliol** possibly married Thomas de Moulton. His sister, **Cecily de Balliol** married John de Burgh and had two daughters. His sister, **Ada de Balliol(pre 1266-?)** married William Lindsay of Lamberton and had one daughter. His sister, **Eleanor de Balliol** married John II Comyn, Lord of Badenoch and had at least three children including John 'The Red' Comyn. His sister, **Maud or Matilda de Balliol** married Bryan FitzAlan, Lord FitzAlan and had at least one daughter Ada who married Sir Gilbert Stapleton. Sir Gilbert is notable as one of the knights that assassinated Piers Gaveston, Earl of Cornwall, a favourite of King Edward II of England.

House of Bruce

Robert I the Bruce (de Brus), King of Scots (1274-1329) was the son of Robert de Brus and Marjorie, Countess of Carrick. He claimed descent through his fourth great-grandfather, David I, King of the Scots.

He defeated King Edward II of England at the Battle of Bannockburn and securing Scotland's independence from England as a basis of gaining full diplomatic independence. He married twice, his first wife was Isabella of Mar, the daughter of Domhnall I, Earl of Mar and his wife Ellen of Wales, the daughter of Llywelyn ab Iorwerth, Prince of Wales. They had one child, a daughter named Marjory who married Walter Steward, 6th High Steward of Scotland. Their son would become King Robert II of Scotland.

His second wife was Elizabeth de Burgh, the daughter of Richard Og de Burgh, 2nd Earl of Ulster and his wife Margarite. They had four children of which three survived. A daughter, Margaret who married William de Moravia, 5th Earl of Sutherland. Another daughter, Maud, married Thomas Isaac and their son, David would succeed his father on the throne. His sister, **Isabel de Brus (1272-1358)** married King Eric II of Norway. They had one child, a daughter, Ingeborg. His sister, **Christina de Brus (1278-1356)** married twice, her first husband was Sir Christopher Seton who was hanged as a traitor by King Edward I of England in 1306. There was no issue from this marriage. Her second husband was Sir Andrew Murray. Sir Andrew was a joint victor of the Battle of Bannockburn with William Wallace. There was no issue from this marriage. His brother, **Nigel de Brus (1279-1306)** was a staunch supporter of his brother Robert's claim to the Scottish throne. He was captured after an assault and hanged, drawn and quartered. He died unmarried and without issue. His brother, **Edward de Brus (1280-1318)** was also an avid supporter of his brother. He also pursed his own claim in Ireland and was proclaimed High King of Ireland. He was eventually defeated and killed in a battle by Sir John de Bermingham. It is believed he died unmarried and without issue despite unsubstantiated rumours to the contrary. His sister, **Mary de Brus (1282-1323)** was captured and betrayed to the English during the first war of Scottish Independence by the Earl of Ross. King Edward I of England ordered her to be imprisoned in an iron or wooden cage and exposed to the public at Roxburgh Castle. She was later released in exchange for hostages after the Battle of Bannockburn. She married twice, her first husband was Sir Neil Campbell and they had a son, John Campbell, Earl of Atholl. Her second husband was Alexander Fraser of Touchfraser and Cowie. There was no issue from this marriage. His brother, **Thomas de Brus (1284-1307)** married Helen Erskine. He was captured while helping his brother in the fight for the crown and was beheaded, like his brother Nigel. His brother, **Alexander de Brus (1285-1307)** died with his brother Thomas.

David II King of Scots (1324-1371) was the son of King Robert I the Bruce and Elizabeth de Burgh. He married, when they we both still very young, Princess Joan of the Tower[5], daughter of King Edward II of England in accordance with the Treaty of Northampton. This treaty was signed after the Battle of Bannockburn, by England and Scotland following the First Scottish War of Independence. There was no issue from this marriage. As David was just 5 years old when he ascended the throne, there was a selection of Guardians of Scotland who ruled on his behalf during his minority.

The Scots were defeated at the Battle of Dupplin Moor, a pretender to the throne, Edward Balliol, supported by King Edward III of England, took the throne, and David and Joan were forced to seek exile in France. When David's supporters regained control of Scotland, he returned to his kingdom and as he had now reached the age of majority, he took over the running of the country. In a later battle, David was wounded and captured by Sir John Copeland and was handed over the King Edward III. Edward imprisoned him in the Tower of London. His imprisonment was not harsh and he was treated well.

David had secret negotiations with Edward and offered him the kingdom of Scotland for his freedom, knowing full well that the Scottish nobility would not agree to this. He was released on the payment of 100,000 marks. David found this a high price to pay because of Scotland's poverty and once again offered Scotland to Edward for cancellation of the ransom. Once again, the Scottish lords refused to accept that. To try to secure an heir, David married again to Margaret Drummond but no heir appeared, he died suddenly and unexpectedly in Edinburgh Castle and buried at Holyrood Abbey. His nephew, Robert, son of his sister Marjorie and her husband Walter Stewart, succeeded him.

---

[5] She was called 'of the Tower' because she was born there, not imprisoned.

House of Stewart/Stuart

Robert III, King of Scots (1337-1406) reigned from 1390 a until his death. He ascended the throne at 57 years of age. His given name was John, but he sought and received permission by parliament to change his regnal name to Robert so as to show continuity from Robert I. His reign was a continued fight with recalcitrant nobles and a restrictive parliament. He married Anabella Drummond, daughter of Sir John Drummond and Lady Mary Montiflex. They had seven children including James who would become a King of the Scots.

His brother, **Walter Stewart, Lord of Fife, 7th High Steward of Scotland (1338-1362)** married Isabella, Countess of Fife. They was no issue from this marriage. His brother, **Robert Stewart, Duke of Albany (1340-1420)** married Margaret, Countess of Menteith. Their son was Murdoch who was executed by the newly returned from exile, James I. Robert was believed to have caused the murder of his nephew, the Duke of Rothesay who was being detained by him.

His brother, **Alexander Stewart, Earl of Buchan 1343-1405)** married Ephemia, the Countess of Ross. He had no legitimate issue. His brother, **David, Earl of Strathearn (1357-1386)** was born in 1357 married Ephemia Lindsey and had a daughter who succeeded to his earldom. He died following a dispute with his old brother Alexander.

His brother, **Walter Stewart, Earl of Atholl (1158-1437)** married Margaret Barclay and had issue. He was an integral part of the conspiracy to assassinate his nephew James I and was tried and executed after three days of terrible torture. His sister, **Isabel Stewart**, no dates known but probably around 1560/1. She married James Douglas 2nd Earl of Douglas. There was no legitimate issue.

James I, King of Scots (1394-1437) spent 18 years in captivity in England as a hostage of King Henry IV of England, when

King Henry V came to the throne, he treated James more like an honoured guest than a prisoner. He married Joan Beaufort, a cousin of King Henry VI. Soon a ransom of 60,000 marks, less a dowry of 10,000 was promised and James returned to Scotland. They had eight children including his successor James.

James' reign, like most Scottish monarchs, was one of intrigue and counter-intrigue and what with England and France arranging diplomatic marriages, his Auld Alliance with France foundered. After running fights, James lodged at Blackfriars Monastery near Perth with his wife. His cousin, Sir Robert Stewart, heir to Walter, Earl of Atholl used his influence to smuggle some of James' opponents into the monastery where James was trapped and killed. The Queen, although wounded, managed to send a message to Edinburgh Castle to make sure that her son, now James II King of Scots was guarded and shielded. The regicides were eventually captured and executed. His brother, **David Stewart, Duke of Rothesay, Earl of Atholl and Earl of Carrick (1378-1402)** was the first ever Duke in the Scottish Peerage. He married Marjorie Douglas, daughter of Archibald the Grim, Earl of Douglas. There was no issue from this marriage.

His main enemy was his uncle, Robert of Albany and was eventually arrested and imprisoned by him, He died in strange circumstances at Falkland Palace and it is believed it was on the orders of his uncle Albany. As mentioned above.

James II, King of Scots (1430-1460) reigned as King from 1437 until his death having ascended the throne upon the murder of his father aged six or seven. He was the son of James I and his wife Joan Beaufort, the daughter of John Beaufort, 1st Earl of Somerset and his wife Margaret Holland. He married Mary of Guelders, daughter of Arnold, Duke of Guelders and Catherine of Cleves, a great aunt of Anne of Cleves, a future consort of King Henry VIII of England. They had seven children of which five survived to adulthood including James who would succeed his father.

James was a great proponent of the use of artillery in warfare and while besieging Roxburgh Castle, which was being held by the English during the Wars of Independence, he attempted to fire a cannon name 'The Lion' when it exploded killing him.

His sister, **Margaret Stewart of Scotland (1424-1445)** married thirteen year old Louis, Dauphin of France the son and heir of King Charles VII of France. She was eleven years old when she became Dauphine of France. Doctors advised against consummation due to the delicate immaturity of Margaret. While Louis went on tour of the kingdom with his father, she continued her studies and amazed many with her intelligence. The marriage remained childless, as Margaret died of inflammation of the lungs aged just 20. His sister, **Eleanor of Scotland (1433-1480)** married Sigismund, Archduke of Austria. There was no issue from this marriage. His sister, **Mary Stewart, Countess of Buchan (1428-1465)** married Wolfert VI of Basemen. There was no surviving issue from this marriage

His sister, **Joan Stewart of Scotland (1440-1486)** was born deaf and dumb and after two marriage attempts she married James Douglas, 1st Earl of Morton, There were two surviving children from this marriage. His sister, **Annabella of Scotland (1433-1509)** married twice, her first husband was Louis of Savoy, Count of Geneva. On the request of King Charles VII of France and for reasons not discovered, the couple separated and divorced and the marriage was annulled.

Her second husband was George Gordon, 2nd Earl of Huntly, but bad luck was not very far from Annabella when she was forced to be legally divorced from her husband due to consanguinity as she and her husband's first wife were with the 3rd and 4th degrees of relation. There was one child from this marriage, although five others are muted but not proved or disproved, named Isabella and she married William Hay 3rd

Earl of Errol.

James III, King of Scots (1451-1488) was not a much-liked monarch and was thought to be unwilling to administer justice with any sense of fairness. He was also eager to have an alliance with England. He married Margaret of Denmark, the daughter of King Christian I of Denmark and had three sons including James, would succeed him. He died during the Battle of Sauchieburn, a fight between James and his recalcitrant nobles and former councillors. He was thrown by a horse and either died from the fall or killed off by enemy soldiers.

His brother, **Alexander Stewart, Duke of Albany (1454-1485)** was created Duke of Albany before he was four years old, presumably when he showed he was going to survive into adulthood. He was also Earl of March, Lord of Annadale and Lord of the Isle of Man. He spent some years in his mother's continental homeland and was captured on his return by the English. He was soon released and went on to be appointed Lord High Admiral and Warden of the Marches. He was later accused of sharp practices and was driven to flee to the court of King Louis XI were he was welcomed. He made several abortive attempts on invading Scotland but achieved nothing. He married twice, his first wife was Lady Katherine Sinclair, daughter of William Sinclair, 3rd Earl of Orkney and had one surviving son, Alexander, who became bishop of Moray. His second wife was Anne de la Tour d'Auvergne. Their only son John inherited the Dukedom of Albany.

James IV, King of Scots (1473-1513) reigned as King from 1488 until his death. He became an effective ruler after defeating a rebellion in 1489 he brought justice to Scotland. He was, for a while, a supporter of Perkin Warbeck, a thorn in the side of King Henry VII of England.[6] In 1497, he laid siege to Norham

---

[6] Perkin Warbeck claimed to be one of the Princes in the Tower, Richard. Duke of York. He was eventually hanged for treason.

Castle in Northumbria using his grandfather's bombard, a cannon or mortar, Mons Meg. He eventually realized that a peace with England was in interest of both kingdoms and went on to cement good relations with England. He decided that a navy was important and created two new dockyards.

He married Margaret Tudor, daughter of King Henry VII of England. The marriage produced two surviving children including James, who succeeded his father. When Scotland and England did go to war, it was because King Henry VIII of England had invaded France and an alliance meant Scotland had to declare war on England, not without a secret smile no doubt. James led an army into Northumbria and was slain at the Battle of Flodden Field. His **brother James Stewart, Duke of Ross (1476-1504)**. It is thought he was also called James because the future James IV was rather delicate as a child. The Duke of Ross died unmarried and with issue. His **brother John Stewart, Earl of Mar** and he died as a child in 1503.

James V, King of Scots (1512-1542) came to the throne aged just 6 days old. He married twice, his first wife was Madeleine of Valois but there was no issue from this marriage. His second wife was Mary of Guise and they had three children of which only one daughter survived to adulthood, Mary, who would become tragically famous as Mary, Queen of Scots. Legend has it that James travelled the countryside dressed as a common man to enable him to see what the average man endures. He was also a great patron of the arts. During the inevitable war with England, his army suffered a serious defeat at the Battle of Solway Moss. He fell ill not long after and died in December 1542. His infant daughter Mary succeeded him. His siblings died young.

Mary, Queen of Scots (1542-1587) ascended the throne in December 1542. She spent the most of the childhood in France as the wife of Louis, the Dauphin of France. She briefly became

Queen of France until her husband's death in 1560. She returned to Scotland in 1561, and four years later she married her first cousin Henry Stuart, Lord Darnley. Their marriage was a stormy one and riven with Darnley's drunken moods. He also wanted to be King Regnant and be a co-ruler with his wife.

This would mean that if he survived his wife he would still be king. He also murdered her Italian private secretary David Rizzio in front of her. Darnley was to die mysteriously in an explosion at the former abbey Kirk o' Field. She had one son with Darnley, James, who would succeed her and eventually ascend the English throne following the death of Queen Elizabeth of England and united both kingdoms under one monarch. Mary married again, her husband was James Hepburn, 4th Earl of Bothwell who many believed to be the murderer on Darnley. There was no issue from this marriage.

Mary was eventually forced to abdicate in favour of her infant son and she fled south to England. She became a nuisance to Elizabeth as she was a possible heir to the English throne but was a Catholic and was a rallying point for disaffected Catholic nobles in England. Her stay in England was really an imprisonment. She either committed treason or was framed or cajoled into it and was tried and executed in 1587.

Her son James became King of the Scots and after the death of Queen Elizabeth I, he became King James VI of Scotland and I of England.

The Kingdom of Belgium

Belgium was part of what was called the Low Countries until they seceded from the Netherlands in 1830, their first King was **King Leopold I of the Belgians (1790-1865)**. He was the son of Francis, Duke of Saxe-Coburg-Saalfeld and Sophia Antonia of Brunswick-Wolfenbüttel. He married twice, his first wife was Princess Charlotte of Wales, daughter of George, Prince of Wales later King George IV of England. She died giving birth. Leopold's second wife was Louise of Orléans, daughter of Louis-Philippe I King of the French and his wife, Maria Amalia of the Two Sicilies. They had four children including the future King Leopold II of the Belgians. His sister, **Princess Sophie of Saxe-Coburg-Saalfeld (1778-1835)** married Emmanuel von Mensdorff-Pouilly. After the marriage, Emmanuel was elevated to Count. They had six sons. His sister, **Princess Antoinette of Saxe-Coburg-Saalfeld (1779-1824)** married Duke Alexander of Württemberg and they had five children including Maria of Württemberg who married Ernest I Duke of Saxe-Coburg-Gotha and became the stepmother of Prince Albert, consort of Queen Victoria of England. His sister, **Princess Juliene of Saxe-Coburg-Gotha-Saalfeld (1781-1860)** married Grand Duke Constantine Pavlovich of Russia. They was no legitimate issue from this marriage. His brother, **Prince Ernest I of Saxe-Coburg-Gotha (1784-1844)** married twice, his first wife was Princess Louise of Saxe-Coburg-Altenburg. They had two children, one Prince Albert became Prince Consort to Queen Victoria of England. His second wife was Maria Duchess of Württemberg. There was no issue from this marriage. His brother, **Prince Ferdinand of Saxe-Coburg-Gotha (1785-1851)** married Maria Antonia Kohary, they had four children one of whom became King Ferdinand II of Portugal.

His sister, **Princess Marie Luise Victoria (1786-1861)** married twice, her first husband was Emich Carl, Prince of Leiningen. There were two children from this marriage. Her second husband was Prince Edward, Duke of Kent. They had one child, Alexandrina Victoria. She was born in 1819 and died in 1901. She was to become **Queen Victoria of Great Britain**.

King Leopold II King of the Belgians (1865-1909) reigned as King of the Belgians from 1865 until 1909. He married Marie Henrietta of Austria. They had four children. Leopold founded the Congo Free State and he extracted a fortune from it by using it as his private property. He was forced to hand it over to the Belgian Government after his cavalier and couldn't-care-less-attitude caused millions of deaths of Congolese. His brother, **Prince Philippe, Count of Flanders (1837-1905)** married Princess Marie of Hohenzollern and they had five children including Albert who was to reign as King Albert I. His sister, **Princess Charlotte of Belgium (1840-1927)** married Maximilian, Archduke of Austria who eventually became Emperor of Mexico. There was no natural issue from this marriage.

King Albert I King of the Belgians (1875-1934) reigned from 1909 until 1934. He married Elisabeth of Austria and they had three children including Leopold III of Belgium.

His brother, **Prince Baudouin of Belgium (1869-1891)** was unmarried and without issue. His sister, **Princess Henriette of Belgium (1870-1948)** married Prince Emmanuel, Duke of Vendome. They had four children. His sister, **Princess Josephine Caroline of Belgium (1872-1958)** married Prince Karl Anton of Hohenzollern. They had four children.

King Leopold III of Belgium (1901-1983) reigned as King of the Belgians from 1934 until 1951. He married twice, his first wife was Princess Astrid of Sweden, they had four children, including two future Belgian Kings. His second wife was Lilian Baels, they had three children. His reign, which covered his country's submission to Nazi Germany after a brief struggle, was one of turmoil and uncertainty. He abdicated in favour of his son Baudouin in 1951.

His brother, **Prince Charles of Belgium, Count of Flanders (1903-1983)**. Despite rumours to the contrary, it is believed he died unmarried and without issue. The talk of a secret marriage has been denied.

His sister, **Princess Marie Jose of Belgium (1906-2001)** married Prince Umberto, Crown Prince of Italy. They had four children. Her husband became King Umberto III of Italy following the abdication of his father King Victor Emmanuel III. She was only Queen of Italy for a month when the Italian government, following a constitutional referendum, dissolved the monarchy and became a republic.

King Baudouin of the Belgians (1930-1993) reigned as King of the Belgians, following his father's abdication, from 1951 until 1993. He married Fabiola de Mora y Aragon. There were no children from this marriage as all five pregnancies sadly ended with miscarriages.

His sister, **Princess Josephine-Charlotte of Belgium (1927-2005)** married Jean, Grand Duke of Luxembourg. They had five children. His brother, **Prince Albert of Belgium (1934-** was born in 1934 and reigned from1993 until 2013 as **King Albert II of the Belgians**. He married Paola, daughter of Word War I Italian flying ace, Fulco, Prince Ruffo de Calabria. They have three children including Prince Philippe the current King His brother, **Prince Alexander of Belgium(1942-2009)** married Princess Lea and there was no issue from this marriage. His sister, **Princess Marie-Christine of Belgium (1951-)** married twice, her first husband was Paul Druker and her second and current husband is Jean-Paul Gourges. She had been outspoken as an anti-monarchist and has worked as an actress. His sister, **Princess Maria-Esmeralda of Belgium (1956-)** married Sir Salvador Moncada. They have three children. She works as a journalist.

The Kingdom of Denmark

Denmark became a recognizable kingdom in the 8th century with a reputation as Vikings and invaders. There were many kings of legend and renown, such as Harald Bluetooth, Sweyn Forkbeard and Cnut the Great King of England. We shall deal with historic kings and begin this section from the House of Oldenburg in the 15th century.

House of Oldenburg

Christian I, King of Denmark, King of Norway and King of Sweden (1426-1481) He reigned as King of Denmark from 1448 until his death. He married his predecessor's widow, Dorothea of Brandenburg. They had five children of whom only three survived into adulthood including John who would succeed him and Frederick, a future King of Denmark and Margaret, a future Queen of Scots. He had no siblings.

John I, King of Denmark, King of Norway and King of Sweden (1455-1513) reigned as King of Denmark from 1481 until his death. He married Christina of Savoy, daughter of the Elector of Saxony. They had three surviving children including Christian who would succeed his father.

His sister, **Margaret of Denmark, later Queen of Scotland (1456-1486)** married King James III of Scotland and they had three children including James who would succeed his father. His **brother Frederick** (see below).

Christian II, King of Denmark, King of Norway and King of Sweden (1481-1559) reigned as King of Denmark from 1513 until 1523. He brought in many reforms that, although accepted at first, began to look like the reforms of an absolute monarch rather than an enlightened one. The crown was offered to Christian's uncle Frederick who deposed him. Fate and the weather stopped Christian recovering his kingdom by scattering his fleet. He was captured by his uncle and imprisoned for the rest of his life. He married Isabella, Archduchess of Austria a sister of the Holy Roman Emperor. They had three children of whom only two survived into adulthood. They were Dorothea of Denmark was born in 1520 and died in 1580. She married the Elector Palatine. There was no issue from this marriage. Christina of Denmark, born in 1522 and died in 1590 who married twice, her first husband was Francesco II Sforza, Duke of Milan, there was no issue from this marriage. Her second husband was Francis I, Duke of Lorraine, they had issue.

Frederick I, King of Denmark and Norway (1471-1533) reigned as King of Denmark from 1523 until his death. He married twice, his first wife was Anna of Brandenburg, daughter of the Elector of Brandenburg. They had two children including Christian who succeeded his father. His second wife was Sophie of Pomerania, daughter of Bogislaw, Duke of Pomerania, they had six children. His siblings have been mentioned above.

Christian III, King of Denmark & Norway (1503-1559) reigned as King of Denmark from 1534 until his death. He married Dorothea of Saxe-Lauenburg and they had five children including Frederick who succeeded his father.

His sister, **Princess Dorothea of Demark, later Duchess of Prussia (1504-1547)** married Duke Albert of Prussia and they had six children. His brother, **Prince John of Denmark, later John II, Duke of Schleswig-Holstein-Haderslev (1521-1580)**. He died unmarried and without issue. His sister, **Princess Elizabeth of Denmark, later Duchess of Mecklenburg-Schwerin (1524-1586)** married twice, her first husband was Magnus II Duke of Mecklenburg-Schwerin, and there was no issue from this marriage. Her second husband was Ulrich II Duke of Mecklenburg-Güstrow. They had one child.

His brother, **Prince Adolf of Denmark, Duke of Holstein-Gottorp (1526-1586)** married Christina of Hesse and they had ten children including Christina who would marry King Charles IX of Sweden. His sister, **Princess Dorothea of Denmark, later Duchess of Mecklenburg-Schwerin (1528-1575)** married Christof, Duke of Mecklenburg-Schwerin but died two years into the marriage and there was no issue. His brother, **Prince Friedrich of Denmark (1532-1556)** was Prince-Bishop of Hildesheim and Bishop of Schleswig. He died unmarried and without issue.

Frederick II King of Denmark & Norway and Duke of Schleswig (1534-1588) reigned as King of Denmark from 1559 until his death. A man of high military ideals he was not happy unless rattling his sabre on some battlefield. He married his own 14 year old half-cousin Sophie of Mecklenburg-Güstrow, he was 37. They had eight children including Charles who would succeed his father and another daughter who would become Queen Consort of England.

His sister, **Princess Anne of Denmark later Electress of Saxony 1532-1585)** married Augustus, Elector of Saxony and they had fifteen children of which only four survived into adulthood. His brother, **Prince Magnus of Denmark, Duke of Holstein, Bishop of Ösel-Wiek, Bishop of Courland and nominal King of Livonia (1540-1583)** had to fight, with the support of the Russian Tsar Ivan IV, known as Ivan the Terrible, for his lands of Livonia. He failed and spent his last days in seclusion Poland and relying on their generosity. He married Maria Vladimirovna of Staritsa, they had two daughters who did not survive to full adulthood. His brother, **Prince John of Denmark, Duke of Schleswig-Holstein-Sonderburg (1545-1622)** married twice, his first wife was Elisabeth of Brunswick-Gruberhagen and they had fourteen children, his second wife was Princess Agnes Hedwig of Anhalt and they had nine children. His sister, **Princess Dorothea of Denmark, later Duchess of Brunswick Lüneburg (1546-1617)** married

William, Duke of Brunswick Lüneburg and they had fifteen children.

Christian IV King of Denmark-Norway (1577-1648) reigned as King of Denmark from 1588 until his death. He was a great reformer king and one of the most popular of the Danish monarchs. He married twice, his first wife was Anne Catherine, daughter of the Margrave of Brandenburg and they had seven children including Frederick who succeeded his father. He married his second wife Kirsten Munk morganatically, so she never became Queen Consort. They had twelve children, the youngest daughter was believed not to be the king's but the daughter of his wife's lover. His sister, **Princess Elizabeth of Denmark, later Duchess of Brunswick Lüneburg (1573-1626)** married Henry, Duke of Brunswick Lüneburg and they had ten children.

His sister, **Princess Anne of Denmark, later Queen Consort of Scotland, England and Ireland (1574-1619)** married King James VI of Scotland & I of England. They had seven children including Charles who succeeded his father. His brother, **Prince Ulrick of Denmark, Duke of Holstein & Schleswig, and Prince-Bishop of Schwerin (1578-1621)** died unmarried and without issue. His sister, **Princess Augusta of Denmark later Duchess of Holstein-Gottorp (1580-1639)** married Duke John Adolf of Holstein-Gottorp and they had eight children. His sister, **Princess Hedwig of Denmark, later Electress of Saxony (1581-1641)** married Christian II, Elector of Saxony. There was no issue from this marriage. His brother, **Prince John of Schleswig-Holstein (1583-1602)** went to Russia to marry the daughter of Boris Godunov but fell ill and died before the marriage.

Frederick III King of Denmark-Norway, Prince-Bishop of Verden and Prince-Archbishop of Bremen (1609-1670) married Sophie Amalie of Brunswick Lüneburg and had eight children including Christian who succeeded his father.

His brother, **Prince Christian, Prince-Elect of Denmark (1603-1647)** married Magdalene Sibylle of Saxony. There was no issue from this marriage. His brother, **Prince Ulrich of Denmark, Duke of Holstein & Schleswig (1611-1633)** Prince-Bishop of Schwerin from 1624 until 1629, died unmarried and without issue.

Christian V King of Denmark-Norway (1646-1699) reigned as King of Denmark from 1670 until his death and was well-liked by his subjects. He married Charlotte Amalie of Hesse-Kassel and they had five children including Frederick who would succeed his father.

His sister, **Princess Anne Sophie of Denmark, later Electress of Saxony (1647-1717)** married John George III, Elector of Saxony and they had two sons, John George, who succeeded his father as Elector and Frederick Augustus who would succeed his brother as Elector and later become King of Poland. His sister, **Princess Frederica Amalia of Denmark, later Duchess of Holstein-Gottorp (1649-1704)** married Christian Albert, Duke of Holstein-Gottorp and had four children. His sister, **Princess Wilhelmina Ernestine of Denmark, later Electress Palatine (1650-1706)** married Charles II, Elector Palatine. There was no issue from this marriage. His brother, **Prince George of Denmark, later Duke of Cumberland (1653-1708)** was never really a power behind the throne and his creation as Lord High Admiral was considered a token title. He married the future Queen Anne of England. His sister, **Princess Ulrika Eleonora of Denmark, later Queen Consort of Sweden (1656-1693)** married Charles XI, King of Sweden and had seven children of which only three survived into adulthood including Charles, a future King of Sweden and Ulrika. A future Queen Consort of Sweden.

Frederick IV King of Denmark-Norway (1671-1730) reigned as King of Denmark from 1699 until his death. He married twice, his first wife was Louise of Mecklenburg-Güstrow. They had five children of which only two survived into adulthood including Christian who succeeded his father.

His brother, **Prince Christian of Denmark (1675-1695)** died unmarried and without issue of Smallpox aged 20. His sister, **Princess Sophie Hedwig of Denmark (1677-1735).** She was proposed as a bride three times but none of them materialized into marriage. She spent her life devoted to charitable and religious pursuits and running her estates. She died unmarried and without issue. His brother, **Prince Charles of Denmark (1680-1705)** never married or had issue. His brother, **Prince William of Denmark (1687-1705)** never married or had issue and died young aged 18.

Christian VI King of Denmark-Norway (1699-1746) reigned as King of Denmark from 1730 until his death. He was an adept politician and his reign is remarkable for the lack of war or sabre rattling to settle international disputes. He married Sophia Magdalene of Brandenburg-Kulmbach and they had two children including Frederick who succeeded his father. His sister, **Princess Charlotte Amalie of Denmark (1706-1782)** never married or had children but was a calming power behind the throne.

Frederick V King of Denmark-Norway (1723-1766) reigned as King of Denmark from 1746 until his death. He married twice, his first wife was Princess Louise of Great Britain, daughter of King George II of Great Britain. They had four children including Christian who succeeded his father. His second wife was Julianna of Brunswick-Wolfenbüttel, they had one son.

His sister, **Princess Louise of Denmark, later Duchess of Saxe-Hildburghausen (1726-1756)** married Ernest Frederick III, Duke of Saxe-Hildburghausen.

Christian VII King of Denmark-Norway (1749-1808) ruled as King of Denmark from 1766 until his death. His reign was dogged by mental illness and the dominance of his personal physician who did his best to increase his power in court. He married his cousin Princess Caroline Matilda of Wales, sister of King George III of Great Britain and had two children including Frederick who succeeded his father. His sister, **Princess Sophia Magdalene of Denmark-Norway, later Queen Consort of Sweden (1746-1813)** married King Gustav III of Sweden and they had two children including Gustav, who succeeded his father. His sister, **Princess Caroline of Denmark-Norway, later Electress of Hesse (1747-1820)** married Prince William I, Elector of Hesse and they had four children. His sister, **Princess Louise of Denmark-Norway, later Landgravine of Hesse-Kassel (1750-1831)** married Landgrave Charles of Hesse Kassel and had seven children. His brother, **Prince Frederick, Hereditary Prince of Denmark (1753-1805)** acted as regent for his half-brother Charles VII from 1772 until 1784. He married Duchess Sophie Frederica of Mecklenburg-Schwerin. They had five children including Charles who would succeed his uncle.

Frederick VI King of Denmark-Norway (1768-1839) was King of Denmark from 1808 until his death. Norway was ceded to Sweden in 1814. He married his cousin Marie of Hesse-Kassel and they had two daughters. As he had no male heir, his nephew succeeded him.

His sister, **Princess Louise Auguste of Denmark, later Duchess of Augustenborg (1771-1843)** married Frederick Christian II, Duke of Schleswig-Holstein-Sonderburg-Augustenborg and they had three children including Caroline Amalie a future Queen Consort of Denmark.

Christian VIII King of Denmark (1786-1848) reigned as King of Denmark from 1839 until his death. He was the son of Hereditary Prince Frederick of Denmark and his wife Sophie Frederica of Mecklenburg-Schwerin. He married twice, his first wife was his cousin Charlotte Frederica of Mecklenburg-Schwerin and they had one son Frederick who succeeded his father. His second wife was Caroline Amalie of Schleswig-Holstein-Sonderburg-Augustenborg. They had no issue.

His sister, **Princess Juliene Sophia of Denmark, later Landgravine of Hesse-Philippsthal-Barchfeld (1788-1850** married Wilhelm, Landgrave of Hesse-Philippsthal-Barchfeld but they had no issue. His sister, **Princess Louise Charlotte of Denmark, later Landgravine of Hesse-Kassel (1789-1864)** married Wilhelm, Landgrave of Hesse-Kassel and they had seven children including Louise, a future Queen Consort of Denmark. His brother, **Hereditary Prince Ferdinand of Denmark (1792-1863)** married his first cousin, once removed, Princess Caroline of Denmark daughter of Frederick, Hereditary Prince of Denmark. There was no issue from this marriage.

Frederick VII King of the Kingdom of Denmark (1808-1863) reigned as King of Denmark from 1848 until his death. He organized a proper Danish Parliament and instituted a constitutional monarchy. His married life was a little more disorganized. He married three times, his first wife was his second cousin Vilhelmine Marie of Denmark, who he divorced after a few years, and his second wife was Mariane of Mecklenburg-Strelitz and again divorced her. His third and last wife was Louise Rasmussen whom he married morganatically. None of these marriages produced children. This caused quite a succession crisis and the throne was passed to a distant cousin. He had no siblings.

House of Schleswig-Holstein

Christian IX King of the Kingdom of Denmark (1818-1906) reigned as King of Denmark from 1863 until his death. He was born a Prince of Schleswig-Holstein-Sonderburg-Glücksburg, a cadet branch of the ruling Oldenburg dynasty. He was elected to the throne as his predecessor had no legitimate issue. He married his second cousin Louise of Hesse-Kassel and they had six children including Frederick who succeeded his father. He was widely known a 'father-in-law of Europe' as four of his children sat on European thrones as either King or Consort.

His sister, **Princess Luise Marie of Schleswig-Holstein-Sonderburg-Glücksburg (1810-1869)**. There is no record extant at the moment of any marriage or issue. His sister, **Princess Frederike of Schleswig-Holstein-Sonderburg-Glücksburg, later Duchess of Anhalt-Bernburg (1811-1902)** married Alexander Karl, Duke of Anhalt-Bernburg, there was no issue from this marriage. His brother, **Prince Karl, Duke of Schleswig-Holstein-Sonderburg-Glücksburg (1813-1878)** married Princess Vilhelmine Marie of Denmark but the marriage produced no offspring. His brother, **Prince Wilhelm of Schleswig-Holstein-Sonderburg-Glücksburg (1816-1893)**. He neither married nor had issue. His sister, **Princess Luise of Schleswig-Holstein-Sonderburg-Glücksburg, later Abbess of Itzehoe (1852-1894)** She became an Abbess and neither married or had issue. His brother, **Prince Julius of Schleswig-Holstein-Sonderburg-Glücksburg (1824-1905)** married, morganatically, Elizabeth von Ziegasar, no issue from this marriage is recorded. His brother, **Prince Johann of Schleswig-Holstein-Sonderburg-Glücksburg (1825-1911)**. There is no record of marriage or issue available. His brother, **Prince Nikolaus of Schleswig-Holstein-Sonderburg-Glücksburg (1828-1849)**. He did not marry or have issue.

Frederick VIII King of the Kingdom of Denmark (1843-1912) reigned as King from 1906 until his death. He ascended the throne aged 63 spending a long time as Crown Prince. He had been excluded from the politics of the country by his father and not taught the art of being a King. When he came to the throne he left the running of the country to his constitutional parliament mainly because of his inexperience and because he suffered poor health. He married Princess Louise of Sweden and they had seven children including Christian who succeeded his father and Haakon who was a future King of Norway

His sister, **Princess Alexandra of Denmark, later Queen Consort of the United Kingdom (1844-1925)** married Albert Edward, Prince of Wales, heir to Queen Victoria of the United Kingdom and they had six children including George who would succeed his father following the death of his elder brother Prince Eddy. (see Kingdom of England for full details).

His brother, **Prince George of Denmark, later King George I of the Hellenes (1845-1913** was born in 1845 and died in 1913. At the age of 17, he was elected the Greek throne by the Greek National Assembly and reigned until his death by assassination. He married Grand Duchess Olga Constantinova of Russia and they had eight children including Constantine who succeeded his father following his assassination. Olga acted as Regent for her son until he became of age. His **sister Princess Dagmar of Denmark, later Tsarina of Russia (1847-1928)** married Tsar Alexander III of Russia and they had six children including Nicholas who succeeded his father. His **sister Princess Thyra of Denmark, later Crown Princess of Hanover (1853-1933)** married Ernest Augustus, Crown Prince of Hanover who was in exile after Hanover was annexed by Prussia. The had six children. His **brother Prince Valdemar of Denmark (1858-1939)** married Princess Marie of Orléans and they had five children.

Christian X King of Denmark and only King of Iceland (1918-1944). He reigned as King of Denmark from 1912 until his death.

He was an authoritarian and a stickler for Royal dignity. His reign spanned two World Wars and he proved a resilient and resolute monarch, he even threatened to don the Star of David if this was forced on Danish Jews during the German Occupation of Denmark in World War 2. He married Duchess Alexandrine of Mecklenburg-Schwerin and they had two children including Frederick who succeeded his father.

His brother, **Prince Carl of Denmark and Iceland, later King Haakon VII of Norway (1872-1957)** reigned as King of Norway from 1905 until his death. He married Princess Maud of Wales, daughter of the future King Edward VII of the United Kingdom and his wife Queen Alexandra. They had one son, Olaf, who succeeded his father.

His **sister Princess Louise of Denmark and Iceland, later Princess of Schaumburg-Lippe (1875-1906)** married Prince Friedrich of Schaumburg-Lippe and despite an unhappy marriage where there spent many months apart, they had three children. His brother, **Prince Harald of Denmark and Iceland (1876-1949)** spent most his life in the Royal Danish Navy achieving the rank of Lieutenant General. He married his first cousin, Princess Helena of Schleswig-Holstein-Sonderburg-Glücksburg and they had five children. His **sister Princess Ingeborg of Denmark and Iceland, later Princess Ingeborg of Västergöland (1878-1958)** married Prince Carl of Västergöland and they had four children including Astrid, later Queen of the Belgians. His sister, **Princess Thyra of Denmark and Iceland (1880-1945)** never married or had any children. His brother, **Prince Gustav of Denmark and Iceland (1887-1944)** never married or had any children. His sister, **Princess Dagmar of Denmark and Iceland (1890-1961)** married Jørgen Castenskjold the son of the Royal Danish Court Chamberlain and they had four children.

Frederick IX King of Denmark (1899-1972) reigned as King of Denmark from 1947 until 1972. He was first engaged to his second cousin Olga, daughter of Prince Nicholas of Greece and Denmark but they never married. He eventually married Princess Ingrid of Sweden and they had three children including Margrethe who succeeded her father.

His brother, **Knud, Hereditary Prince of Denmark 1900-1976)** married his first cousin Princess Caroline-Mathilde of

Denmark and they had three children.

Margrethe II Queen Regnant[7] of Denmark (1940-) and is the first reigning Queen since her namesake in the 14th Century. She married a French Diplomat Count Henri de Laborde de Monpezat in 1967 when she was Crown Princess and as husband of the heir to the throne Henri was created Prince Henrik of Denmark and then Prince Consort when his wife ascended to the throne. They had two children, Frederick, the Crown Prince and Heir and Joachim. At the time of writing, Queen Margrethe II is still on the throne.

---

[7] A Queen can be Regnant which means she rules in her own right or Consort which means she is the wife of a reigning King.

Principality of Liechtenstein

The name began when one Hugh, took the name of Liechtenstein from a Castle that was situated south of Vienna. The family had property in the vicinity of this castle.

In the 13th century, the family split into three lines, the Liechtenstein, the Rohrauer and the Petroneller. Over the years, the last two lines became extinct and a lot of land was lost. Liechtenstein became a principality in 1627.

Karl I, Prince of Liechtenstein (1569-1627) was the first Prince of Liechtenstein and founder of the Princely House of Liechtenstein. He reigned as sovereign Prince from 1608 until his death. He was the son of Hartmann II, Baron of Liechtenstein and his wife Countess Anna Maria of Ortenburg. He married Anna Maria Šemberová and they had four children including Karl Eusebius who succeeded his father.

His brother, **Maximilian of Liechtenstein (1578-1645)** was a senior officer in Imperial Hapsburg service and attained the rank of Field Marshal. He also acted as regent, together with his brother Gundaker, for his nephew Karl Eusebius. He married Catherine Šembera of Czernahora and Boskovice. There was no issue from this marriage. His brother, **Gundakar of Liechtenstein (1580-1658)** acted as Regent, with his brother Maximilian until Karl Eusebius came of age. He was a wealthy nobleman and was rich enough to lend money to the state. He married twice, his first wife was Countess Agnes of East Frisia. They had six children of which only four survived to adulthood. His second wife was Elizabeth Lucretia, Duchess of Cieszyn, they had three surviving children.

Karl Eusebius, Prince of Liechtenstein (1611-1684) inherited the throne aged 16 and was served by his uncles as Regents until he came of age. After the Thirty Years War, he did a praiseworthy job in restoring his lands to a good economic state. He married Johanna Beatrix, Princess of Dietrichstein and Nikoburg, They had nine children including Johanna who married Maximilian II, Prince of Liechtenstein and Johann Adam who succeeded his father as Hans-Adam I, Prince of Liechtenstein.

His sister, **Princess Anna Maria of Liechtenstein 1597-1640).** There is no record of marriage or issue found. His sister, **Princess Franziska of Liechtenstein** was born in 1604 and died in 1655. No record of marriage or issue found. His brother, **Prince Heinrich of Liechtenstein** died young.

Hans-Adam I, Prince of Liechtenstein (1662-1712) reigned as sovereign Prince from 1699 until his death. He married Edmunda Maria Theresia, Princess of Dietrichstein-Nikolsburg. They had seven children but left no direct male heirs as both his sons predeceased him. He was succeeded by a cousin.

His **sister Johanna Beatrix, Princess of Liechtenstein (1650-1672)** married Maximilian II, Prince of Liechtenstein. There is no record of any issue.

Joseph Wenzel I, Prince of Liechtenstein (1686-1772) reigned as sovereign Prince three times, in 1712 until 1718 in his own right and secondly and thirdly as regent for two future princes. Anton Florian and Joseph Johann Adam. He married Princess Anna Maria Antonie of Liechtenstein, the daughter of Anton Florian. They had five children but none survived early childhood. There are no records of siblings.

Anton Florian, Prince of Liechtenstein (1656-1721) reigned as sovereign Prince from 1718 until his death. He was the son of Prince Hartmann III of Liechtenstein and Countess Sidonie Elizabeth of Salm-Reifferscheidt. He married Eleonore Barbara Catharina, Countess of Thun-Hohenstein. They had eleven children including Joseph Johann Adam who succeeded him.

His sister, **Anna Maria of Liechtenstein (no dates known),** married William Rudolph of Trauttmasdorff and had issue. His brother, **Philipp Erasmus of Liechtenstein (no dates known)** married Christine Theresia of Löwenstein-Wertheim and had issue.

Joseph Johann Adam Prince of Liechtenstein (1690-1732) reigned as sovereign Prince from 1721 until his death. He married three times, his first wife was his cousin Gabrielle, Princess of Liechtenstein who was a daughter of Hans-Adam I. They had no surviving issue. His second wife was Marianne Countess of Thun-Hohenstein who died 20 days after the wedding. His third wife was Maria Anna, Princess of Oettingen-Spielberg, they had three children including Johann Nepomik Karl who succeeded his father.

His sister, **Anna Maria Antoine, Princess of Liechtenstein (1699-1753)** married Joseph Wenzel I Prince of Liechtenstein. His sister, **Maria Eleonore, Princess of Liechtenstein (1703-1757)** married Count Friedrich August von Harrach-Rohrau. They had sixteen children including Maria Josepha who married Johann Nepomik Karl, Prince of Liechtenstein.

Johann Nepomik Karl, Prince of Liechtenstein (1724-1748) reigned as sovereign Prince from 1732 until his death, He married Maria Josepha, Countess of Harrach-Rohrau, they had two daughters, he died aged 24 leaving no male descendants.

His brother, **Karl Anton, Prince of Liechtenstein (1713-1715)** died young. His brother, **Joseph Anton, Prince of Liechtenstein (1720-1723)** died young. His sister, **Maria Theresia, Princess of Liechtenstein (1721-1753)** No further details are extant.

Franz Joseph I, Prince of Liechtenstein (1726-1781) reigned as sovereign Prince from 1772 until his death. He was a cousin of previous Princes. He married Marie Leopoldine von Sternberg, they had eight children including Aloys and Johann who succeeded their father.

His brother, **Karl Borromäus, Prince of Liechtenstein (1730-1789)** married Marie Eleonore, Princess of Oettingen-Spielberg and had issue. His brother, **Philipp Joseph, Prince of Liechtenstein (1734-1757)** was killed in action in Prague in 1757. He died unmarried and without issue. His brother, **Johann Joseph Simplicius, Prince of Liechtenstein (1724-1781)** died unmarried and without issue in 1781. His sister, **Maria Amalia Susanna, Princess of Liechtenstein (1737-1787)** married Johannes Siegmund Frederick von Khevenhüller-Metsch and had issue. His sister, **Maria Anna Theresia, Princess of Liechtenstein (1738-1814)** married Emanuel Philibert, Graf von Waldstein and had issue. His sister, **Franziska Xaveria Maria, Princess of Liechtenstein (1739-1821)** married Charles-Joseph, 7th Prince of Ligue and had issue. His sister, **Maria Christina Anna, Princess of Liechtenstein (1741-1819)** married Franz Ferdinand, Graf Kiusty von Wichnitz and had issue. She was the twin of the following sister. His sister, **Maria Theresia Anna, Princess of Liechtenstein (1741-1766)** married Karl Joseph Graf Palffy ab Erdod, Chancellor of Hungary. They had issue. His brother, **Josef Leopold Sebastian Emanuel, Prince of Liechtenstein (1743-1771)**. He died unmarried and without issue.

Aloys I, Prince of Liechtenstein (1759-1805) was the son of Franz Joseph I and his wife Marie Leopoldine von Sternberg. He started a military career but it had to be cut short because of his ill-health. He was a great lover of forestry and gardens and imported many trees for his arboretums. It was during his reign that the last execution in its history was carried out when Barbara Erni, a notorious thief and confidence trickster was beheaded for theft.

He married Karoline, Gräfin[8] von Manderscheid-Blankenheim. There was no issue from this marriage and Aloys was succeeded by his brother Johann.

His sister, **Leopoldina Maria Anna, Princess of Liechtenstein (1754-1823)** married Karl Emanuel, Landgrave[9] of Hesse-Rheinfels-Rotenburg and had issue. His sister, **Maria Antonia Aloysia, Princess of Liechtenstein (1756-1821)** became a nun and died unmarried and without issue. His brother, **Philipp Joseph Aloys, Prince of Liechtenstein (1762-1802)** died unmarried and without issue. His sister, **Maria Josepha, Princess of Liechtenstein (1768-1845)** married Nikolaus, Prince Esterházy von Galántha and had issue. His brother Johann succeeded him to the title.

Johann I Joseph, Prince of Liechtenstein (1760-1836) reigned as sovereign Prince from 1805 until its death. He had a successful military career rising in rank to Field Marshal. He fought in the Austro-Turkish War, the French Revolutionary War and the Napoleonic Wars. He expanded agriculture and forestry schemes and was instrumental in streamlining governmental administration. He married Landgravine Josepha of Fürstenberg-Weitra and they had fourteen children including Aloys who succeeded his father.

Aloys II, Prince of Liechtenstein (1796-1858) reigned as sovereign Prince from 1836 until his death. He married Countess Franziska Kinsky of Wchinitz and Tettau. They had eleven children including Johann and Franz who became sovereign Princes in their own right.

His sister, **Maria Sophia, Princess of Liechtenstein (1798-1869)** married Vincenz, Graf von Esterházy von

---

[8] Graf and Gräfin are a title that translates to Count and Countess.
[9] Landgrave and Margrave are titles given by the Holy Roman Emperor to Lords who control the edges of the Holy Roman Empire not unlike the Marcher Lords of England.

Galántha. There was no issue from this marriage. His sister, **Maria Josepha, Princess of Liechtenstein (1800-1884)** died unmarried and without issue. His brother, **Franz de Paula, Prince of Liechtenstein (1802-1887)** married Countess Julia Potocka and had issue. His great grandson who eventually become Franz Joseph II of Liechtenstein. His brother, **Karl Johann, Prince of Liechtenstein (1803-1871)** married Rosalie d'Hemricourt, Gräfin von Grünne and had issue. His sister, **Henrietta, Princess of Liechtenstein (1806-1886)** married Joseph, Graf Hunyady von Kethély and had issue. His brother, **Frederick Adalbert, Prince of Liechtenstein (1807-1885)** married Johanna Sophie Christiane Löwe, one of the most famous German opera singers of her day. They was no issue. His brother, **Eduard Franz, Prince of Liechtenstein** was born in 1809 and died in 1864. He married Countess Honoria Choloniowa-Choloniewska and had issue. His sister, **Ida Leopoldine Sophie, Princess of Liechtenstein (1811-1884)** married Karl, Fürst Paar Freiherr auf Hartburg und Krottenstein and had issue. His brother, **Rudolf Maria Franz Placidus, Prince of Liechtenstein (1816-1848)** died unmarried and without issue.

Johann II, Prince of Liechtenstein (1840-1920) reigned as sovereign Prince from 1858 until his death. His reign as sovereign Prince is the longest precisely documented tenure without a Regent employed. After World War I, Liechtenstein became a constructional monarchy and the army was abolished as a unnecessary expense. He never married or had issue and was succeeded by his brother Franz.

His sister, **Maria Franziska, Princess of Liechtenstein (1834-1909)** married Ferdinand, Graf von Trauttmansdorff-Weinberg and had issue. His sister, **Carolina Maria Josepha, Princess of Liechtenstein (1836-1885)** married Alexander, Fürst[10] von Schönburg-Hartenstein and had issue. His sister,

---

[10]Fürst translates approximately to Prince.

Sophie Maria Gabriela, Princess of Liechtenstein (1837-1899) married Charles, 6th Prince of Löwenstein-Wertheim-Rosenburg and had issue. His sister, **Aloysia Maria Gabriele, Princess of Liechtenstein (1838-1920)** married Heinrich, Graf von Fünfkirchen. There was no issue from this marriage. His sister, **Ida Maria, Princess of Lichtenstein (1839-1921)** married Adolf Joseph, Fürst von Schwatzenburg and had issue. His sister, **Henrietta Maria Norberta, Princess of Liechtenstein (1843-1931)** married her first cousin Prince Alfred of Liechtenstein and had issue that eventually inherited the Principality by the male line. His sister, **Anna Maria, Princess of Liechtenstein (1846-1924)** married Georg Christian, Prince of Lobkowicz and had issue. His sister, **Therese Maria, Princess of Liechtenstein (1850-1938)** She married Prince Arnulf of Bavaria and had issue. This line is now extinct.

Franz I, Prince of Liechtenstein (1853-1938). He reigned a sovereign Prince from 1929. He married Elisabeth von Gutmann but had no issue and was succeeded by his first cousin, twice removed Franz Josef. His siblings are mentioned above.

Franz Josef II, Prince of Liechtenstein (1906-1989) reigned as sovereign Prince from 1938 until his death. He married Countess Georgina von Wilczek and have five children including Hans-Adam who succeeded his father.

His sister, **Maria Theresia Henriette, Princess of Liechtenstein (1908-1973)** married Artur, Graf Strachwitz von Gross-Zauch und Camminetz and had issue. His brother, **Karl Alfred, Prince of Liechtenstein (1910-1985)** married Archduchess Agnes Christina of Austria and had issue. His brother, **Georg Hartmann, Prince of Liechtenstein (1911-1998)** married Maria Christine, Duchess of Württemberg and had issue. His brother, **Ulrich Dietmar, Prince of Liechtenstein (1913-1978)** died unmarried and without issue. His sister,

Maria Henrietta Theresia, Princess of Liechtenstein (1914-2011) was born in 1914 and died in 2011. She married Peter, Graf von Eltz and had issue. His brother, **Aloys Heinrich, Prince of Liechtenstein (1917-1963)** died unmarried and without issue.

His brother, **Heinrich Hartneid, Prince of Liechtenstein (1920-1993)** married Amalie, Gräfin von Podstatzki-Lichenstein and had issue.

Hans-Adam II, Prince of Liechtenstein (1945-) has been sovereign Prince since 1989. He married Countess Marie Kinsky of Wchinitz and Tettau and have four children.

His brother, **Philipp Erasmus, Prince of Liechtenstein (1946-)** married Fernade de L'Arbre de Malander and had three sons. His brother, **Nikolaus, Prince of Liechtenstein (1947-)** married Princess Margaretha of Luxembourg and had four children. His sister, **Nora, Princess of Liechtenstein (1950-)** married Vicente Sartorius y Cabeza de Vaca, 3rd Marquis of Mariño. They had one daughter. His brother, **Franz Joseph Wenceslas, Prince of Liechtenstein (1962-1991)** died in suspicious circumstances in 1991. A completely unsubstantiated rumour says he committed suicide over his homosexuality. He died unmarried and without issue.

County, Duchy & Grand Duchy of Luxembourg

Luxembourg was originally part of the Kingdom of Germany and later of the Holy Roman Empire. It was ruled by Counts until it was elevated to a Duchy in 1354. It finally became the world's only sovereign extant Grand Duchy in 1815.

Siegfried, Count of Luxembourg(922-998) married Hedwig of Nordgau. They had eleven children including Henry who would become Count of Luxembourg. As Siegfried's parentage is disputed, there is not a lot known about his siblings.

Henry I, Count of Luxembourg (964-1026) married and died without issue. The County passed to his nephew.

His brother, **Frederick of Luxembourg (965-1019)**. It is understood that he married Ermentrude of Glieberg and had nine children. Their son Henry would succeed his uncle as Count of Luxembourg. His brother, **Dietrich I of Metz (?-984)** was bishop of Metz from 964 until his death. He founded the Abbey of St Vincent in Metz. He died unmarried and without issue. His sister, **Cunigunde of Luxembourg, Saint Cunigunde (975-1040)** was the wife of Saint Henry II, Holy Roman Emperor. She was canonized in 1200 by Pope Innocent III.

Henry II, Count of Luxembourg, Henry VII, Duke of Bavaria (1007-1047) reigned as Count of Luxembourg from 1026 until his death. He died unmarried and without issue. He had no known siblings.

Giselbert, Count of Luxembourg (1007-1059) reigned as Count of Luxembourg from 1047 until 1059. He was the son of Frederick of Luxembourg and a grandson of Count Siegfried of Luxembourg.

His brother, **Frederick of Luxembourg, Duke of Lower Lorraine (1003-1065)** married twice, his first wife was, Gerberga of Boulogne, they had issue. His second wife was Ida of Saxony, there was no issue of this marriage. His brother, **Aldalbero III of Luxembourg (1010-1072)** was Bishop of Metz and led a life of prayer and piety. He died unmarried and without issue. His sister, **Ogive of Luxembourg (990-1036)** married Baldwin IV Count of Flanders. They had one son, Baldwin, who succeeded his father as Count of Flanders. His sister, **Ermengarde of Luxembourg (1000-1057)**. It is believed she married Welf II of Altdorf, Lord of Lechrain. There was no known issue from this marriage. His sister, **Oda of Luxembourg (no dates known)** she became Canoness at Remiremont and the Abbess at Saint Remy in Luneville. His sister, **Giselle of Luxembourg (1019-1058)** married Radulfe, Lord of Aalst. There was no known issue of this marriage.

Conrad I, Count of Luxembourg (1040-1086) was the son of Giselbert and an unknown wife. He was Count of Luxembourg from 1059 until 1086. He married Clementia the supposed daughter of Peter-William VII, Duke of Aquitaine. They had six children including two future Counts of Luxembourg. Conrad was involved in an argument with the Archbishop of Trier over one of the many Abbeys he had founded. The Archbishop excommunicated Conrad and only reinstated him after a heavy penalty. Conrad also had to go on a pilgrimage to Jerusalem. He died in Italy on the way back.

His brother, **Herman of Luxembourg (c.1041-1088)** was count of Salm having founded the House of Salm. There is no record of any marriage or issue. His brother, **Adalberon of Luxembourg (1046-1098)** was Canon at Metz and died in Antioch He died unmarried and without issue. His sister, **Jutta of Luxembourg (no dates known)** married Udo of Limbourg. There is no known issue of the marriage.

Henry III, Count of Luxembourg (?-1096) died unmarried and without issue. He was succeeded by his brother **William**

William I, Count of Luxembourg (1081-1131). He was the brother of Henry III and the son of Conrad I. He was the first Count of Luxembourg to use his title on documents. He married Mathilde of Northiem and had three children including Conrad, his successor. Like his predecessors, he argued with the Archbishop of Trier and was excommunicated for it. Apart from his brother Henry III whom he succeeded his siblings were:

His sister, **Mathilde of Luxembourg (no dates known)** married Godefroy, count of Bleisgau. There was no known issue. His brother, **Rodolphe of Luxembourg (no dates known)** He was Abbot of Saint-Vannes in Verdun. He died unmarried and without issue. His sister, **Erminsinde of Luxembourg (1075-1142)** married twice, her first husband was Albert II, count of Egisheim. Her second husband was Godefroy, count of Namur. They were the parents of Henry IV, Count of Luxembourg.

Conrad II, Count of Luxembourg (?-1136) reigned as Count of Luxembourg from 1131 until 1136. He married Ermengarde the daughter of Count Otto II of Zutphen. As Conrad died without a male heir, the County reverted back to the Holy Roman Empire for a decision. The Emperor did not want it to go to Conrad's nearest male relative, his brother-in-law Henry III, count of Grandpre.

Henry was a French noble and the Emperor was worried Luxembourg would be annexed the Kingdom of France He granted it to Henry of Namur, a cousin of Conrad's

His brother, **William of Luxembourg** (no dates recorded) was count of Gleiburg. But as I stated above, Conrad II had no male heir so William must have died before 1136. His sister, **Luitgarde of Luxembourg (1120-1170)** married Henry III, Count of Grandpre.

Henry IV, called 'the Blind', Count of Luxembourg (1112-1196) was the son of Godfrey I Count of Namur and Erminsinde of Luxembourg. He married twice, his first wife was Laurette of Alsace, daughter of Thierry Count of Flanders. They separated and were without issue. His second wife was Agnes of Guelders with whom he had a daughter. Once gain there was no male heir to the County and it reverted to the Holy Roman Empire on Henry's death.

His sister, **Elisabeth (no dates known)** married Gervais Count of Rethel. His sister, **Flandrina** married Hugh of Epinoy. No dates recorded. His brother, **Albert** died around 1127. His sister, **Clementia** married the Duke Conrad I of Zahringen. No dates recorded. His sister, **Alice** married Baldwin IV, Count of Namurs. No dates recorded. His sister, **Beatrice** married Ithier, Count of Rethel. No dates recorded.

Otto I, Count of Burgundy (1169-1200) was Count of Luxembourg for a year until he was assassinated for his regional conflicts.

Henry V, the Blond, the Great, Count of Luxembourg (1216-1281) was Count of Luxembourg from 1247 until 1281. He married Margaret of Bar, they had seven children including Henry a future Count of Luxembourg.

His sister, **Sophie (1190-1227)** married Frederick of Isenburg, there was issue from this marriage. His sister, **Matilda (1190-1234)** married William III Count of Julich. No known issue. His brother, **Henry IV Duke of Limburg (no dates known)** He married Imgard of Berg. They had issue. His brother, **Waleran** was born in 1200 and died in 1242. He married Elizabeth of Bar. No known issue. His sister, **Catherine (1215-1255)** married Matthias II Duke of Lorraine. There was issue from this marriage. His brother, **Gerhard, Count of Durbuy (1223-1298).** He married Mechthilde of Cleves and had issue.

Henry VI, Count of Luxembourg (1240-1288) was the son of Henry V and his wife Margaret of Bar. He married Beatrice d'Avesnes and they had three children including Henry who succeeded him. He was killed at the Battle of Worringen.

His brother, **Waleran I, Count of Ligny and Roussy (?-1288)**. He died at the Battle of Worringen. His sister, **Isabelle of Luxembourg (1247-1298)** married Guy of Dampierre and had issue. His sister, **Philippa of Luxembourg (1252-1311)** married John II Count of Holland and had issue.

Henry VII, Holy Roman Emperor, King of Italy and Germany and Count of Luxembourg (1275-1313) was the first Holy Roman Emperor from the House of Luxembourg. He married Margaret of Brabant. They had three children including John who succeeded him.

His brother, **Baldwin of Luxembourg (1285-1354)** became Archbishop-Elector of Trier. He died unmarried and without issue. His brother, **Walram of Luxembourg** of which no birth date is extant. He died at the siege of Brescia in 1311.

John 'the Blind' King of Bohemia and Count of Luxembourg (1296-1346) was count of Luxembourg from 1309 until his death. He married Elizabeth of Bohemia and they had six children. Charles who would become Holy Roman Emperor and Wenceslas his son with his second wife Beatrice of Bourbon, who would be Count of Luxembourg and the first Duke. John was killed at the Battle of Crecy whilst fighting King Edward III of England and his son Edward the Black Prince, Prince of Wales. John insisted in being allowed to take part in the battle although he had been blind for the past decade. His horse was tethered between two of his knights and they galloped in to battle swords swinging. They were all cut down.

When the Prince of Wales came across John's body on the field of battle, he took the three feathers and the motto of Ich Dien (I serve) as his personal badge. The badge has belonged to every Prince of Wales since.

His sister, **Marie of Luxembourg (1304-1324)** married King Charles IV of France. They had no surviving issue. She miscarried her first pregnancy. She was pregnant again when she and her husband were on their way to Avignon to see the Pope. She fell out of the bottom of the coach in which they were travelling and went into labour. The child died premature and Marie died several hours later. She was 20 years of age. His sister, **Beatrix of Luxembourg (1305-1319)** married King Charles I of Hungary. She died aged just 14 in child birth.

Dukes of Luxembourg

Wenceslas I, Duke of Luxembourg (1337-1383) was the son of John 'the Blind' and his second wife Beatrice of Bourbon. When Wenceslas' older brother, Charles became Holy Roman Emperor, he gave the county of Luxembourg to him and in 1355 raised its status to a Duchy. Wenceslas was the first Duke of Luxembourg. He married Joanna, Duchess of Brabant. There was no issue from this marriage.

His sister, **Margaret of Bohemia (1313-1341)** married Henry XIV, Duke of Bavaria and had issue. His sister, **Bonne of Bohemia (1315-1349)** married King John II of France and they had nine children, including Charles who succeeded his father. His brother, **Charles of Bohemia** was born in 1316 and died in 1378. He became **Charles IV, King of Bohemia and Holy Roman Emperor**. His brother, **John Henry of Bohemia (1322-1375)**. His marriage and issue records are not very extant. His sister, **Anne of Bohemia (1323-1338** married Otto, Duke of Austria when she was seven years old. She died at fifteen long before she and her husband could have children.

Wenceslas 2nd Duke of Luxembourg, King of Bohemia, King of Germany, Elector and Margrave of Brandenburg (1361-1388) was the son of Holy Roman Emperor Charles IV and his third wife, Anna von Schweidnitz. He married twice, his first wife was Joanna of Bavaria who died after being mauled by one of his much-loved deerhounds. His second wife, Sofia of Bavaria was a first cousin, once removed, of his first wife. Both marriages were childless. Wenceslas was described as a man of great knowledge but ruled with a mixture of laziness and cruelty and relied on favourites and yes-men for advice. He died of a heart attack while hunting in the woods surrounding his castle.

His sister, **Margaret of Bohemia (1335-1349)** married King Louis I of Hungary. She died while still a minor so the marriage was without issue. His sister, **Catherine of Bohemia (1342-1373)** married twice, her first husband was Rudolf IV of Austria. The marriage was childless. Her second husband was Otto V of Bavaria, this marriage was also childless. His sister, **Elisabeth of Bohemia (1358-1395)** married the seventeen year old Albert III, Duke of Austria when she was eight years old and died at fifteen without issue. His sister, **Anne of Bohemia (1366-1394)** married King Richard II of England. The marriage was without issue and Anne died of the plague and was buried in Westminster beside her husband. His brother, **Sigismund of Bohemia (1368-1431)** became Holy Roman Emperor, King of Hungary, King of Bohemia and Margrave of Brandenburg. He married twice, his first wife was Mary of Hungary, there was no issue from this marriage. His second wife was Barbara Celje. They had a daughter Elizabeth. His brother, **John of Gorlitz (1370-1396)** married Richardis Catherine of Sweden and Mecklenburg. They had one daughter, Elizabeth, Duchess of Gorlitz and Luxembourg. His sister, **Margaret of Bohemia (1373-1410)** married John III Burgrave of Nuremberg, they had one daughter.

Jobst of Morovia, King of Germany, Margrave of Morovia, Elector of Brandenburg and Duke of Luxembourg (1351-1411) was the son of Emperor Charles IV and Margaret of Troppau.

He married twice, Elizabeth of Opole and Agnes of Opole who were aunt and niece. There was no issue from these marriages. This line of descent became extinct upon his death in 1411.

Elizabeth of Gorlitz, Duchess of Gorlitz and Luxembourg (1390-1451) was the daughter of John of Gorlitz and Richardis Catherine of Sweden. The Duchy was mortgaged to Elizabeth by her uncle Sigismund but being unable to repay the loan, Elizabeth was left to run the Duchy. She married twice, her first husband was Antoine, Duke of Brabant. There were no surviving issue of this marriage. Her second husband was John III Duke of Bavaria-Straubing. The marriage was childless.

The next Dukes and Duchesses of Luxembourg were a disparate lot. We will leave them behind to quarrel and complain and move on to the Dukes of Luxembourg of the House of Valois-Burgundy.

Philip the Good, Duke of Luxembourg and Duke of Burgundy (1396-1467) He was a second cousin, once removed of Elizabeth, Duchess of Luxembourg and had usurped the ducal throne. He was the son of John the Fearless, Duke of Burgundy and Margaret of Bavaria. He married three times, his first wife was Michelle of Valois, there was no issue from this marriage. His second wife was Bonne of Artois again this marriage produced no issue. His third wife was Isabella of Portugal, they had one son who was Charles the Bold who would succeed to his father's titles. His sister, **Marie of Burgundy (1393-1463)** married Adolph I, Duke of Cleves. She became the great grandmother of John III, Duke of Cleves whose daughter Anne of Cleves would become Queen Consort to King Henry VIII of England.

His sister, **Margaret of Burgundy (1394-1441)** married twice, her first husband was Louis de Valois, Dauphin of France, heir to King Charles VI of France. Following his death she married Arthur III, Duke of Brittany. There was no issue from either marriage. His sister, **Anne of Burgundy (1404-1432)** married John of Lancaster, Duke of Bedford son of King Henry IV of England. His sister, **Agnes of Burgundy (1407-1476)** was born in 1407 and died in 1476. She married Charles I, Duke of Bourbon and went on to have eleven children.

Charles the Bold, Duke of Burgundy, Duke of Luxembourg (1433-1477). He died at the Battle of Nancy after a lifetime and reign of difficulties and struggles to build, it is believed, a kingdom for himself. He married three times, his first wife was the twelve year old Catherine of France. He was seven years old at the time and as Catherine died aged eighteen there was naturally no issue from this marriage. His second wife was Isabella of Bourbon. This marriage produced one daughter Mary, who went on to marry Maximilian I, Holy Roman Emperor. His third wife was Margaret of York, the daughter of Richard Plantagenet, 3rd Duke of York. She was also the sister to two kings of England, Edward IV and Richard III. At her wedding to Charles she wore a magnificent crown covered with pearls and enamelled white roses for the House of York.

The crown can still be seen at Aachen Cathedral in Germany. It is probably the last surviving medieval English crown in the world.

Mary I of Burgundy, Duchess of Burgundy and **Duchess of Luxembourg (1457-1482)**. She was also called Mary the Rich because of the vast wealthy estates her father left her at his death. She reigned as Duchess of Luxembourg from 1477 until her death. She was the only child of Charles the Bold and his wife Isabella of Bourbon. She married Emperor Maximilian I Holy Roman Emperor. They had two surviving children including a son Philip who succeeded his mother. As she was an only child. She had no siblings.

Philip I, King of Castile, called 'The Handsome' Duke of Luxembourg (1478-1506) reigned as Duke of Luxembourg from 1482 until his death. He inherited all of his mother's titles and lands. He married Joanna of Castile, the second daughter of Queen Isabella I of Castile and King Ferdinand II of Aragon. She was sister to Catherine of Aragon who married Arthur, Prince of Wales and after his death, King Henry VIII of England. They had six children including Charles who succeeded to his fathers titles. When Philip died, his wife Joanna refused to let him be entombed for quite a while, she would open the casket now and then and weep.

His sister, **Margaret, Arch-Duchess of Austria, Duchess of Savoy (1480-1530)** married twice, her first husband was John, Prince of Asturias. John died six months into the marriage and there was no issue. Her second husband was Philibert II, Duke of Savoy. There was no issue from this marriage.

Charles III 'The Golden One' Holy Roman Emperor, King of the Romans, King of Italy. King of Spain, Lord of the Netherlands, Count Palatinate of Burgundy and Duke of Luxembourg (1500-1556) reigned as Duke of Luxembourg from 1506 until 1555. He was the son of King Philip I of Castle and his wife, Queen Joanna 'the Mad' of Castile. Nearly all of Charles' reign was spent in the 'Italian Wars' against France. He was also well-known in opposing the 'Protestant Reformation' on the continent that was beginning to undermine the Catholic faith. He expanded his over-seas territories in South America and the Philippines. He was a supporter of Ferdinand Magellan and his round the world voyage. It was during his reign that the Society of Jesus (The Jesuits) was formed by St Ignacio de Loyola.

Tired and suffering from gout he retired from life and abdicated his throne, giving his Spanish empire to his son Philip and the Holy Roman Empire to his brother Ferdinand. He had an enlarged lower jaw, a deformity that grew worse in later Hapsburg generation. It became known as the Hapsburg

Jaw. This deformity was caused by a long history of interbreeding which was rife and done mainly to enable the family to keep control over its lands. Charles retired to a monastery and died there of Malaria in 1558.

His sister, **Eleanor, Archduchess of Austria (1498-1558)** was the daughter of King Philip I of Castile and his wife, Queen Joanna 'the Mad' of Castile. She married twice, her first husband was King Manuel I of Portugal who was her uncle by marriage. They had two children, a son, Infante Charles of Portugal who died young and a daughter, Infanta Maria of Portugal who died unmarried and childless. Her second husband was King Francis I of France. There was no issue from this marriage. His sister, **Isabella Archduchess of Austria (1501-1526)** married King Christian II of Denmark, Sweden & Norway. They had three surviving children, a son, Prince John who died young, a daughter, Dorothea of Denmark who married Frederick II, Elector Palatine. There were no children from this marriage. Their third daughter was Christina of Denmark who married Francis I, Duke of Lorraine. They had three children, a son, Charles, who married Princess Claude of France and had nine children, a daughter, Renata who married William V, Duke of Bavaria and had ten children and their third daughter, Dorothea who married Eric II, Duke of Brunswick-Lüneburg-Calenberg, They had no issue.

Philip II, King of Spain, Duke of Luxembourg (1547-1598) was the son of Charles V, Holy Roman Emperor and his wife, Isabella of Portugal. During his reign, Spain became the foremost Western European power. Under his leadership many new overseas territories were founded, including the Philippine Islands. His reign had its negative side. He was responsible in 1581, for precipitating the Declaration of Independence with created the Dutch Republic and, of course, the disastrous Spanish Armada invasion of England.

He married four times, his first wife, and also his double

first cousin, was Maria Manuela, Princess of Portugal. They had one son, Carlos, Prince of Asturias, who died young, unmarried and without issue. His second wife was his double first cousin, once removed, Queen Mary I of England and Ireland. With this marriage he became, in the right of his wife, King of England and Ireland. They spent most of their marriage ruling their own countries. Mary died in 1558 and Philip's claim on the English throne ended. His third wife, Elisabeth of Valois was the eldest daughter of King Henry II of France and his wife, Catherine de' Medici.

This marriage produced five daughters. Of the five, only two survived into adulthood. Infanta Isabella Clara Eugenia of Spain who was born in 1566 and died in 1633 married Albert VII, Archduke of Austria and Catherine of Spain, born in 1567 and died in 1597. She married Charles Immanuel I, Duke of Savoy. Philip's fourth and last wife was Anna of Austria. The marriage produced five children of which only one survived. This was Philip who would succeed his father.

His sister, **Maria of Austria (1258-1603)** was the daughter of Charles V, Holy Roman Emperor and his wife Isabella of Portugal. She married Maximilian II, Holy Roman Emperor. Maria and Maximilian had sixteen children of which nine survived to adulthood. They included two Holy Roman Emperors

His sister, **Joanna of Austria (1535-1573)** married her double first cousin Infante John of Portugal. They had one son, Sebastian who died unmarried and without issue.

Isabella Clara Eugenia, Archduchess of Austria and Albert VII Archduke of Austria were co-rulers of Luxembourg from 1598 to 1621.

Philip IV King of Spain and Duke of Luxembourg (1605-1665). He was noted as a great supporter of the arts especially Diego Velazquez, Lope de Vega and Pedro Calderon de la

Barca.

He married twice, his first wife was Elisabeth of France and had eight children or which two survived into adulthood. They were Balthaser Charles, Prince of Asturias, born in 1629 and died in 1646. He died young, unmarried and without issue. Their only surviving daughter was Infanta Maria Theresa of Spain born in 1638 and died in 1683. She married King Louis IV of France and had issue. His second wife was Mariana of Austria. They had five children of which one survived to adulthood. She was Margaret Theresa of Spain. She was born in 1651 and died in 1673. She became the first wife of Leopold I, Holy Roman Emperor.

His sister, **Anne of Austria (1601-1666)** married King Louis XIII of France. She was mother of King Louis XIV of France and his brother Philippe, Duke of Orléans.

Louis VIII and Anne were never close, they married very young, they were both 11 years old and were expected to consummate their marriage at 14, Louis refused. She had four stillborn children before she fell pregnant with Louis in 1638, she was 37 years old at the time.

It is said that Louis was caught in a storm and had to spend the night at Anne's house which was nearby. With the birth of Louis and later his brother Philippe the Bourbon line was deemed secure. His sister, **Marie Anne Archduchess of Austria, Infanta of Spain (1606-1646)** married Ferdinand III, Holy Roman Emperor. The had three children.

His brother, **Charles, Archduke of Austria(1607-1632)**. He died unmarried and without issue. His brother, **Cardinal-Infante Ferdinand (1609-1641)**. He also died unmarried and without legitimate issue.

Charles II of Spain, Duke of Luxembourg, also called 'the Bewildered' (1661-1700) was the son of Philip IV of Spain and his second wife, Mariana of Austria. A possessor of the famous 'Hapsburg Jaw, his reign was marred by economic stagnation in Spain. Spanish power world-wide had declined and they also had to contend with the Spanish Inquisition. He married twice, his first wife was Marie Louise d'Orléans the daughter of Philippe I, Duke of Orléans and she was the niece of King Louis IV of France, the Sun King. There was no issue from this marriage and Marie Louise died, deeply distressed, aged 26. Charles was broken-hearted.

The need to produce an heir forced Charles into his second marriage with Maria Anne of Neuburg, daughter of Philip William, Elector of the Palatinate. There was no issue from this marriage causing the rumour that Charles was impotent. As his life neared its end, his fragile health deteriorating, he began to fantasize. At one time he demanded that all the bodies of his family be exhumed so he could look at the bodies. This demand was ignored. He died in Madrid aged 39. His surviving siblings are mentioned above.

Philip V of Spain, Duke of Luxembourg (1683-1746) was the son of Louis, the Dauphin of France and Maria Anna Victoria of Bavaria. He was a grand-nephew of the last Duke of Luxembourg. He reigned as King of Spain from 1700 until 1724 when he abdicated in favour of his son Louis. After Louis' death, 7 months later, he resumed the throne and reigned until his death in1746. He married twice. His first wife was Maria Luisa of Savoy daughter of Victor Amadeus II, Duke of Savoy and Anna Marie d'Orléans, the youngest daughter of Philippe I, Duke of Orléans and his Henrietta of England, daughter of King Charles I of England.

Philip and Maria had four children of which only two sons survived into adulthood. They both succeeded their father, Louis as mentioned above and Ferdinand who reigned after his father's death. His second wife was Elisabeth Farnese of Palma, daughter of Odoardo Farnese and his wife Dorothea Sophie of Neuburg, they had seven children including Charles, who became Charles III, King of Spain.

His brother, **Louis, the Dauphin of France, Duke of Burgundy (1682-1712)** was heir to his father who was heir to King Louis XIV of France. He married Marie Adelaide of Savoy. They had two children. Neither Dauphin succeeded, it was to be the son of Louis who would succeed his great grandfather as King Louis XV of France. His brother, **Charles of France, Duke of Berry (1686-1714)** married Maria Louise Elisabeth d'Orléans and had issue.

Maximilian II Elector of Bavaria and Duke of Luxembourg (1662-1726) reigned as Duke of Luxembourg from 1712 until 1713. He was the son of Frederick Maria, Elector of Bavaria and his wife Henriette Adelaide of Savoy. He was a first cousin, once removed of his predecessor Philip V. He married twice, his first wife was Maria Antonia of Austria, daughter of Emperor Leopold I Holy Roman Emperor. They had three children but none survived into adulthood.

His second wife was Theresa Kunegunde Sobieska, the daughter of King John III Sobieska of Poland. They had ten children including Charles Albert, born in 1697 who would become Elector of Bavaria, King of Bohemia and Holy Roman Emperor. His sister, **Maria Anna Victoria, Duchess of Bavaria (1660-1690)** married Louis, the Dauphin of France, son and heir to King Louis XIV of France and became the second woman in France after the Queen as Dauphine of France. They had three children including Louis, who would succeed Louis XIV as King Louis XV. Maria was considered something of a drab figure at the court of the Sun King. She was not the most attractive of women and was shunned and ignored by the rest of the Versailles glitterati. She was always stating that she could not perform any royal functions after the death of the Queen as she was now First Lady of France, because of illness and this angered the King who considered her to be a hypochondriac.

At her death, her autopsy showed a plethora of internal disorders that vindicated her completely.

His brother, **Joseph Clemens of Bavaria (1671-1723)** was Archbishop-Elector of Cologne and served as Prince-Bishop of Liege, of Regensburg, of Freising and Hildesheim. Despite being a proposed groom for Elisabeth Charlotte, the daughter of Philippe d'Orléans of France, brother of Louis XIV, he died unmarried and without issue. His sister, **Violante Beatrice Duchess of Bavaria (1673-1713)** became Grand Princess of Tuscany upon her marriage to Grand Prince Ferdinando of Tuscany who was also Governor of Siena. Ferdinando was the son of Grand Duke Cosimo III of Tuscany and his wife Marguerite Louise d'Orléans. There was no issue from this marriage.

Charles VI, Holy Roman Emperor, King of Bohemia, Hungary, Croatia, Archduke of Austria and Duke of Luxembourg (1685-1740) was a second cousin to his predecessor Maximilian II. He was the son of Emperor Leopold I Holy Roman Emperor and Princess Eleonor Magdalena of Neuburg. He married Elizabeth Christine of Brunswick-Wolfenbüttel, daughter of Louis Rudolph, Duke of Brunswick-Lüneburg and Princess Christine Louise of Oettingen-Oettingen. They had four children of which two survived into adulthood including Maria Theresa who married Francis III Duke of Lorraine who later became Francis I Holy Roman Emperor. They had sixteen children including Archduchess Maria Antonia who as Marie Antoinette would marry the future King Louis XVI of France and died on the scaffold of the guillotine during the French Revolution. His sister, **Maria Antonia of Austria (1669-1692)** was the daughter of Leopold I Holy Roman Emperor and Margaret Theresa of Spain. Her birth was the result of the inbreeding rife in the Hapsburg family in the sixteenth and seventeenth centuries. Her father Leopold was her mother's maternal uncle and paternal cousin once removed.

Her maternal grand parents, King Philip IV of Spain and

Queen Mariana were uncle and niece. This inbreeding seemed important to keep Hapsburg property and land in the family. She married Maximilian II Emmanuel, Elector of Bavaria but no children survived into adulthood. His brother, **Joseph I, Holy Roman Emperor (1678-1711)** married Wilhelmina Amalia of Brunswick-Lüneburg. They had three children of which two survived into adulthood including Maria Amalia who married Charles VII Holy Roman Emperor. His sister, **Maria Elisabeth Archduchess of Austria (1678-1741)**. She was successor to Prince Eugene of Savoy as Governor of the Austrian Netherlands, a forceful administrator she suspended the East India Company in 1727 and finally closed in it 1731. She died suddenly at the age of 61 unmarried and without issue.

His sister, **Maria Anna Archduchess of Austria (1683-1754)** became Queen Consort of Portugal when she married King John V of Portugal, she was also Regent of Portugal during the illness of her husband. He died in 1750 and she handed control of the country over to he son Joseph, the new King. They had six children of which four survived into adulthood.

His sister, **Maria Magdalena Archduchess of Austria (1389-1743)**. After a failed marriage proposal, Maria retired to a life of peace and seclusion and died unmarried and without issue at 54. The next few Dukes were related and their siblings have been accounted for,

Grand Dukes of Luxembourg

William I King of the Netherlands and Grand Duke of Luxembourg (1772-1843) reigned as Grand Duke from 1815 until his death. He was the son of William V, Prince of Orange and his wife Wilhelmina of Prussia, daughter of Prince Augustus William of Prussia and his wife Luise of Brunswick-Wolfenbüttel. It was Napoleon Bonaparte's escape from Elba that prompted William to elevate the Netherlands from a

Principality of the Netherlands to a Kingdom to have a stronger backing against any assault. A move that was confirmed at the Congress of Vienna. He married Wilhelmina of Prussia, the daughter of King Frederick William II of Prussia and his wife Frederica Louisa. They had six children of which only three survived into adulthood including their son William who would succeed his father. He reigned until 1840 when because of heavy constitutional changes, and the loss of Belgium from his rule, he abdicated the throne and his son William succeeded to the title. After abdicating he had a morganatic marriage to Henrietta d'Oultremont. There was no issue of this marriage.

His sister, **Louise Princess of Orange-Nassau (1770-1819)** married Prince Karl Georg Augustus of Brunswick-Wolfenbüttel as a gesture of gratitude to her father-in-law for his help given to her father during the Dutch Rebellion. There were no children from this marriage as her husband was mentally restricted as well as blind. She spent her marriage with him solely as his carer.

His brother, **Frederick Prince of Orange-Nassau (1774-1799)** chose a military career and spent most of his young life fighting for the Holy Roman Empire. He died unmarried and without issue of a fever in Padua Italy aged just 24.

William II King of the Netherlands and Grand Duke of Luxembourg (1792-1849) is supposed to have had a string of relationships with both men and women but after an aborted engagement to Princess Charlotte of Wales, daughter of George, Prince of Wales he married Anna Pavlovna of Russia, daughter of Emperor Paul I of Russia and his wife Empress Maria Feodorovna. They had five children including William, who succeeded his father.

He entered the British Army in 1811 and was aide-de-camp to Arthur Wellesley 1st Duke of Wellington and fought in the Peninsular Wars. His courage and pleasant nature endeared him to the British people. He fought along side Wellington again a commander of the Allied Corp during the Battle of Waterloo where he was wounded. His brother, **Frederick, Prince of Orange-Nassau (1797-1881)** married his first cousin Louise, daughter of King Frederick William III of Prussia and had four children. His sister, **Pauline, Princess of Orange-Nassau (1800-1806)**. Died in infancy. His sister, **Marianne Princess of Orange-Nassau (1810-1883)** married her first cousin Prince Albert of Prussia and had five children of which three survived into adulthood.

William III King of the Netherlands and Grand Duke of Luxembourg (1817-1890) was not a man who could be intellectually stretched, and preferred everything military and forbade intellectual discussion at home much to the consternation of his first wife, Sophie of Württemberg and also to Queen Victoria in her letters to Sophie called him a 'uneducated farmer'. They had three children including two heirs to the throne that predeceased their father. His second wife was Emma of Waldeck & Pyrmont with whom he had one daughter whose descendants now rule the Netherlands.

His brother, **Alexander, Prince of the Netherlands (1818-1848)** was the son of King William II of the Netherlands and his wife Anna Pavlovna. He spent his early years in the military and despite two approaches of marriage to the future Queen Victoria and Isabella of Spain, following a decline in his health, he died aged 29, unmarried and without issue. His brother, **Henry, Prince of the Netherlands (1820-1879)** married twice, his first wife was Amalia of Saxe-Weimar-Eisenach, the daughter of Prince Bernhard of Saxe-Weimar-Eisenach and Princess Ida of Saxe-Meiningen, there was no issue from this marriage. His second wife was Princess Marie of Prussia, the daughter of the Prussian Field Marshal, Prince Frederick Charles of Prussia and his wife, Princess Maria Anna of Anhalt-Dessau. This marriage was also childless.

His sister, **Sophie, Princess of Netherlands (1824-1897)**

married Charles Alexander, Grand Duke of Saxe-Weimar-Eisenach. They had four children of which three survived to adulthood.

Adolphe, Grand Duke of Luxembourg (1817-1905) reigned as Grand Duke from 1890 until his death, He was the son of William, Duke of Nassau and his wife Princess Louise of Saxe-Hildburghausen, and he was a nephew of his predecessor William III. He married twice, his first wife was Grand Duchess Elizabeth Mikhailovna of Russia, the daughter of Grand Duke Mikhail Pavlovich of Russia and his wife Princess Charlotte of Württemberg. There were no surviving issue from this marriage. His second wife was Princess Adelheid-Marie of Anhalt-Dessau. They had four children of which only two lived into adulthood including William who succeeded father.

His sister, **Theresa, Princess of Nassau-Weilburg (1815-1871)** married Duke Peter of Oldenburg and had eight children of which four survived to adulthood. His sister, **Marie, Princess of Nassau (1825-1902)** married Herman, Prince of Wied and had three children of which two survived until adulthood. His sister, **Helene, Princess of Nassau (1831-1888)** married George Victor, Prince of Waldeck and Pyrmont. They had seven children, including Princess Emma who married King William II of the Netherlands as mentioned above. His brother, **Nikolaus Wilhelm, Prince of Nassau (1832-1905)** had many children from morganatic marriages. His sister, **Sophia, Princess of Nassau (1836-1913)** married Oscar II, King of Sweden-Norway and had four children including Gustav who succeeded his father as King Gustav V of Sweden.

William IV, Grand Duke of Luxembourg (1852-1912) was the son of his predecessor Adolphe. He married Infanta Marie Anne of Portugal and had six children including Marie-Adelaide who succeeded him.

His sister, **Hilda of Nassau (1864-1952)** married

Frederick II, Grand Duke of Baden, there was no issue from this marriage.

Marie-Adelaide, Grand Duchess of Luxembourg (1894-1924) reigned from 1915 until 1919. She was named heir by her father Adolphe, her predecessor because if the lack of a male heir. She reigned throughout the First World War. During this time Germany occupied Luxembourg and Marie-Adelaide seemed to acquiesce and seemed to get on with the occupiers. After the war Marie-Adelaide was accused of being pro-German and did not wish to be ruled by such a person. Marie-Adelaide abdicated in 1919 in favour of her younger sister Charlotte. Marie-Adelaide did not marry or have issue.

Charlotte, Grand Duchess of Luxembourg (1896-1985) reigned from 1919 until 1964. She was the daughter of Adolphe and the sister of Marie-Adelaide her predecessor who abdicated in her favour. The Luxembourg government decided to keep itself as a Grand Duchy and Charlotte was welcomed back from London, where she had spent the War, to ascend the throne. She married Prince Felix of Bourbon-Parma, a first cousin of her mother's side.

With the marriage of Charlotte and Felix the lineal descent was changed from Grand Ducal Highness to Royal Highness. They had six children including Jean who succeeded his mother.

Her sister, **Hilda, Princess of Luxembourg (1897-1979)** married Adolph Schwarzenberg, there was no issue from this marriage. Her sister, **Antonia, Princess of Luxembourg (1899-1954)** married Rupprecht, Crown Prince of Bavaria and had issue. Her sister, **Elisabeth, Princess of Luxembourg (1901-1950)** married Prince Ludwig Philipp of Thurn und Taxis and had issue. Her sister, **Sophie, Princess of Luxembourg (1902-1941)** was born in 1902 and died in 1941. She married Prince Ernst Heinrich of Saxony and had issue.

The current Grand Duke is Henri, son of Jean who abdicated in 2000.

Principality of Monaco

The House of Grimaldi have ruled Monaco since 1297, first as Lords and then Princes. They originated from Genoa and fled to Monaco in 1271. François Grimaldi captured the Rock of Monaco disguised as a monk to enable him to gain access to the castle. He wore a sword under his habit. He was assisted by his cousin and stepson Rainier, Lord of Cagnes.

I have begun this section from 1662 when the Lords of Monaco were designated Sovereign Princes of Monaco which was approved by King Philip IV of Spain and King Louis XIII of France due to their holdings in Italy.

Louis I, Prince of Monaco (1642-1701) reigned as Prince of Monaco from 1662 until his death. He was the grandson of Honoré II Lord & Prince of Monaco. He married Catherine Charlotte de Gramont, daughter of Antoine III de Gramont, Marshal of France. They had six children including Antoine, who would succeed his father,

His sister, **Princess Maria Ippolita Grimaldi of Monaco (1644-1694)** married Carlo Emanuele Filiberto de Simiane, Prince of Montafia and had issue. His sister, **Princess Giovanna Maria Grimaldi of Monaco (1645-?)** married Andrea Imperiali, Prince of Francaville and had issue. His sister, **Princess Teresa Maria Grimaldi of Monaco (1648-1723)** married Sigismundo d'Este, Marquis of San Martino and had issue.

Antoine I, Prince of Monaco (1661-1731) reigned as Prince of Monaco from 1701 until his death. He married Marie de Lorraine-Armagnac and had six legitimate children of whom only three survived into infancy including Louise who succeeded her father.

His sister, **Princess Maria Teresa Carlotta Grimaldi of Monaco (1662-1738)** lived as a Visitandine Nun in Monaco and died unmarried and without issue. His sister, **Princess Anna**

Hippolyte Grimaldi of Monaco (1667-1700) married Jacques de Crussol, Duke of d'Uzès, there is no record of any issue. His brother, **Prince François Honoré Grimaldi of Monaco (1669-1748)** became Archbishop of Besançon and died unmarried and without issue. His sister, **Princess Jeanne Maria Grimaldi of Monaco (no dates known)** lived as a Visitandine Nun and died unmarried and without issue.

Louise Hippolyte Grimaldi, Sovereign Princess of Monaco (1697-1731) reigned as Princess of Monaco from February until December 1731. She married Jacques Goyan de Matignon, Count of Thorigny, Duke of Valentenois and Prince of Monaco in the right of his wife. They had nine children including Honoré who succeeded his parents. Louise died of smallpox and Jacques was so distraught he neglected the country until forced to abdicate in 1733 in favour of his son. He spent the last few years of his life in Paris.

Her sister, **Princess Margherita Camilla Grimaldi of Monaco (1700-1750)** Louis de Gand Vilain, Prince d'Isenghein, Marshal of France. There is no recorded issue.

Honoré III Grimaldi, Prince of Monaco (1720-1795) reigned as Prince of Monaco from 1733 until 1793. He married Maria Caterina Brignole, daughter of Guiseppe Brignole Sale, 7th Marchese di Groppoli They had two children including Honoré who succeeded his father. His only sibling died in infancy.

From 1793 Monaco was run by the Nation Convention and annexed by France. This lasted until 1814 and the fall of Napoleon. It was then that the Grimaldi Dynasty resumed the throne.

Honoré IV Grimaldi, Prince of Monaco (1758-1819) reigned as Prince of Monaco from 1814 until his death. He married Louise d'Aumont and they had two sons including Honore who succeeded his father.

His brother, **Prince Joseph Grimaldi of Monaco (1763-**

1816) married Marie Theresa de Choiseul and they had two children. Marie Theresa was one of the last people executed during the French Revolution before the downfall of Robespierre.

Honoré V Grimaldi, Prince of Monaco (1778-1841) he reigned as Prince of Monaco from 1819 until his death. He never married and did not have any legitimate issue. He was succeeded by his only sibling Floristan.

Floristan I Grimaldi, Prince of Monaco (1785-1856) reigned as Prince of Monaco from 1841 until his death. He married Maria Caroline Gibert de Lametz and had two children including Charles who succeeded his father.

Charles III Grimaldi, Prince of Monaco (1818-1889) reigned as Prince of Monaco from 1856 until his death. He married Countess Antoinette de Merode and had one son, Albert who succeeded his father.

His sister, **Princess Florestine Grimaldi of Monaco (1833-1897)** married Wilhelm, 1st Duke of Urach and had two children.

Albert I Grimaldi, Prince of Monaco (1848-1922) reigned as Prince of Monaco from 1889 until his death. He married twice, his first wife was Lady Mary Hamilton, daughter of the Scottish Peer the 11th Duke of Hamilton. They had one son Louis who succeeded his father. His second wife was Alice Heine, there was no issue from this marriage.

Louis II Grimaldi, Prince of Monaco (1870-1949) reigned as Prince of Monaco from 1922 until his death. He married Ghislaine Dommanget a former French comedy actress and although there was no issue from this marriage, Louis controversially adopted his illegitimate daughter Charlotte and made her his heir. Charlotte married Count Pierre de Polignac, they had two children including Rainier who, with the blessing of his mother and probably because of her adoption furore, succeeded his grandfather. He had no siblings.

Rainier III Grimaldi, Prince of Monaco (1923-2005) reigned as Prince of Monaco from 1949 until his death. He married the American movie actress Grace Kelly and had three children including the current **Prince of Monaco, Albert II**

His sister, **Princess Antoinette of Monaco, Baroness of Massy (1920-2011)** had a long term relationship with Monegasque lawyer and tennis champion Alexandre-Athenase Noghès. They had three children out-of-wedlock that were legitimised upon their parent's eventual marriage.

Kingdom of the Netherlands

House of Orange-Nassau

I have chosen to begin this section from the first King, William I as he is the first to bear the title of King of the Netherlands. Before him there were Stadtholders, Princes and Bonapartes.

I would suggest that you read up about **William 'the Silent', Prince of Orange, the Father of the Nation**. He is believed to be the first Head of State to be assassinated by a handgun.

William I, King of the Netherlands (1772-1843) reigned as King of the Netherlands from 1815 until 1840. He was the son of William V, Prince of Orange and Wilhelmina of Prussia. He created the Netherlands a Kingdom after pressure the members of the Congress of Vienna following Napoleon Bonaparte's escape from Elba. He was a constitutional monarch and his dislike of changes to the constitution, and his threat to marry a Roman Catholic Belgian, two things at that time abhorrent to the Netherlands Government, caused him to abdicate in favour of his son William. He married his cousin Frederica Wilhelmine of Prussia, daughter of King Frederick William II of Prussia and his wife Queen Frederica Louise. They had six children of which only four survived including William who succeeded his father.

His sister, **Louise, Princess of Orange-Nassau (1770-1819)** married Prince Charles George Augustus of Brunswick Wolfenbüttel. There was no issue from this marriage. His brother, **Willem Georg Frederick, Prince of Orange-Nassau (1774-1799)** chose a military career in the armies of the Holy Roman Empire and died of fever at Padua, unmarried and without issue.

William II, King of the Netherlands (1792-1819) reigned as King from 1840 until his death. His early years were spent in the British Army where he fought in the Peninsular Wars and later became aide-de-camp the Arthur Wellesley, 1st Duke of Wellington. He fought at the Battle of Waterloo where he was wounded. He was initially betrothed to Princess Charlotte of Wales, daughter of the Prince Regent and his estranged wife, Princess Caroline of Brunswick. It was because of her mother's insistence and Charlotte's apprehension of living in the Netherlands that the marriage was called off. He eventually married Anna Pavlovna of Russia, daughter of Emperor Paul I of Russia and his wife Sophia Dorothea of Württemberg. They had five children including William who succeeded his father.

His brother, **Frederick, Prince of the Netherlands (1797-1881)** married his first cousin Princess Louise of Prussia and they had four children.

His sister, **Marianne, Princess of the Netherlands (1810-1883)** married her first cousin Prince Albert of Prussia, they had five children. As Albert was continually unfaithful so Marianne left him to live with her lover and former coachman, Johannes von Rossum. They had a child after she had divorced Albert. Both Johannes and her son, also named Johannes, predeceased her and she had them interred in a church she had built, she joined them aged seventy three.

William III, King of the Netherlands (1817-1890) reigned as King from 1849 until his death. William was not a happy monarch, he baulked at the constitutional changes inaugemented by his father. He married twice, his first wife was his cousin Sophie of Württemberg. It was an unhappy marriage because of the many differences between King and Queen. They had three sons of which two survived into adulthood but predeceased their father. His second wife was Emma of Waldeck and Pyrmont, they had one daughter, Wilhelmina who succeeded her father.

His brother, **Prince Alexander of the Netherlands, Prince of Orange-Nassau (1818-1848)** served in the army for most of his early career, he became a Lieutenant-General and Inspector of the Cavalry. King William IV of Great Britain wanted Alexander to marry his niece Princess Alexandrina Victoria of Kent, the future Queen Victoria of Great Britain but nothing came of it. It was also proposed that he marry Isabella II of Spain, this also came to nought. He therefore never married and had no issue. His brother, **Prince Henry of the Netherlands, Prince of Orange-Nassau (1820-1879)** served as Governor of Luxembourg from 1850 until his death. He married twice, his first wife was Amalia Maria de Gloria Augusta of Saxe-Weimar-Eisenach. His second wife was Marie Elisabeth Louise Frederica of Prussia. Both marriages were childless.

His sister, **Princess Sophie of the Netherlands (1824-1897)** married Charles Alexander, Grand Duke of Saxe-Weimar-Eisenach and they had issue including Karl who succeeded his father.

Wilhelmina, Queen of the Netherlands (1880-1962) reigned as Queen from 1890 until 1948. Her reign of almost 58 years covered both World Wars and the decline of the Netherlands colonial power. She married Henry, Duke of Mecklenburg-Schwerin. They had one daughter, Juliana who succeeded her mother when Wilhelmina abdicated in her favour in 1948.

Her brother, **William, Prince of Orange (1840-1879)**. It was planned for him to marry Queen Victoria's daughter Princess Alice but this failed. His other attempts at marriage were refused by his father as unsuitable and he died unmarried and without issue.

Her brother, **Alexander, Prince of Orange (1851-1884)**. Although marriages were discussed he died aged 32 unmarried and without issue.

Juliana, Queen of the Netherlands (1909-2004) reigned as Queen from her mother's abdication in 1948 until her own in favour of her daughter in 1980. She spent her formative years, during the war in Canada where her mother had a Government in Exile. She married Prince Bernhard of Lippe-Biesterfeld and they had four daughters including Beatrix who succeeded her mother when Juliana abdicated in her favour in 1980. Juliana was an only child so she had no siblings.

Beatrix, Queen of the Netherlands (1938-) reigned as Queen from 1980 until her abdication in 2013. She married Claus von Amsberg who became Prince Consort of the Netherlands upon Beatrix's accession to the throne. They had three sons including Willem Alexander, the present King who took over from his mother when she abdicated.

Her sister, **Princess Irene of the Netherlands, Princess of Orange-Nassau and Princess of Lippe-Biesterfeld (1939-)** married Carlos, Duke of Palma and had four children. Her sister, **Princess Margriet of the Netherlands (1943-)**. As a descendent of King George II of Great Britain, she is in line to the British throne, so she assumed British nationality as well as Dutch. She married Pieter van Vollenhoven and they had four children. Her sister, **Princess Christine of the Netherlands (1947-)** married Jorge Guillermo and they had three children. They divorced in 1996.

Willem Alexander, King of the Netherlands (1967-) assumed the Crown of the Netherlands on 30 April 2013 when his mother, Queen Beatrix, abdicated in his favour. He married Máxima Zorrequieta Cerruli, who became Queen Máxima of the Netherlands upon her husband's accession. They have three daughter including Catharina-Amalie, Crown Princess of Orange, who is next in line to the throne.

His brother, **Prince Friso of the Netherlands (1968-2013)** married Mabel Wisse Smit and due to controversy over the marriage, he is classed as a member of the Dutch Royal Family but not a member of the Dutch Royal House and therefore he nor any descendants are eligible for the throne. They have two daughters. In February 2012, Prince Friso was buried in an avalanche and was badly injured and in a coma. He died in August 2013.

His brother, **Prince Constantin of the Netherlands (1969-)** married Petra Laurentien Brinkhorst and they have three children. Upon his mothers abdication he and his family are no longer considered members of the Dutch Royal House but remain members of the Dutch Royal Family.

Kingdom of Norway

Norway was continually annexed by Denmark and Sweden during the course of its long history. In addition, is mention in other sections of this book.

However, there were many times when it was an autonomous independent state and it is those times we shall concentrate on here. In 1905, it again achieved independence.

House of Schleswig-Holstein

Haakon VII, King of Norway (1875-1957) reigned as king from 1905 until his death. He was the son of King Frederick VIII and his wife Princess Louise of Sweden. As a prince of Norway he was called Carl but took the name Haakon when elected to the Norwegian throne. He married Princess Maud of Wales, daughter of the Edward, Prince of Wales and Princess Alexandra, the future King and Queen of the United Kingdom.

They had one son, Olav, who succeeded his father as king of Norway. For his siblings see Kingdom of Denmark.

Olav V, King of Norway (1903-1991) reigned as King of Norway from 1957 until his death. He married Princess Märtha of Sweden and had three children including Harald who would succeed his father as King. He had no siblings.

Harald V, King of Norway (1937-) married Sonja Haraldsen, the daughter of a clothing manufacturer and they had two children. Their daughter Princess Märtha Louise of Norway was born in 1971. She married author Ari Behn and they had three children. They live in Islington London England. Their son, Crown Prince Haakon of Norway was born in 1940.

The Kingdom of Spain

House of Trastamara

It was the marriage of Ferdinand II of Aragon and Isabella I of Castile that began the unification of Spain as a Kingdom and Empire. It was Joanna, the daughter of Ferdinand and Isabella who tentatively ruled as the monarch of a united Spain.

Joanna I, (the Mad) Queen of Spain (1479-1555) reigned from 1504 until 1555. She married Philip the Handsome, the son of Maximilian I, Holy Roman Emperor and his wife Mary of Burgundy. They had six children including Charles who would co-rule with and finally succeed his mother. After the death of her husband she became mentally ill and was eventually confined to a nunnery.

Her sister, **Isabella of Aragon, Princess of Asturias (1470-1555)** married twice, her first husband was Prince Afonso, Prince of Portugal. After his death she married Prince Manuel, the future King Manuel I of Portugal. She died giving birth to her only child, Miguel, Crown Prince of Portugal and Spain who was to die himself in infancy. Her brother, **John, Prince of Asturias (1478-1497)** married Margaret of Hapsburg, daughter of Maximilian I, Holy Roman Emperor. His son with Margaret was stillborn. Her sister **Maria of Aragon, later Queen of Portugal (1482-1517)** married King Manuel I of Portugal, the widower of her eldest sister Isabella and had eight children including two Kings of Portugal. She had a twin sister **Anna** who died at birth. Her sister, **Catarina (Catherine) of Aragon, later Queen of England (1485-1536)** married twice, her first husband was Arthur, Prince of Wales, eldest son of King Henry VII of England. After his early death, she married Arthur's younger brother Henry, Duke of York the future King Henry VIII of England and gave birth to the future Queen Mary I of England.

House of Hapsburg

Charles I, King of Spain and Charles V, Holy Roman Emperor (1500-1558) reigned as King of Spain from 1516 until his death. He was the son of Queen Joanna 'the Mad' and Philip 'the Handsome'. He married Princess Isabella of Portugal and had three children who were legal issue including Philip who would succeed him and two children who were deemed illegitimate.

His sister, **Infanta Eleanor of Castile, Archduchess of Austria and later Queen Consort of Portugal and France (1498-1558** married twice, her first husband was her uncle by marriage, King Manual I of Portugal. They had two children, the Infante Charles who died in early childhood and the Infanta Marie, Duchess of Viseu who died unmarried and without issue aged 56. His sister, **Infanta Isabella of Castile, later Queen Consort of Denmark, Norway and Sweden (1501-1526)** married King Christian II of Denmark & Norway, and later Sweden. They had two daughters. His brother, **Infante Ferdinand, King of Bohemia, Hungary, Croatia and Holy Roman Emperor (1503-1564)**.He inherited the Emperorship when his brother Charles abdicated it. He married Princess Anne of Bohemia & Hungary inheriting the Kingships from Anne's brother. They had ten children including Maximilian who succeeded his father as Holy Roman Emperor. His sister, **Infanta Mary of Castile, later Queen Consort of Bohemia & Hungary (1505-1558)** married King Louis II of Bohemia & Hungary, the marriage was childless with the royal titles going to Mary's brother Ferdinand. His sister, **Infanta Catherine of Castile, Archduchess of Austria and later Queen Consort of Portugal (1507-1578)** married her first cousin King John III of Portugal and had nine children of which only two survived into adulthood.

Philip II, King of Spain and one-time King of England and Ireland (1527-1598). He was the son of Charles I of Spain and

Isabella of Portugal. He was married four times, his first wife was his double first cousin Maria Manuela, Princess of Portugal. They had one son, Carlos who died unmarried and without issue aged 23. His father then arranged for him to marry Queen Mary I of England and Ireland with the hope of uniting England and Spain under a continual Catholic monarchy. Philip spent most of his time in Spain. Mary was to die before producing any issue. When Elizabeth I came to the English throne and Philip made overtures to her with a view to marriage but was rebuffed. His third wife was Princess Elizabeth of Valois, daughter of King Henry II of France and Catherine de' Medici. They had two surviving children, Infanta Isabella of Spain. His second daughter was Infanta Catherine of Spain. Desperate for a male heir he married his fourth wife was Anne of Austria, his niece and they had five children of which only Philip survived into adulthood and succeeded his father.

His sister, **Infanta Maria of Spain, later Holy Roman Empress (1528-1603)** married Maximilian II, Holy Roman Emperor and had seven children including Rudolph who succeeded his father as Holy Roman Emperor. His sister, **Infanta Joanna of Spain and later Princess of Portugal (1535-1573)** married Prince John of Portugal, heir to the Portuguese throne and they had one son.

Philip III, King of Spain (1578-1621) married his cousin, Margaret of Austria and they had five children, including Philip who would succeed his father.

His brother, **Infante Carlos, Prince of Asturias (1545-1568)**. He was considered mentally unstable and imprisoned by his father dying six months after his incarceration unmarried and childless. His sister, **Infanta Isabella of Spain, later Archduchess of Austria (1566-1633)** married Albert VII, Archduke of Austria. They had three children who all died in infancy. His sister, **Infanta Catherine of Spain, later Duchess of Savoy (1567-1597)** married Charles Emmanuel I, Duke of

Savoy, they had four children including Victor Emmanuel who succeeded his father as Duke.

Philip IV, King of Spain and King of Portugal (1621-1640) reigned as King of Spain from 1621 until his death. He married twice, his first wife was Elisabeth of France, daughter of King Henry IV of France and his wife Marie de' Medici. They had eight children of which only two survived infancy and one who survived to adulthood. His heir Balthazar died in his teenage years. His second wife was Mariana of Austria, his niece. They had five children of which only two survived into adulthood including Charles who succeeded his father.

His sister, **Infanta Anne of Austria, later Queen Consort of France & Navarre (1601-1666)** married King Louis XIII of France and had two children including Louis who would reign as King Louis XIV of France. She is central in the novel The Three Musketeers by Alexander Dumas.

His sister, **Infanta Maria Anna of Spain, later Holy Roman Empress and Queen Consort of Hungary & Bohemia (1606-1646)** married Ferdinand III, Holy Roman Emperor and they had three children including Mariana who married her uncle Philip.

His brother, **Infante Charles, Archduke of Austria (1607-1632).** He was at one time heir to the throne but the birth of a son to his brother ended this. He died unmarried and without issue aged 25.

His brother, **Cardinal-Infante Ferdinand, Archduke of Austria**[11] **(1609-1641).** He was created a Cardinal but never took holy orders. He was Governor of the Spanish Netherlands and Archbishop of Toledo. He died unmarried and without issue.

Charles II, King of Spain (1661-1700). He was the last Hapsburg ruler of Spain. He was a possessor of the 'Hapsburg

---

[11] Many of the offspring of the Spanish Hapsburgs bore Austrian titles as Hapsburg was an Austrian dynasty.

Jaw' the tell-tale sign of massive inbreeding. He married twice, his first wife was Marie Louise of Orléans, a granddaughter of King Louis XIII of France. His second wife was Maria Anna of Neusburg. There was no issue from either marriage. Charles designated Philip Duke of Anjou, his grand-nephew and son of his half-sister Maria Theresa of Spain as his heir.

His sister, **Infanta Maria Theresa of Spain, later Queen Consort of France & Navarre** was born in 1638 and died in 1683. They had six children of whom only one, Louis, the Grand Dauphin, survived to adulthood. His sister, **Infanta Margaret Theresa of Spain, later Holy Roman Empress, Queen of Germany, Hungary & Bohemia (1651-1673)** married Leopold I, Holy Roman Emperor. They had one surviving child, a daughter, who married Maximillian II Emmanuel, Elector of Bavaria.

House of Bourbon

Philip V, King of Spain (1683-1746) was the son of Louis, The Grand Dauphin of France and his wife Maria Anne Victoria of Bavaria, he was also the great grandson of King Philip IV of Spain. He reigned as King of Spain from 1700 until 1724. He married twice, his first wife was Maria Luisa of Savoy, his second cousin, they had four sons including Louis and Ferdinand, future Kings of Spain. His second wife was Elisabeth of Palma, they had seven children including Charles, a future King of Spain. Philip abdicated in favour of his son Louis in 1724.

His brother, **Louis de France, Duke of Burgundy, later Dauphin of France (1682-1712)** married his second cousin, Princess Maria Adelaide of Savoy. They had two children including Louis, the future King Louis XV of France. His brother, **Charles de France, Duke of Berry, Count of Ponthieu (1686-1714)** married his first cousin Marie Louise Elisabeth d'Orléans. They had children but none survived.

Louis I, King of Spain (1707-1724) reigned as King of Spain for only seven months when he died from Smallpox aged 17. He married Louise Elisabeth d'Orléans but there was no issue. He father resumed the throne and reigned until his death in 1746.

His brother, **Ferdinand VI, King of Spain** reigned as King of Spain from 1746 until 1759. He married the Infanta Barbara of Portugal but there was no issue from this marriage. He was succeeded by his brother Charles. His brother, **Charles III, King of Spain** reigned as King of Spain from 1759 until 1788. He married Maria Amalia of Saxony, daughter of the Elector of Saxony. They had seven surviving children including Charles, who would succeed his father.

Charles IV, King of Spain (1748-1819) he was the son of King Charles III of Spain. He abdicated in favour of his son in 1808. He married Maria Luisa of Parma and they had six children including Ferdinand who would succeed his father.

His sister, **Infanta Maria Josepha, Princess of Naples & Sicily (1744-1801)** died unmarried and without issue aged 57. His sister, **Infanta Maria Luisa of Spain, Princess of Naples & Sicily, later Holy Roman Empress, German Queen, Queen of Hungary & Bohemia and Duchess of Tuscany (1745-1792)** married Leopold II, Holy Roman Emperor and had 12 children including Francis who would succeed his father. His brother, **Infante Philip of Spain, Prince of Naples & Sicily and Duke of Calabria (1747-1777)**. He never enjoyed good health and was subject to epileptic fits. He died aged 30 unmarried and without issue. His brother, **Infante Ferdinand of Spain, Prince of Naples & Sicily and King of the Two Sicilies (1751-1825)** married twice, his first wife was Maria Carolina of Austria daughter of Francis I, Holy Roman Emperor. They had nine children including Francis who succeeded his father. His second wife was Lucia Migliaccio, Duchess of Floridia, there was no issue from this marriage. His sister, **Infanta Maria Christina, Princess of Naples & Sicily later Queen of Sardinia (1779-1849)** married Charles Felix, King of Sardinia. There were no issue from this marriage. His brother, **Infante Gabriel of Spain, Prince of Naples & Sicily (1752-1788)**. He married Infanta Mariana of Portugal and they had one child. His brother, **Infante Antonio Pascual of Spain, Prince of Naples & Sicily (1755-1817)** married his niece, Maria Amalia of Spain. There was no issue from this marriage.

Ferdinand VII, King of Spain (1784-1833) was the son of King Charles IV of Spain. He was King of Spain twice, firstly from March to May 1808 and secondly from 1813 until his death. Both of these reigns were controversial because of Ferdinand's misinterpretation of Napoleon's intentions. Napoleon took the throne and gave it to his brother **Joseph** only to decide that Ferdinand was probably safe enough at a later date to assume the throne again. He married four times, his first wife was his cousin, Maria Antonia of Naples, there was no issue from this marriage, his second wife was another niece, Maria Isabella of Portugal. They had two daughters but neither of them survived infancy. His third wife was Princess Maria Amalia of Saxony. There was no issue from this marriage. His fourth wife was yet another niece, Maria Christina of the Two Sicilies. They had two daughters including Isabella who would reign briefly as Queen of Spain.

His sister, **Infanta Carlotta Joaquin of Spain, later Queen Consort of Portugal (1775-1830)** was born in 1775 and died in 1830. She married King John VI of Portugal and they had nine children including Miguel a future King of Portugal and Maria Isabel a future Queen Consort of Spain. His sister, **Infanta Maria Louisa of Spain, Duchess of Lucca and later Queen Consort of Etruria (1782-1824)** married Louis, King of Etruria and they had two children including Charles who would succeed his father.

His brother, **Infante Charles of Spain, Count of Molina (1788-1855)** married Maria Francisco of Portugal. They had three children.

His sister, **Infanta Maria Isabella of Spain, later Queen of the Two Sicilies (1789-1855)** married Francis I, King of the Two Sicilies they had twelve children including Ferdinand who would succeed his father.

His brother, **Infante Francisco de Paula of Spain (1794-1865)** married his niece, the Princess Luisa Carlotta of Naples & Sicily. They had eleven children including Francisco who would become King Consort of Spain after his marriage to his double first cousin Isabella.

Isabella II, Queen of Spain (1830-1904) was the daughter of King Ferdinand VII of Spain. She ascended the throne aged three under the regency of her mother and reigned as Queen from 1833 until she was forced to abdicate after the 'Glorious Revolution' in 1869, formally abdicating in 1870. She married her cousin Francisco, Duke of Cadiz and they had four children including Alfonso who would succeed his mother.

Her sister, **Infanta Luisa Fernanda of Spain, later Duchess of Montpesier (1832-1897)** married Prince Antoine d'Orléans, Duke of Montpesier. They had three children.

From 1868 until the formal abdication of Isabella, an interim government ruled Spain until a suitable candidate was chosen from the House of Savoy.

<u>*House of Savoy*</u>

Amadeo I, King of Spain (1845-1890) was elected to the throne by the government Cortes Generales. He reigned from 1870 until 1873. He was the son of King Victor Emmanuel II of Italy and Adelaide of Austria. His reign was very troublesome with the growing republican attitude in the country. He abdicated and returned to Italy. He married twice and had issue.

After Amadeo abdicated and the 1st Spanish Republic was instituted from 1873 until 1874. It was decided very quickly to restore the House of Bourbon to the throne as a country in governmental turmoil was a country ripe for conquest.

House of Bourbon (Restored)

Alfonso XII, King of Spain (1857-1885) was the son of Queen Isabella II of Spain. He married twice, his first wife was Mercedes of Orléans a near cousin. She died of typhoid fever shortly after the honeymoon. His second wife was Marie Christina of Austria and they had three children including Alfonso who would succeed his father.

His sister, **Isabella of Spain, Princess of Asturias (1851-1931)** married Prince Gaeton of Bourbon-Two-Sicilies. They had no children and her husband committed suicide three years into the marriage.

His sister, **Infanta Maria de la Paz of Spain (1862-1946)** married her first cousin Prince Louis Ferdinand of Bavaria. They had three children.

His sister, **Infanta Eulalia of Spain** was born in 1864 and died in 1958. She married her first cousin Infante Antonio of Spain, Duke of Gallieria. They had two children.

Alfonso XIII King of Spain was born in 1886 and died in 1941, he was the son of King Alfonso XII of Spain. He reigned from 1886 until he abdicated in 1931. He married Victoria Eugenie of Battenburg and they had six children including Infante Juan Carlos who was the father of the present King of Spain.

His sister, **Infanta Mercedes of Spain, Princess of Asturias** was born in 1880 and died in 1904. She married Prince Carlos of Bourbon-Two Sicilies and had three children.

His sister, **Infanta Maria Teresa of Spain** was born in 1882 and died in 1912. She married Prince Ferdinand of Bavaria and four children.

2nd Spanish Republic & Spanish State

In 1936 General Franco took over as President of Spain until his death and bequeathed his role of head of state to the grandson of Alfonso XIII who now reigns as **King Juan Carlos I of Spain.**

Kingdom of Sweden

Sweden, at various times, was part of Denmark and Norway so I have started with kings of Sweden who had a sense of independent control over the country.

House of Vasa

Gustav I, King of Sweden (1496-1560) reigned as King from 1523 until his death. He was a member of the Vasa line of Nobles and was the son of Erik Johansson Vasa, Lord of Rydboholm Castle and his wife Cecilia. Gustav was called the founder of modern Sweden and 'father of the nation'. He married three times, his first wife was Catherine of Saxe-Lauenburg, daughter of Magnus I, Duke of Saxe-Lauenburg. The marriage was a stormy one as Catherine spoke little Swedish and Gustav little German, it produced only one child Eric who would succeed his father as King of Sweden. Following her death in 1535, rumour abounded that Gustav had killed her with the silver hammer he used to summon servants with but this is now believed to be just that, a rumour. Gustav married again a year later to Margaret Leijonhufvud a member of a Swedish noble family and they had eight children including two sons, John and Charles who would subsequently become Kings of Sweden. His last wife was 17-year-old Catherine Stenbock, daughter of another Swedish nobleman. There was no issue from this marriage.

Many of Gustav's siblings either died young or in early adulthood and not much information of them is extant. Only one has been recorded in any detail.

His sister, **Margareta Eriksdotter Vasa (1497-1536)** married twice, her first husband was Joakim Brahe and they had one son, Per. Her husband was executed alongside her father following a rebellion against the king. Her second husband was John VII of Hoya who died in the Count's Feud in 1535. They had two children, and their son John would later become bishop of Osnabrück.

Eric XIV, King of Sweden (1533-1577) reigned as King of Sweden from 1560 until 1568. He was the son of Gustav I and his first wife Catherine of Saxe-Lauenburg. Although he showed some intelligence and artistic ability in his early years, he soon developed signs of mental instability which eventually turned into insanity. He was deposed in 1568 and imprisoned. He was later poisoned by arsenic. He married Karin Månsdotter and they had four children. None of whom succeeded him. He was succeeded by his brother John.

His sister, **Princess Katharina Vasa of Sweden (1539-1610)** married Edzard II, Count of Ostfriesland and became an ancestor of Queen Victoria. His sister, **Princess Cecilia of Sweden (1540-1627)** married Christopher II, Margrave of Baden-Rodemachern. There was no issue from this marriage. His brother, **Prince Magnus of Sweden, Duke of Östergötland (1542-1595)**. He never married or had issue. His sister, **Princess Anna Marie of Sweden (1545-1610)** married George John I, Count Palatine of Veldenz and they had eleven children of which only seven survived infancy. His sister, **Princess Sofia of Sweden (1547-1611)** married Magnus II, Duke of Saxe Lauenburg and had one child. His sister, **Princess Elisabet of Sweden (1549-1598)** married Christopher, Duke of Mecklenburg-Gadebusch and had one child. His brother, **Prince Charles of Sweden** (see below King Charles IX of Sweden).

John III, King of Sweden (1537-1592) reigned as king from 1568 until his death. He had been given the throne by the self-same nobles who deposed Eric. John was worried that if Eric was still imprisoned there may be an attempt to free him and put him back on the throne. To prevent this, John told Eric's guards that if there is any real or suspected attempt to free the ex-king they should kill Eric immediately. As mentioned above, he was poisoned. John married twice, his first wife was Catherine Jagellonica and they had two children including Sigismund who succeeded his father. His second wife was Gunilla Bielke, a cousin and they had one son. Gunilla did not really want to marry the king, she had been brought up in court as a companion to the king's daughter. But pressure from her family and a slap around the face by the angry king forced her to comply. For John's sibling, see above.

Sigismund III Vasa, King of Sweden, King of Poland and Grand Duke of Lithuania (1566-1632) reigned as King of Sweden from 1592 until he was deposed in favour of his uncle Charles. Sigismund married twice, his first wife was Archduchess Anna of Austria, daughter of Archduke Charles II of Austria and they had five children including Vladislaus a future King of Poland. His second wife was his first wife's sister, Constance, they went on to have seven children including John Casimir another future King of Poland.

His sister, **Princess Anna Vasa of Sweden (1568-1625)** was born in 1568 and died unmarried and without issue in 1625.

His brother, **John, Duke of Östergötland (1589-1618)**. He died massively in debt in 1618. A complete wastrel, forever changing his titles and lands and never really getting the best from any of them. He married his cousin Princess Marie Elizabeth of Sweden, daughter of King Charles IX. There was no issue from this marriage. He had one illegitimate son with his mistress.

Charles IX, King of Sweden (1550-1611) reigned as king from 1604 until his death. He was the son of Gustav I and his second wife Margaret Leijonhufvud. He took the throne when his nephew Sigismund was deposed. His reign was continually interrupted by warfare fuelled by the need to hold on to and to obtain land. He married twice, his first wife was Maria of the Palatinate-Simmern, daughter of Louis VI, Elector Palatine. They had six children of which only one survived into adulthood. His second marriage was to Christina of Holstein-Gottorp and they had four children including Gustav who would succeed his father. See Eric XIV for siblings.

Gustav II Adolph, King of Sweden (1594-1632) reigned as king from 1611 until his death. He managed to change Sweden from a backwater little kingdom into a Great Power. He was a military commander par excellence and was called 'The Golden King' and 'The Lion of the North'. He married Maria Eleonora, daughter of the Elector of Brandenburg and they had one daughter Christina, who succeeded him. He died at the Battle of Lützen and was succeeded by his six-year-old daughter.

His sister, **Princess Catherine of Sweden, later Countess Palatinate of Kleeburg (1584-1638)** married John Casimir of Palatinate-Zweibrüken and they had five children who survived infancy. His sister, **Princess Maria Elizabeth of Sweden (1596-1618)** married John, Duke of Östergötland, they had no children. His brother, **Prince Charles Philip, Duke of Södermanland (1601-1622)** married Elisabet Ribbing a noblewoman and had one daughter.

Christina, Queen of Sweden (1626-1689) reigned as Queen Regnant from 1632 until 1654. She was constantly asked by her ruling council to marry and produce an heir. She was secretly engaged to Charles Gustav for a while but nothing came of this. It is said that she abdicated because of the constant pressure to provide an heir. She abdicated the throne in favour of her one-time amour and cousin Charles Gustav and renounced the state religion of Lutheranism and embraced the Catholic religion. Because she dressed in men's clothing, had a deep voice and masculine behaviour, it was believed she was a Hermaphrodite and other, because many of her ladies-in-waiting shared her bed, believed her to be a lesbian. After abdicating the Swedish throne she attempted, unsuccessfully, to become Queen of Naples and it is said she had a French Marquis murdered in front of her for betraying her plans. She eventually went to live in Rome and is one of the few women to be allowed burial in St Peter's Basilica. She was played by Greta Garbo in the 1933 film *Queen Christina*. There were no siblings.

House of Palatine-Zweibrüken

Charles X Gustav, King of Sweden (1622-1660) reigned as king from 1654 until his death. He was the son of John Casimir, Count Palatinate and Catherine of Sweden the daughter of King Charles IX of Sweden. His reign was dogged by wars against Poland and Denmark in pursuit of land and power. He married Hedwig Eleonora of Holstein-Gottorp and had one son, Charles who would succeed him. He died of pneumonia after insisting on continually reviewing his troops in the field while carrying symptoms of a cold.

His sister, **Countess Palatine Christina Magdalena of Zweibrüken and Royal Princess of Sweden from 1654 (1616-1662)** married Frederick VI, Margrave of Baden-Durlach and became the great grandmother of King Adolf Frederick of Sweden. His sister, **Countess Palatine Maria Eufroyne of Zweibrucken and Royal Princess of Sweden from 1654 (1625-1687)** married Count Magnus De la Guardie and they had eleven children of which only three survived into adulthood. His sister, **Countess Palatine Eleonora Catherine of Zweibrucken and Royal Princess of Sweden from 1654 (1626-1692)** married Frederick, Landgrave of Hesse-Eschwege. They had six children or which only three survived into adulthood. His brother, **Adolph John I, Count Palatine of Kleeburg and Royal Prince of Sweden from 1654 (1629-1689)** married twice, his first wife was Countess Elizabeth Beate Brahe of Wisingborg and they had only one son who died at five months of age. His second wife was the younger sister of his first wife, Countess

Else Elizabeth Brahe and they had nine children of which only six survived into adulthood including Adolph and Gustav who would, in turn, succeed their father.

Charles XI, King of Swede (1655-1697) reigned as king from 1660 until his death. He ascended the throne on the death of his father aged only 5. During his minority his mother acted as regent. He married Ulrike Eleonora, daughter of King Frederick III of Denmark. They had seven children, of which only three survived into adulthood, including Charles who would succeed his father. He had no siblings.

Charles XII, King of Sweden (1655-1697) reigned as king from 1660 until his death. He ascended the throne on the death of his father aged five-years-old. His mother acted as his regent until he achieved the age of seventeen when he was crowned king. He died on the battlefield unmarried and without issue and was succeeded by his sister Ulrica Eleanor.

His sister, **Princess Hedvig Sophia of Sweden (1681-1708)** married Frederick IV, Duke of Holstein-Gottorp and had one son Charles Frederick who succeeded his father. Hedvig became the grandmother of Tsar Peter III of Russia.

Ulrica Eleanor, Queen Regnant & Consort of Sweden (1688-1741). When her brother King Charles XII died without an heir, thought was given to the son of his sister Hedwig, Charles Frederick. Ulrica argued that she was her brother's closet living relative and cited the precedent of Queen Christina. She won her case and ruled as Queen from 1718 until 1720, when she abdicated in favour of her husband. She married Frederick, Landgrave of Hesse-Kassel and they had one son. She abdicated in his favour and was Queen Consort from 1720 until his death.

House of Hesse

Frederick I, King of Sweden, Landgrave of Hesse-Kassel (1676-1751) reigned as king from 1720 until his death. As Ulrica had handed over most of her powers to the government his reign was quite powerless and it was the Russian Tsarina Elizabeth who insisted the throne go to Adolph Frederick of Holstein-Gottorp a distant cousin of his wife.

His sister, **Princess Sophie Charlotte of Hesse-Kassel (1678-1749)** married Frederick William, Duke of Mecklenburg-Schwerin. There was no issue from this marriage.

His brother, **Prince William of Hesse-Kassel (1682-1760)** succeeded his father as Landgrave. He married Dorothea Wilhelmina of Saxe-Zeitz and they had two children.

His sister, **Princess Marie Louise of Hesse-Kassel (1688-1765)** married Johan Willem Frisco, Prince of Orange and had two children. His son William succeeded his father as prince of Orange and married Princess Anne of Great Britain, daughter of King George II.

His brother, **Prince Maximilian of Hesse-Kassel (1689-1753)** married Landgravine Friederike of Hesse-Darmstadt and they had eight children.

His brother, **Prince George of Hesse-Kassel (1691-1755)**. His life was dedicated to a military career and he died unmarried and without issue.

House of Holstein-Gottorp

Adolph Frederick, King of Sweden (1710-1771 reigned as king from 1751 until his death. He was descended from King Gustav I on his mother's side and obtained the Swedish throne through the machinations of Empress Elizabeth of Russia, a relative and, of course, a power to reckon with. He was, up to his elevation to the crown, prince-Bishop of Lübeck and administrator of the lands in Holstein-Gottorp whilst his nephew, the future Tsar

Peter III of Russia was in his minority. He married Louisa Ulrika of Prussia, daughter of King Frederick William I of Prussia and his wife Sophia Dorothea of Hanover daughter of the Elector of Hanover and future King George I of Greta Britain. They had five children of which four survived into adulthood including Gustaf and Charles, future Kings of Sweden. He died after consuming a meal of Lobster, Caviar, Sauerkraut, Kippers and Champagne.

His sister, **Hedwig Sophie Auguste of Holstein-Gottorp (1705-1764)** was born in 1705 and died in 1764. She became Abbess of Herford and died unmarried and without issue. His sister, **Frederica Amalia of Holstein-Gottorp (1708-1782)** became a nun at Quedlinburg and died unmarried and without issue. His sister, **Anne of Holstein-Gottorp (1709-1758)** married Prince Wilhelm of Saxe-Gotha-Altenburg. There are no records of issue extant at the time of writing. His brother, **Frederick August, of Holstein-Gottorp Duke of Oldenburg (1711-1758)** married Princess Ulrike of Hesse-Kassel and had three children. His sister, **Joanna Elisabeth of Holstein-Gottorp (1712-1760)** married Charles August, Prince of Anhalt-Zerbst and became the mother of Russia's Catherine the Great. His **brother, George Ludwig of Holstein-Gottorp (1719-1763)**. His life was spent pursuing his army career, he was an officer in the Prussian Army and a Field Marshal in the Imperial Russian Army. He married Sophie Charlotte of Schleswig-Holstein-Sonderburg-Beck and they had three children.

Gustaf III, King of Sweden (1746-1792) reigned as king from 1771 until his death. A proponent of absolute monarchy he attempted to reign with minimal input from the government (Riksdag). This and his emulation of the French monarchy in spending money like water brought him few friends and many enemies. He married Princess Sophia Magdalena of Denmark, daughter of King Frederick V of Denmark and they had two children. Only their son Gustav survived into adulthood and succeeded his father. Despite receiving many threats to his life he decided to attend a masked ball at the Stockholm Royal Opera House. Being masked, it enabled a Swedish Army officer with many grievances against the king to get close enough to Gustav to shoot him in the back. He was mortally wounded but survived for nearly two weeks before succumbing to his would. For his brother Charles (see Charles XIII below)

His brother, **Prince Frederick Adolf of Hesse-Kassel, Duke of Östergötland (1750-1803).** Despite his many plans to marry he never did, he spent his time spending money and having love affairs. He had no legitimate issue.

His sister, **Princess Sophia Albertina of Hesse-Kassel** was born in 1753 and died in 1829. She was the last Princess-Abbess of Quedlinburg and, of course, died unmarried and without issue.

Gustaf IV Adolph, King of Sweden (1778-1837) reigned as king from 1792 until his abdication in 1809. He married Frederica of Baden and they had three children. He was rumoured to be the biological son of a Finnish nobleman and when his ineptitude and lack of diplomacy caused a coup d'état and abdication it was decided that the abdication would include his entire immediate family, probably because of his supposed illegitimacy. His only sibling died in infancy. The crown was passed to Gustav's uncle Charles.

Charles XIII, King of Sweden (1748-1818) reigned as king from 1809 until his death. As the uncle of the previous monarch he never really expected to assume the throne. He seemed to rely on others to give him ideas. He married his cousin Hedwig Elizabeth of Holstein-Gottorp and they had two children who died in infancy. He and his wife went on to live separate lives leaving Charles free to have a string of mistress and at least one extramarital child. As he had no heirs, he took the unusual step of adopting two sons. The first was Charles August, Crown

Prince of Sweden. He predeceased his adoptive father after falling off his horse. He never married or had issue. His second adoptive son succeeded him as king (see below).

House of Bernadotte

Charles XIV John, King of Sweden (1763-1844) reigned as king from 1818 until his death. He was adopted by the ailing King Charles XIII as his heir. He was born Jean Baptiste Bernadotte and changed his name upon adoption. He was a Frenchman by birth and a Marshal of France. He married Désirée Clary, a former Fiancé of Napoleon Bonaparte and they had one son Oscar who succeeded his father. He died of a suspected stroke in 1844.

His brother, **Jean Bernadotte, 1st Baron Bernadotte (1754-1813)** was born in 1754 and died in 1813. He married Maria Anne Charlotte Saint-Pau, there is no record of any children.

Oscar I, King of Sweden (1799-1859) reigned as king from 1844 until his death. During the reign of his father, when he was Crown Prince, he held the post of Viceroy of Norway. He father, like all kings, thought his son was plotting against him and seeking the throne, brought him home. His father arranged for Oscar to marry one of four princesses. In the end he married Princess Josephine of Leuchtenburg and they had five children including Charles and Oscar who would, in time, become kings of Sweden. He had no siblings.

Charles XV, King of Sweden (1826-1872) reigned as king from 1859 until his death. He married Princess Louise, daughter of Prince Frederick of the Netherlands and they had two children.

Charles' son and heir Carl died in infancy and his daughter Louise became Queen of Denmark when she married King Frederick VIII of Denmark. He was succeeded by his brother Oscar.

Oscar II, King of Sweden (1829-1907) reigned as king from 1872 until his death. A great lover of art and music, he encouraged education throughout Sweden. He married Sophia, daughter of Wilhelm, Duke of Nassau and had five children including Gustaf who would succeed his father.

His brother, **Prince Gustaf of Sweden, Duke of Uppland (1827-1852)** was a very competent musician and composer and many of his songs are still remembered and sung at occasions in Sweden. He never married or had issue and died of Typhoid Fever aged 25. His sister, **Princess Eugenie of Sweden (1830-1889)** was born in 1830 and died in 1889. She never married or had issue and because unmarried adult women were giving legal majority she was able to live an independent life. His brother, **Prince Albert of Sweden, Duke of Dalarna (1831-1873)** was born in 1831 and died in 1873. He had a great interest in trains and locomotives and even had one named after him. He married Princess Therese of Saxe-Altenburg but there was no issue from this marriage.

Gustaf V, King of Sweden (1858-1950) reigned as king from 1907 until his death. He had to face allegations of sympathizing with the Nazi's and rumours of homosexuality. He married Princess Victoria, daughter of Grand Duke Frederick I of Baden and Princess Louise of Prussia. They had three children including Gustav who succeeded his father.

His brother, **Prince Oscar of Sweden, Count of Wisborg and Duke of Gotland (15-859-1953)** married Ebba Munck af Fulkila and they had five children. His brother, **Prince Carl of Sweden, Duke of Västergötland (1861-1951)** married Princess Ingeborg of Denmark and had four children including Astrid who would become Queen of the Belgians. His brother, **Prince Eugen of Sweden, Duke of Närke (1865-1947)**. He died unmarried and without issue.

Gustaf VI Adolf, King of Sweden (1882-1973) reigned as king from 1950 until his death. He ascended the throne at the age of 67 and, at the time, was the oldest heir apparent to a crown. He married twice, his first wife was Princess Margaret of Connaught, daughter of Prince Arthur, Duke of Connaught and was a granddaughter of Queen Victoria. They had five children including Gustaf who predeceased him leaving his son Carl as heir to the throne.

His brother, **Prince Wilhelm, Duke of Södermanland (1884-1965)** married Grand Duchess Marie Pavlovna of Russia and had one son. His brother, **Prince Erik, Duke of Västmanland (1889-1918)**. He never married or had issue and died in the Spanish Flu epidemic of 1918.

Carl XVI Gustaf, King of Sweden (1946-) is the current King of Sweden. He married Silvia Sommerlath and they have three children including Victoria the present Crown Princess and heir to the throne. It is King Carl XV Gustaf who presents the Nobel Prizes each year.

His sister, **Princess Margaretha of Sweden (1934-2008)** was born in 1934. She married John Ambler, a British businessman and they had three children. His sister, **Princess Birgitta of Sweden (1937-)** was born in 1937 and married Prince Johan Georg of Hohenzollern. They had three sons. His sister, **Princess Désirée of Sweden (1937-)** was born in 1938 and she married Baron Nils August Silfverschiöld. They had three children. His sister, **Princess Christina of Sweden (1943-)** married Tord Magnuson and they had three children.

That is a list of monarchies in Europe that are still extant. There are two other monarchies within the boundaries of Europe, Andorra and Vatican City. But as we are dealing with siblings, they shall be left alone.

Royal Siblings of Former Kingdoms

Emperors of Austria 1804 - 1918

Austria was settled in ancient times by Celtic tribes until absorbed into the Roman Empire. During the Middle Ages the family of the Habsburgs began their rise to power acquiring land and building, gradually, their own empire. The roots of this family began to spread through other ruling families and in later years sat on many of the most illustrious thrones in Europe. This continual intermarrying, to keep the land and property in Habsburg control, created a physical deformation called 'the Habsburg Jaw' causing the face to have a large lumpy appearance in both male and female members of the family. Heads of the Habsburg family invariably were elected Holy Roman Emperors. The idea of a Habsburg Empire is really a self-imposed soubriquet, it was really just control over several disparate areas. But as an influential family they warrant mention as well as other rulers of Austria.

Francis I, Emperor of Austria, Archduke of Austria and last Holy Roman Emperor as Francis II (1768-1835) reigned as Emperor from 1804, when he founded the Empire after he dissolved the Holy Roman Empire, until his death. He married four times, his first wife was Elisabeth of Württemberg and had one daughter who died in infancy. His second wife was Maria Theresa of Naples, daughter of the King of the Two Sicilies and had nine children including Ferdinand who would succeeded his father. His third wife was Maria Ludovika of Austria-Este and his fourth wife was Caroline Augusta of Bavaria, there was no issue from either of these last two marriages.

His sister, **Maria Theresa, Archduchess of Austria, Princess of Tuscany, later Queen Consort of Saxony (1767-1827)** married Anton I, King of Saxony and they had four children, none of which survived infancy.

His brother, **Ferdinand, Archduke of Austria, Duke of**

Tuscany, Prince-Elector and Grand Duke of Salzburg and Grand Duke of Würzburg (1769-1824)** married twice, his first wife was his double first cousin Princess Luisa of Naples & Sicily. They had five children of which only two survived. His second wife was Maria Ferdinande of Saxony but there was no issue from this marriage. His brother, **Charles, Archduke of Austria, Duke of Teschen (1771-1847)** was a Field-Marshal in the Austrian Army. He married Princess Henriette of Nassau-Weiburg and had seven children including Maria Theresa who would become Queen of the Two Sicilies.

His brother, **Alexander Leopold, Archduke of Austria, Palatine of Hungary (1772-1795)** greatly interested in science and pyrotechnics and decided to put on a surprise firework display for the arrival of his sister in law the Empress Maria Theresa. He manufactured the fireworks himself and as he prepared to send up a rocket, a door was opened, causing a draught of air which threw the lighted rocket onto a pile of gunpowder and Alexander and his servants were all killed in the ensuing explosion. He died unmarried and without issue. His brother, **Joseph, Archduke of Austria later Palatine of Hungary (1776-1847)** married three times, his first wife was Grand Duchess Alexandra Pavlovna of Russia, daughter of Tsar Paul I of Russia and they had one stillborn daughter. His second wife was Princess Hermine of Anhalt-Bernburg and they had two children. His third wife was Duchess Maria Dorothea of Württemberg and had five children including Maria Henriette who would become Queen-Consort of Belgium. His sister, **Maria Clementia, Archduchess of Austria (1777-1801)** married Francis I, Hereditary Prince of Naples and had one daughter Carolina who would marry Charles, Duke of Berry, son of King Charles X of France and have two children. His brother, **Anton Victor, Archduke of Austria, Viceroy of Lombardy-Venetia, last Archbishop-Elect of Cologne and Prince-Bishop of Münster (1779-1835)** unmarried and without issue. His brother, **Johann, Archduke of Austria (1782-1859)** was Commander of the Austrian Army. He was an avid mountaineer and nature lover. He also had a great interest in technology and agriculture. He married Anna Maria Plochi, the daughter of a local postmaster and they had one son. His brother, **Rainier Joseph, Archduke of Austria, Viceroy of Lombardy-Venetia, Prince Royal of Hungary & Bohemia (1783-1853)** married Princess Elisabeth of Savoy and they had three children including Adelaide who would become Queen of Sardinia. His brother, **Louis, Archduke of Austria, Prince Imperial of Austria and Prince Royal of Hungary & Bohemia and Prince of Tuscany (1784-1864)** a career soldier and achieved, through merit, the rank of Feldmarschel Leutnant. He died unmarried and without issue. His brother, **Rudolf, Archduke of Austria, Prince Imperial of Austria, Prince Royal of Hungary & Bohemia (1788-1831)** became a Cardinal and Archbishop of Olomouc and died unmarried and without issue.

Ferdinand I, Emperor of Austria, King of Hungary, Croatia, Bohemia, Lombardy-Venetia (1793-1875) He reigned from 1835 until his abdication in 1848 due to his inability to govern because of his mental incapability. He married Maria Ann of Savoy, daughter of King Victor Emmanuel I of Sardinia, there was no issue from this marriage. He abdicated following the 1848 revolutions in favour of his nephew Franz Joseph.

His sister, **Marie Louis, Archduchess of Austria, Princess of Hungary & Bohemia** was born in 1791 and died in 1847. She married three times, her first husband was Napoleon Bonaparte, Emperor of France and they had one son, Napoleon. This story is well known and documented. Her second husband was Adam Albert von Neipperg and had three children. Her last husband was her Chamberlain, Charles de Bombelles, there was no issue from the marriage. His sister, **Maria Carolina, Archduchess of Austria, later Queen-Consort of Naples & Sicily (1752-1814)** married Ferdinand IV, King of Naples and they had eight children including Maria Theresa who married

Francis II, Holy Roman Emperor. His sister, **Maria Leopoldina, Archduchess of Austria, Empress-Consort of Brazil and Queen-Consort of Portugal (1797-1831)** married Emperor Pedro I of Brazil and had four children). His sister, **Clementina, Archduchess of Austria (1798-1881)** married Leopold, Prince of Salerno and they had one daughter. His sister, **Marie Caroline, Archduchess of Austria (1801-1832)** married Frederick Augustus, Crown Prince of Saxony, there was no issue from this marriage. His brother, **Franz Karl, Archduke of Austria (1802-1878)** married Princess Sophie of Bavaria and they had five children including Franz Joseph who succeeded his uncle as Emperor of Austria and Maximilian a future Emperor of Mexico. His sister, **Maria Anna, Archduchess of Austria (1738-1789)** was born in 1738 and died in in 1789. She was physically disabled with a fused spine and died unmarried and without issue.

Franz Joseph I, Emperor of Austria (1830-1916) reigned as Emperor from 1848 until his death. He married Elisabeth of Bavaria and they had four children including Rudolf, the crown Prince and heir to the throne. Rudolf predeceased his father in a renowned joint suicide with his mistress Baroness Mary Vetseva. Refused permission to marry, he shot his mistress and then himself at his hunting lodge at Mayerling. Mystery still surrounds this event and many believe they were murdered to stop any embarrassment to the throne. A motion picture was made starring Omar Sharif. Franz Joseph himself survived an assassination attempt in 1853 when he was attacked by an Hungarian nationalist who tried to stab him in the neck. His high collar, specifically designed for this sort of attack saved him from serious injury and his assailant was struck down.
His reign coincided with the beginning of the First World War. The sabre rattling that was part of European politics at that time was exacerbated by the assassination of his nephew Archduke Franz Ferdinand and his wife in Sarajevo. His brother,

Maximilian, Archduke of Austria, Prince Imperial of Hungary & Bohemia and later Maximilian I, Emperor of Mexico (1832-1867) was created Emperor of Mexico with the support of Napoleon III of France and several Mexican families. Although not formally recognized as Emperor by many other countries, he reigned for three years until arrested and executed by firing squad by Republicans. He married Princess Charlotte, daughter of King Leopold I of the Belgians but there was no issue from this marriage.

His brother, **Karl Ludwig, Archduke of Austria (1833-1896)** married three times, his first wife was Princess Margaretha of Saxony, there was no issue from this marriage. His second wife was Princess Maria Annunciate of Bourbon-Two Sicilies and they had four children including Franz Ferdinand who would be assassinated, together with his wife, by Gavrilo Princip in Sarajevo thereby instigating the First World War. His third wife was Infanta Maria Theresa of Portugal, this marriage produced two daughters. His brother, **Ludwig Victor, Archduke of Austria (1842-1919)**. He never married or had issue and despite doing his best to keep his homosexuality and transvestitism under cover he came out into the open after a brawl at a public bathhouse. He was sent away from Vienna and spent the rest of his long life doing philanthropic work and becoming a patron of the arts.

Karl Ludwig I, Emperor of Austria (1887-1922) succeeded his great uncle as Emperor and reigned from 1916 until 1918. At the end of the First World War his did not abdicate but, in his own words was 'withdrawing himself from state affairs'. He spent the rest of his life trying to restore the monarchy on the grounds that he did not abdicate. He married Princess Zita of Bourbon-Parma and they had eight children. Karl Ludwig was beatified by Pope John Paul II for his 'holiness in his political actions' and since then has been known as The Blessed Charles of Austria, this is the first step on the road to Sainthood.

Kingdom of Bavaria

Bavaria began as a small settlement that was elevated into a Duchy in the 500's as part of the Holy Roman Empire. It became an independent kingdom in 1806 when the Holy Roman Empire was abolished. It is now a state (Bundesland) of the Federal Republic of Germany. The first King of Bavaria had been the Elector of the Palatinate under the Holy Roman Empire and became its king when the Empire was dissolved.

House of Wittelsbach

Maximilian I Joseph, King of Bavaria (1756-1825) reigned as King of Bavaria from 1806 until his death. He had previously been Prince-Elector of Bavaria under the Holy Roman Emperor. He was the son of Count-Palatine Frederick Michael of Zweibrüken-Birkenfeld and his wife Maria Francisca of Sulzbach. He fond of walking through the streets of Munich, which was extensively enlarged and improved under his kingship, to talk to and meet his subjects. During one of these walkabout he led a rescue operation after a glassmakers workshop had collapsed and managed to pull out the glassmakers fourteen year old orphaned apprentice, Joseph von Fraunhofer. He directed the glassmaker to give Joseph time to study and provided books for him to read. Joseph was to go on and become one of the most famous optical scientists in history and invented the Spectroscope and spectroscopy.

Maximilian married twice, his first wife was Auguste Wilhelmine Marie of Hesse Darmstadt, they had five children including Ludwig who would succeed him as King. His second wife was Karoline Friederike Wilhelmine of Baden. They had eight children.

His brother, **Karl III August Christian, Duke of Zweibrüken** was born in 1746 and died in 1795. He married Maria Amalia of Saxony, daughter of Frederick Christian,

Elector of Saxony and Maria Antonia Walpurgis of Bavaria, daughter of Charles VII, Holy Roman Emperor. There was no issue from this marriage. His sister, **Maria Amalia Auguste of Bavaria (1752-1825)** married Frederick Augustus I, King of Saxony. They had four children of which only one survived into adulthood. Princess Maria Augusta who died unmarried and without issue aged 80. His sister, **Maria Anna of Bavaria (1753-1824)** married Duke Wilhelm of Bavaria and they had three children of which only two survived.

Ludwig I, King of Bavaria (1786-1868) reigned as king from 1825 until his abdication in 1848 following the revolutions in the German States. Ludwig had a great love or art and architecture and, of course, women. He rebuilt monasteries and initiated the building of the Ludwig Canal between the Rivers Main and Danube. The first German railway was also built during his reign. He married Therese of Saxe-Hildburghausen and had nine children of which eight survived into adulthood including Maximilian who succeeded his father.

He is famous for his liaisons with beautiful women including Lady Jane Digby an English eccentric and adventuress and the most famous of all, Lola Montez and whatever ever Lola wanted, Lola got, except the love of the Bavarian people. She actually did wear diamonds on the soles of her shoes. Lola was the unmaking of Ludwig and her excessive demands and spending together with the 1848 riots, he abdicated in favour of his son.

His sister, **Auguste Amalia Ludovika Georgia, Princess of Bavaria (1788-1851)** was originally promised in marriage to Charles, heir to the Grand Duchy of Baden but this was broken at the command of Emperor Napoleon I of France. She eventually married Eugène Beauharnais, only son of Josephine de Beauharnais, future wife of Napoleon Bonaparte, and her husband Alexander, viscomte de Beauharnais. Eugène was a stepson of Napoleon. Eugène and Auguste had a very happy marriage and had seven children including Josephine was married King Oscar I of Sweden, Auguste who married Queen Maria II of Portugal and Amélie who married Pedro I Brazil and became Empress of Brazil. His sister, **Caroline Auguste, Princess of Bavaria later Empress of Austria (1792-1873)** was born in 1792 and died in 1873. She married twice, her first husband was William I of Württemburg and her second was Francis I, the last Holy Roman Emperor. They was no issue from either marriage. His brother, **Karl Theodor Maximilian Augustus, Prince of Bavaria (1795-1875)** was a soldier and achieved the rank of Field Marshal. A brave but inept commander, he married twice morganatically so any issue had no right or claim to any Bavarian titles. His sister, **Elisabeth Ludovika, Princess of Bavaria and later Queen of Prussia (1801-1873)** married Frederick William IV, King of Prussia, there was no issue from this marriage. His sister, **Amalie Auguste, Princess of Bavaria and later Queen of Saxony (1801-1877)** was the twin of her sister Elisabeth Ludovika. She married King John I of Saxony and had nine children of which only six survived into adulthood including two sons who would become Kings of Saxony. His sister, **Sophie, Princess of Bavaria and later Archduchess of Austria (1805-1872)** married Franz Joseph I Archduke of Austria and they had six children including Franz Joseph who succeeded his father. Their son Maximilian was proclaimed Emperor of Mexico and ended his life in front of a firing squad. His sister, **Marie Anne Leopoldine Elizabeth Wilhelmine, Princess of Bavaria and later Queen of Saxony (1805-1877)** married Frederick Augustus II, King of Saxony. There was no issue from this marriage. His sister, **Marie Ludovika Wilhelmine, Princess of Bavaria (1808-1892)** married Maximilian Joseph Duke in Bavaria. They had ten children including Elisabeth who became Empress of Austria.

Maximilian II King of Bavaria (1811-1864) reigned as King from 1848 until his death. He was a great advocate of art and literature and a friend of Hans Christian Andersen. Always in bad health he was compelled to go abroad a lot and when he was home he would spend most of the time in the country. He married Marie Friederike Hedwig of Prussia and had two sons Ludwig and Otto who would both reign after him.

His sister, **Mathilde Karoline Friederike, Princess of Bavaria (1813-1862)** married Ludwig III, Grand Duke of Hesse and by Rhine. They had no issue. His brother, **Otto Friedrich Ludwig. Prince of Bavaria and later 1st King of Greece (1815-1867)** married Duchess Amalia of Oldenburg, there was no issue from this marriage. His brother, **Luitpold Karl Ludwig, Prince of Bavaria and Regent of Bavaria (1821-1912)** acted as Regent during the illnesses of his two nephews Ludwig and Otto when kings. He married Archduchess Augusta of Austria-Tuscany and had four children including Ludwig who would become King of Bavaria. His sister, **Adelgarde Auguste, Princess of Bavaria and later Duchess of Modena (1823-1914)** married Francis V, Duke of Modena and had one daughter that died in infancy. His sister, **Hildegard Luise Charlotte, Princess of Bavaria and later Archduchess of Austria and Duchess of Teschen (1825-1914)** married Archduke Albert of Austria and Duke of Teschen. They had three children. They were Maria Theresa who married Duke Philipp of Württemburg and they had five children, Karl, who died of smallpox when he was a year old and their tragic daughter Mathilde. She got ready for a visit to the theatre and put on a gauze dress for the occasion and just before leaving decided that she would like to smoke a cigarette, a habit forbidden by her father. As she was smoking, her father approached her and she quickly hid the cigarette behind her causing it to set light to her flimsy flammable dress. She died in front of her whole family from second and third degree burns aged only eighteen. His sister, **Alexandra Amalie, Princess of Bavaria (1826-1875)** died unmarried and without issue. His brother, **Adalbert Wilhelm Georg Ludwig, Prince of Bavaria (1828-1875)** was born in 1828 and died in 1875. He married the Infanta Amalia of Spain and had five children.

Ludwig II, King of Bavaria (1845-1886) reigned as king from 1864 until just before his death. He was variously called the 'Swan King' and the 'Fairy Tale King'. A great fan of Richard Wagner whom he would quote at various times. He is also famous for building extravagant and expensive castles like Schloss Neuschwanstein, a fairy-tale castle built on an Alpine crag that became the inspiration for Cinderella's Castle in Disneyland etc. He was engaged to his cousin Duchess Sophie Charlotte in Bavaria, a granddaughter of King Louis-Philippe of France. After repeated postponements of the wedding, Ludwig cancelled the engagement and never married or had issue. He is known to have had several close relationships with men and is believed to have had homosexual tendencies.

He was eventually deposed because of his unwillingness to cut back spending extravagantly and his disinterest in the governing and the financial state of Bavaria. He was thought to be mentally deficient and was placed in the control of Dr. Bernhard von Gudden one of the signatories of his deposition.

He was taken to Castle Berg near Lake Starmberg and technically imprisoned. One day, either the king or the doctor suggested a stroll by the lake, they went off without any attendants. Later that night after a gale and heavy rain their bodies were found drowned in a shallow part of the lake.

The cause of their death is still not known, maybe he was attacked by the doctor with the aim of relieving the state of his burden and was overcome by the struggle, or Ludwig decided to commit suicide and take his tormenter with him. He was succeeded by his only sibling, his brother Otto.

Otto, King of Bavaria (1848-1916) reigned as king from 1886 until 1913. He was always called melancholic, which then was a by-word for mental debility. His uncle Luitpold was once again called in to act as Prince Regent as Otto was incapable of ruling and actually thought that the Prince Regent was King!. When Luitpold died in 1912, his son Ludwig assumed the regency and with the government connivance assumed the crown in 1913. Otto died unmarried and without issue aged 68 of a bowel obstruction.

Ludwig III, King of Bavaria (1845-1921) reigned as king from 1913 until 1918 when Bavaria became part of the newly formed German republican government after the First World War. He married Maria Theresia of Austria-Este, his step-cousin and they had thirteen children The monarchy was dissolved in 1918.

Kingdom of Bulgaria

The Bulgarian people originated from people who lived on the steppes north of the Black Sea. They would renowned as fierce warriors and exceptional horsemen. In the 5th century AD the these people split into two separate groups with one heading westwards to the regions around the Danube. These people became members of the Kingdom of Bulgaria.

The monarchs of Bulgaria ruled from the beginning of the Bulgarian Empire in 681 until the monarchy was abolished in 1946. We will deal with its swansong period from 1878 until its end.

House of Battenburg

Alexander of Battenburg, Prince of Bulgaria (1857-1893) reigned as Prince of Bulgaria from 1879 until his forced abdication in 1886. He was the son of Prince Alexander of Hesse and by Rhine. He is also the nephew of Tsar Alexander II of Russia and it was the Tsar that recommended Alexander to the proposed principality vacancy. The vacancy was under the control of the Ottoman Empire. And not wanting to upset the Russian Tsar they agreed. As his reign progressed he was prompted to assume absolute power with the connivance of his Russian uncle. He was soon forced to abdicate and as a take over by the Russians seemed possible, the Ottomans offered the throne to a member of the House of Saxe-Coburg-Gotha. After his abdication, he married an Austrian actress and singer, Johanna Loisinger and had two children. He claimed the title Prince of Tarnovo and went into exile.

His sister, **Princess Marie of Battenburg (1852-1923)** married Gustav, Prince of Erbach-Schönberg and had four children including Alexander who succeeded his father to the title. His brother, **Prince Louis of Battenburg, 1st Marquis of Milford Haven (1854-1921)** joined the British Royal Navy at the age of 14 and rose through the ranks to become the First Sea

Lord.

During the First World War, the Royal Family and its adherents were advised to drop their German titles and adopt British ones because of the amount of anti-German feeling. King George V changed the family name from Saxe-Coburg-Gotha to Windsor and subsequently Prince Louis was given the title of Marquis of Milford Haven and changed his name from Battenburg to Mountbatten. He complained that at a stroke of a pen he was no longer a royal prince, but only an English lord. He married Princess Victoria of Hesse and by Rhine, a granddaughter of Queen Victoria and they had four children.

Alice, who was born in 1885 and died in 1969, married Prince Andrew of Greece and Denmark and was the mother of the Duke of Edinburgh, consort to Queen Elizabeth II of Great Britain. Louisa who was born in 1889 and died in 1965 married King Gustav VI Adolph of Sweden. George who was born in 1892 and died in 1938 married Countess Nadejela Mikhailovna de Torny. Their youngest son, Louis was born in 1900 and died in 1979. He married Edwina Ashley. His involvement in the Second World war was immense. He was the last Viceroy of India and was close to the Royal Family, especially the Prince of Wales. He was given the title Earl Mountbatten of Burma. He was an uncle to the Duke of Edinburgh and a second cousin of the Queen and probably because of this he was targeted by the Provisional Irish Republican Army and assassinated by bomb in 1979. His brother, **Prince Henry of Battenburg (1858-1896)** spent his career in the Army rising to the rank of Colonel. He became a member of the British Royal Family when he married Princess Beatrice, the youngest daughter of Queen Victoria. They had four children including Victoria Eugenie who married King Alfonso XIII of Spain. His brother, **Prince Francis Joseph of Battenburg (1861-1924)** proposed marriage to Consuelo Vanderbilt the daughter of William Vanderbilt the American Railroad Millionaire but was refused as she disliked him right from the start. She eventually married the 9th Duke of

Marlborough. He proposed to and was accepted by Princess Ana Petrovic-Njegos of Montenegro, there was no issue from this marriage.

House of Saxe-Coburg-Gotha

Ferdinand I, Prince of Bulgaria and later Tsar of Bulgaria (1861-1948) reigned as Prince from 1887 until independence of Bulgaria and assumed the title of Tsar until his abdication in 1918. He was the son of Prince August of Saxe-Coburg-Gotha and a first cousin of Queen Victoria. Although thought to be rather ineffective he is said to have made quite a success of his reign. He married twice, his first wife was Princess Maria Louise of Bourbon-Palma. They had four children including Boris who succeeded his father. His second wife was Eleonore Reuss, there were no children from this marriage.

Bulgaria was one of the countries that attacked Serbia following the assassination of Archduke Franz Ferdinand and instigated the First World War and afterwards Ferdinand abdicated in favour of his son to save the monarchy.

His brother, **Philipp, Prince of Saxe-Coburg-Gotha (1844-1921)** joined the Hungarian Army as a Major and was married to Princess Louise of Belgium. They had two children. His brother, **Ludwig August, Prince of Saxe-Coburg-Gotha and a Duke in Saxony (1845-1907)** was an Imperial Brazilian Admiral. He married Princess Leopoldina of Brazil, the daughter of Emperor Pedro II of Brazil and they had four children. His sister, **Clotilde, Princess of Saxe-Coburg-Gotha (1846-1927)** married Archduke Joseph Karl of Austria and had seven children of which only three survived into adulthood.

His sister, **Amalia, Princess of Saxe-Coburg-Gotha (1848-1894)** married Maximilian Emanuel, Duke of Bavaria and had three children.

Boris III, Tsar of Bulgaria (1894-1943) as Tsar from 1918 until his death, He ascended the throne following the abdication of his father. During the Second World War Bulgaria was neutral with, perhaps, a leaning towards Nazi Germany. Hitler got more and more frustrated with Boris because he would not declare war on the Soviet Union or deport Bulgarian Jews to Labour Camps. He died after returning from a visit to Hitler propagating a rumour that he was poisoned on Hitler's orders because of his refusal to follow Hitler's advice.

He married Princess Giovanna, daughter of King Victor Emmanuel III of Italy and they had two children including Simeon who succeeded his father.

His brother, **Kiril Prince-Regent of Bulgaria, Prince of Prelav (1895-1945)**. As Simeon was just a child when he ascended the throne, Kiril assumed the regency and was under continual pressure from Nazi Germany to do what Boris had refused to do and declare war on the Soviet Union. Kiril only went as far as letting the Germans use their railway system and station troops on the Bulgaria/Soviet border. This was enough for the Soviet Union and accepted these actions as an act of aggression and invaded Bulgaria in 1944. The Soviet Union backed a military coup in 1945 which ended with Kiril and his cabinet members being sentenced to death and executed. Kiril never married or had issue. His sister, **Eudoxia, Princess of Bulgaria (1898-1985)** was arrested and tortured following the 1945 military coup but was released and went to live in Germany. She never married or had issue. His sister, **Nadezhda, Princess of Bulgaria (1899-1958)** was born in 1899 and died in 1958. She married Duke Albrecht Eugen of Württemburg and had five children.

Simeon II Tsar of Bulgaria later Simeon Saxe-Coburg-Gotha (1937-) ascended the throne aged 6 years. He reigned until 1946 when a plebiscite was taken and it was decided that Bulgaria should become a Soviet established republic and the monarchy was abolished. Simeon never signed an abdication papers so he considers himself a 'monarch in exile' and has spent the years since as a businessman and financial adviser. Now aged 76 he lives in semi-retirement. He married Margareta Gomez-Acebo y Cejeula and they have five children. His sister, **Princess Maria Louise of Bulgaria (193)** was born in 1933 and married twice. Her first husband was Prince Karl of Leiningen and they had two sons. Her second husband was Bronislaw Tomasz Andvzej Chrobot. They had two children. The monarchy was abolished.

Kingdom of France

The history of the **Kingdom of France** is a long and illustrious one. The most renowned king was Clovis. He was born in 466 and died in 511. He reigned as King of the Franks from 509 until his death. He was the first King of the Franks to unite all the Frankish tribes under one ruler and set the template for what would become France. I have started this list with Philip Augustus as he was the first to call himself King of France.

House of Capet

Philip II Augustus, King of France (1165-1223) was the monarch to style himself as King of France. The Kingdom of France originated as West Francia, the western part of the Carolingian Empire. He reigned as King of France from 1180 until his death. Philip was the son of King Louis VII and his third wife Adela of Champagne. He was successful in expanding the land owned directly by the crown as well as raising the influence of the monarchy. He broke up the powerful Angevin Empire and reorganized the government as well as increasing the prosperity of the country. He married three times, his first wife was Isabella of Hainault, and she gave birth to a son Louis who succeed his father. His other issue, twins, died at birth. His second wife was Ingebord of Denmark there was no issue from this marriage as Philip strove to annul it. His third wife was Agnes of Merania with whom he had a son and daughter.

His sister, **Marie of France (1148-1198)** was the daughter of King Louis VII of France and his first wife, Eleanor of Aquitaine. She married Henry I Count of Champagne and had issue including Marie who married Baldwin I of Constantinople and bore the title Empress of Constantinople. His sister, **Alix of France (1151-1197)** married Theobald, Count of Blois. They had seven children. His sister, **Margaret of**

France (1158-1197) was born in 1158 and died in 1197. She married twice, her first husband was Henry, the Young King of England, son of King Henry II of England. There was no issue from this marriage. Her second husband was Bela III, King of Hungary. There was also no issue from this marriage. His sister, **Alys of France (1160-1220)**. Although for a time engaged to King Richard I of England, she married William IV, Count of Ponthieu. They had a daughter. His sister, **Agnes of France (1171-1204)** three times, her first husband was Alexios II Komnenos with no issue, her second husband was Andronicus I Komnenos, Byzantine Emperor. There was no issue from this marriage. Her last husband was Theodore Branas. They had issue.

Louis VIII 'the Lion', King of France (1187-1226) reigned as king from 1223 until 1226. His rule was only three years long but it was quite eventful. When he ascended the throne he still continued to seek revenge on the Angevin rulers of England because when he was Prince Louis, he was asked by the rebelling English nobles and barons to come to England and take the throne from King John of England who was involved in the First Barons War with them. He landed with a substantial force and soon occupied London. Unfortunately John died and the baron's preferred his son, an English born king to rule, so the nine year old boy was crowned King Henry III of England. Louis remonstrated for a while but with 10,000 crowns in his pocket he withdrew back to France with a promise not to seek the English crown again. But the rebuttal was still a thorn in his side.

He married, at the age of twelve, Blanche of Castile, the daughter of Alfonso VIII King of Castile and Eleanor of England, daughter of King Henry II of England and Queen Eleanor of Aquitaine. They had thirteen children of which only six survived into adulthood including Louis who succeeded his father.

His sister, **Marie of France (1198-1238)** was born in 1198 and died in 1238. She was betrothed twice before she actually married anyone. Her first betrothal was to Prince Alexander Stewart, the future King Alexander II of Scotland. They were both only two years old and the betrothal was discarded when it was deemed more advantageous for Alexander to marry Joan, daughter of King John of England. Her second proposal was also scuppered by King John. She was destined to marry Arthur I, Duke of Brittany, son of Geoffrey of Brittany, son of King Henry II and older brother of John.

Although King Richard the Lion-Heart had designated Arthur his heir he changed his mind on his deathbed and chose John to reign after him. John still worried about the possibility of Arthur taking the crown from him had the 16 year old murdered, some say he was slain by John's own hand in a fit of anger. Whatever happened this ended any chance of betrothal. She finally married Philip, Count of Namur who had been imprisoned during a war with France and bought his freedom by marrying Marie. There was no issue from this marriage.

Her second marriage was to Henry I, Duke of Brabant, this marriage was probably the only one she had any choice in. They had two daughters, Marie who died young and Elizabeth who married twice, firstly Count Dietrich of Cleves and following his death, Gerhard II, Count of Wassenberg.

His brother, **Philip of France (1200-1235)** married Matilda II Countess of Boulogne. He became, by right of his wife, Count of Boulogne, Count of Mortain, Count of Aumale and Count of Dammartin. The couple had two children, a son, Alberic and a daughter Joan.

Louis IX 'the Saint', King of France (1214-1270) was born in 1214 and died in 1270. He was the son of King Louis VIII of France and his wife Blanche of Castile. He was a devout religious king and went on two crusades, the seventh and the eighth. He was also a great patron of the arts and built Sainte-

Chapelle in Paris to house what he believed to be the Holy Crown of Thorns and a fragment of the True Cross.

He married Margaret of Provence, the daughter of Alfonso II, Count of Provence and his wife Gersende II de Sabran Countess of Forcalquier. They had eleven children of which only nine survived to adulthood including Philip who succeeded him. He died during the eighth crusade while at Turin. He was canonized by Pope Boniface VIII in 1297. He is the only French monarch to achieve sainthood.

His brother, **Robert I called 'the Good' Count of Artois (1216-1250)** married Matilda of Brabant, daughter of Henry II, Duke of Brabant and his wife Marie of Hohenstaufen. They had two children, a daughter Blanche who married twice, her first husband was Henry I of Navarre and had one surviving daughter Joan, their son Theobald fell to his death from the battlements of the castle at Estella. Joan married King Philip IV of France.

His brother, **Alphonse, Count of Toulouse & Poitiers (1220-1270)** married Joan of Toulouse, daughter of Raymond VII, Count of Toulouse. There were no children from this marriage.

His sister, **St Isabella of France (1225-1270)** refused the hand of Hugh X, Count of Lusignan and Conrad IV of Germany and founded the monastery of the Poor Ladies of St Clare of Assisi at a site give to her by her brother in the Forest of Rouvray now called the Bois de Boulogne. She died unmarried and without issue.

His brother, **Charles of France, King of Naples and King of Sicily (1226-1285)** his brothers in the seventh crusade and returned in 1250. He married twice, his first wife was Beatrice of Provence, daughter of Raymond Berenguer IV Count of Provence and his wife Beatrice of Savoy. They had seven children. His second wife was Margaret of Burgundy. There was no issue from this marriage.

Philip III the Bold, King of France (1245-1285) as King of France from 1270 until his death. He increased the size of the Crown Lands of France by acquiring many territories including the County of Toulouse. He also accompanied his father on the Eighth Crusade in 1270 and ascended the throne the same year following his fathers death in Tunis.

He married twice, his first wife was Isabella of Aragon, the daughter of King James I of Aragon and Yolande of Hungary, daughter of King Andrew II of Hungary. They had five children of which three survived. Their second son, Philip succeeded his father on the throne. His second wife was Maria of Brabant, daughter of Henry III, Duke of Brabant and his wife Adelaide of Burgundy. They had three children, their youngest daughter, Margaret, went on to marry King Edward I of England and became his second wife.

His sister, **Isabella of France (1241-1271)** married Theobald II, King of Navarre because her father wished to make peace with the Kingdom of Navarre, Theobald was eighteen years old and Isabella was thirteen. There was no issue from this marriage and Isabella is believed to have died in childbirth. Before he ascended the throne, Theobald was Count of Champagne and Brie, which to me is a very civilized luncheon. His brother, **Louis of France (1244-1260)** was born in 1244 and died in 1260 He died after a short illness aged 15 and was unmarried and without issue. His brother, **John Tristan, Count of Valois (1250-1270)**. His father had wanted John to enter the Dominican Order but John resisted this successfully and married Yolande II. Countess of Nevers. He was Count of Valois and Count of Crépy in the gift of his father and Count of Nevers, Auxerre and Tonnerre in the right of his wife. There was no issue from this marriage and John died of dysentery while on the Eighth Crusade. His brother, **Peter I, Count of Alençon (1251-1284)** married Joanne de Châtillon. There was no issue from this marriage. He died fighting for his uncle, Charles I of Anjou.

His sister, **Blanche of France (1253-1323)** married Ferdinand de la Cerda, Infante of Castile, and had two children. She died in the Cordeliers Convent in Paris after her son's right to the Castilian throne was usurped by an uncle. His sister, **Margaret of France (1254-1271)** was born in 1254 and died in 1271 She was betrothed to Henry IV, Duke of Brabant but this was cancelled owing to Henry's imbecility. After Henry was disposed, she married his brother John I, Duke of Brabant. Margaret died in childbirth and the child a few days later. His brother, **Robert, Count of Clermont (1256-1317)** married Beatrice of Burgundy and had six children including his son Louis, the first Duke of Bourbon. During his first joust in 1279, he suffered head injuries that caused him to remain an invalid for the rest of his life.

His sister, **Agnes of France (1260-1327)** married Robert II, Duke of Burgundy and had eleven children of which eight survived until adulthood, including two Dukes of Burgundy and a daughter, Margaret, who married King Louis X of France.

Philip IV 'the Fair' King of France (1268-1314) reigned as King of France from 1285 until his death. Relying entirely on advisors and civil servants he transformed France from a feudal to a centralized country. He is also best known as the King who destroyed the Knights Templar and having their Grand Master, Jacques De Molay burnt at the stake for heresy. He said that they were guilty of committing abominable and other vile practices. I believe the real reason was that he was heavily in debt to the Templar's and was envious of their immense wealth. He married Joan of Navarre and also became King of Navarre and Count of Champagne. They had four children including three sons who became Kings of France and a daughter, Isabella who married King Edward II of England. She was known as 'The She-Wolf of France'

His brother, **Louis of France (1265-1276)** died aged 12 or 13 and is believed to have been poisoned by his Step-Mother,

Maria of Brabant. His brother, **Charles of Valois (1270-1325)** married three times, his first wife was Margaret, Countess of Anjou, the daughter of King Charles II of Naples and became Count of Anjou in the right of his wife. They had six children including Philip of Valois destined to become the first Valois King of France. His second wife was Catherine I of Courtney, titular Empress of Constantinople. They had four children. His third marriage was to Mahaut of Châtillon, they also had four children and one, Blanche would marry Charles IV, Holy Roman Emperor. His brother, **Louis, Count of Evreux (1276-1319)** Margaret of Artois. They had five children including a daughter Joan, who married Charles IV, Holy Roman Emperor. His sister, **Blanche of France (1278-1305)** had four betrothals before her actual marriage. Her first betrothal was to John I, Marquis of Namur, her second betrothal was to Edward, Prince of Wales, the future King Edward II of England. Her third betrothal was to his father, King Edward I who tried to take her from his son because of her renowned beauty. He married her sister instead. Her fourth betrothal was to John II, Count of Holland. All the above proposals were most likely diplomatic machinations. She eventually married Rudolph I, Duke of Austria. They had no surviving issue. His sister, **Margaret of France (1279-1318)** was born in 1279 and died in 1318. She married King Edward I of England as his second wife. They had three children.

Louis X 'the Quarreller' King of France (1289-1316) reigned as King of France from 1314 until 1316. He was a great proponent of all men are born free and decided that the serfs could take their freedom on the payment of a designated amount of money. He married twice, his first wife was Margaret of Burgundy, and they had one daughter Joan who was born in 1312 and died in 1349. She married King Philip III of Navarre and had seven children including Marie who married King Peter IV of Aragon and Blanche who married King Philip VI of

France. His second wife was Clementia of Hungary who gave birth to Louis' successor, John, whose reign lasted just a few months until he was usurped by his uncle Philip.

Louis was also a keen player of jeu de paume or real tennis. He even built the first indoor court as he disliked player the game outside. It was after a lengthy and exhausting game that Louis drank a large amount of cooled wine and died later of pneumonia or pleurisy.

His brother, **Philip later King Philip V of France (1293-1322)** married Joan II, Countess of Burgundy. They had four children. His brother, **Charles, later King Charles IV of France (1267-1328)** married Blanche of Burgundy. They had one daughter. His sister, **Isabella of France, often called 'The She-Wolf of France' (1295-1358)** was born in 1295 and died in 1358 In 1308 she married King Edward II of England and had issue including Edward who would succeed his father. His brother, **Charles IV** was the last Capetian King of France. The next kings were from the House of Valois.

House of Valois

Philip VI 'the Fortunate' King of France (1293-1350) reigned as King of France from 1328 until his death. He was the son of Charles, Count of Valois and his wife Margaret of Anjou and a grandson of King Philip III of France. He married twice, his first wife was Joan of Burgundy, daughter of Robert II, Duke of Burgundy. They had two children, John who succeeded his father and Philip of Valois, Duke of Orléans. His second wife was Blanche of Navarre and they had one daughter Joan who died on her way to her wedding and was therefore unmarried and childless at her death.

His sister, **Isabelle of Valois (1292-1309)** married John III, Duke of Brittany. There was no known issue. His sister, **Joan of Valois (1294-1342)** was born in 1294 and died in 1342. She married William I, Count of Hainault and had eight children of which five attained adulthood. Their daughter Philippa of Hainault married King Edward III of England as was mother to Edward the Black Prince. She also begged her husband to have mercy on the Burghers of Calais after he besieged the town, as depicted by the famous statuary in Calais by Auguste Rodin. His sister, **Margaret of Valois (1295-1342)** was born in 1295 and died in 1342. She married Guy I, Count of Blois-Châtillon and had three children. His brother, **Charles II, Count of Alençon (1297-1346)** married twice, his first wife was Jeanne de Joigny, there was no issue from this marriage. His second wife was Maria de La Cerda y Lara, they had five children. He died at the Battle of Crecy. His sister, **Catherine of Valois (1303-1346)** married Philip Prince of Taranto and Emperor of Constantinople. They had five children. His sister, **Joan of Valois (1304-1363)** was born in 1304 and died in 1363. She married Robert III, Count of Artois, they had five children of which only two survived to adulthood. His sister, **Isabella of Valois (1305-1349)** was born in 1305 and died in 1349. She became a nun and eventually Abbess of Fontrevault and died unmarried and without issue. His sister, **Marie of Valois (1309-1332)** married Charles, Duke of Calabria at the age of fourteen. She was his second wife. There was no issue from his first marriage. His second marriage to Marie produced five children, the first at sixteen years of age. She endeared herself to the lesser nobles of Florence when she was able to persuade her husband to allow the genteel woman to wear clothes that they could afford and not to try and keep up appearance with wealthier women of court. Marie died aged 23. His sister, **Isabella of Valois (1313-1348)** married Peter I, Duke of Bourbon and had eight children, including Jeanne of Bourbon who married King Charles V of France and was mother of King Charles VI of France. His sister, **Blanche of Valois (1317-1348)** married Charles IV, Holy Roman Emperor and gave birth to two children.

John II 'the Good' King of France (1319-1364) reigned as King of France from 1350 until his death. John was King when the Hundred Years War flared up again. Edward, the Black Prince had taken his army on a great chevauchée which is a horse charge through the countryside, raiding, pillaging, burning and causing great havoc, which is aimed to re stock supplies and to unnerve the enemy. John chased after them and the two armies met a couple of miles from Poitiers. John had 19 of his knight dress exactly like him to confuse the enemy and after failing peace talks the to sides clashed. John was captured by a French exile, Denis de Morbecque, who recognised him after his helmet was dislodged. He was taken to the Black Prince and eventually removed to England and lodged in the Tower.

His ransom was set by Treaty at 3 million crowns and John, leaving his son Louis as hostage with the English left for France to raise the money. Louis, thinking he was helping escaped from the Tower but to the dismay of his people and for the sake of 'good faith and honour' John returned to England to take up his part as hostage and he was welcomed back by cheering crowds. His incarceration was not a unhappy one and he was very well looked after and treated as the King he was. He died in 1364 in the Savoy Palace. He body was returned to France and interred at Saint Denis Basilica.

He married twice, his first wife was Bonne of Bohemia, daughter of King John I (the Blind) of Bohemia. They had nine children of which seven survived to adulthood including Charles who would succeed his father. His second wife was Joan I , Countess of Auvergne, they had no surviving issue.

His brother, **Philip of Valois, Duke of Orléans (1336-1376)** married Blanche of France, daughter of King Charles IV of France. There was no issue from this marriage.

Charles V 'the Wise' King of France (1338-1380) reigned as King of France from 1364 until his death. As a young prince, he was given the province of Dauphiné to rule. This meant that he could use the title Dauphin until he ascended the throne when the Dauphiné was absorbed into the Crown Lands of France. Since then every male heir-apparent carried the title Dauphin until their coronation.

He was Regent during his father John's imprisonment in England and had the odious task of raising the enormous ransom asked. He had to do this by raising heavy taxes and other ways that all but depleted the treasury. When he came to the throne, through skilful management, he soon was back in the black. He married Joan of Bourbon, daughter of Peter I, Duke of Bourbon and Isabella of Valois. They had nine children of which only three survived into adulthood including John and Charles, two future Kings of France.

His brother, **Louis of Valois, Duke of Anjou (1339-1384)** married Marie of Blois, daughter of Charles, Duke of Brittany and his wife Joanna of Dreux. They had three children. His brother, **John, Duke of Berry (1340-1416)** married twice, his first wife was Joan of Armagnac and had issue. His second wife was Joan II, Countess of Auvergne. This marriage produced no children. His brother, **Philip II of Valois, Duke of Burgundy (1342-1404)** married Margaret III, Countess of Flanders. They had nine children of which only six survived into adulthood. His sister, **Joan of Valois (1343-1373)** married Charles II, 'the Bad', King of Navarre and issue including Joanna of Navarre who married King Henry IV of England. They had no issue. His sister, **Marie of Valois (1344-1404)** married Robert I, Duke of Bar and had issue. Two of their sons died at the Battle of Agincourt. His sister, **Isabelle of Valois 1348-1382)** married Gian Galeazzo Visconti, Duke of Milan and had issue.

Charles VI 'the Mad' King of France (1368-1422) reigned as King of France from 1380 until his death. He married Isabeau of Bavaria and had twelve children of which only eight survived to adulthood. Charles descended gradually into madness until at one point the believed he was made of glass and would shatter if touched. It was this king who after the Battle of Agincourt made King Henry V of England his heir and gave his daughter Catherine of Valois in marriage to him. His son Charles, the Dauphin did succeed him.

His brother, **Louis I, Duke of Orléans (1372-1407)** married Valentia Visconti and had nine children of which five survived to adulthood including Charles who was the father of King Louis XII of France and John, Count of Angoulême, grandfather of King Francis I of France. Louis acted as regent for his increasing ill brother and it was his continued disagreement with the Kings cousin, John 'the Fearless', Duke of Burgundy over who should oversee the upbringing of the Kings children that led John to instigate Louis' murder in the streets of Paris. A group of 15 armed men attacked Louis and his supporters and stabbed him to death.

Charles VII, King of France (1403-1461) reigned as King of France from 1422 until his death. The story of him being assisted to the throne with the aid of St. Joan of Arc is well-known and not for here. He married his second cousin Marie of Anjou and they had fourteen children of which seven survived into adulthood including a son Louis who succeeded his father.

His sister, **Isabella of Valois (1389-1409)** married twice, her first husband was King Richard II of England, there was no issue from this marriage. After Richard's suspicious death, King Henry IV of England wanted her to marry his son Prince Hal, the future Henry V, she refused and went back into mourning. Henry then let her return to France where she married her second husband, Charles, Duke of Orléans and a daughter was born from this marriage.

His sister, **Joan of Valois (1391-1433)** married John IV, Duke of Brittany and they had seven children of which only four survived into adulthood. His sister, **Mary of Valois (1393-1438)** became a nun and eventually Prioress of the Convent of Poissy. His sister, **Michelle of Valois (1395-1422)** married

Philip the Good, Duke of Burgundy. There was no surviving issue from this marriage. His sister, **Catherine of Valois (1401-1438)** married twice, her first marriage was to King Henry V of England and gave birth to the future King Henry VI of England. Her second marriage was to Owen Tudor and had two sons, Edmund and Jasper. And it is through their son Edmund that Owen Tudor's grandson became King Henry VII of England and began the Tudor Dynasty.

Louis XI called 'the Prudent, the Cunning, the Universal Spider, King of France (1423-1483) reigned as King of France from 1461 until his death. As Dauphin of France he openly rebelled against his father but as with all Royal parents he forgave his son and presented him with the province of Dauphiné to rule. His continued acts of intrigue and his intense diplomatic machinations earned him, amongst others, the soubriquet *l'universelle aragne*, the Universal Spider, for his web spinning of plots and conspiracies

He married twice, his first wife was Margaret of Scotland, daughter of King James I of Scotland and his wife Joan Beaufort. There were no issue from this marriage. His second wife was Charlotte of Savoy daughter of Louis, Duke of Savoy and his wife Anne of Cyprus. Charlotte was only nine years old when she married her twenty-seven year old husband and it was advice of doctors that the marriage not be consummated for a while. The marriage was not consummated until she was fourteen and she went on to have eight children of which only three survived into adulthood including Charles who would succeed his father.

His sister, **Catherine of Valois (1428-1446)** married Charles the Bold, Duke of Burgundy. There was no issue from this marriage. His sister, **Yolande of Valois (1434-1478)** was born in 1434 and died in 1478. She married Amadeus, Duke of Savoy. They had ten children of which only three survived to adulthood. His sister, **Joan of Valois (1435-1482)** married John

II, Duke of Bourbon. There was no issue from this marriage. His sister, **Magdalena of Valois (1443-1495)** married Gaston of Foix, Prince of Viana and had issue.

Charles VIII the Affable, King of France (1470-1498) reigned as King of France from 1483 until his death. He married Anne, Duchess of Brittany while she had been married by proxy to Maximilian I, Holy Roman Emperor and as he was involved elsewhere he did not pursue his claim of Anne. The was advantageous to Charles as it brought Brittany into French hands and stopped France being completely surrounded by Hapsburg lands. There were four children from the marriage but none survived into adulthood.

His sister, **Anne of France (1461-1522)** married Peter II, Duke of Bourbon and had one daughter Suzanne. His sister, **Joan of France (1464-1505)** was born in 1464 and died in 1505. She was briefly married to King Louis XII of France. Following the annulment of this marriage, she spent the rest of her life dedicated to the Catholic Church and was canonized after her death.

Louis XII, called 'the Father of his People' King of France (1462-1515) reigned as Orléans King of France from 1498 until his death. He was a cousin of the preceding monarch who died without a living heir and he was also a great grandson of King Charles V of France. He married, prior to ascending the throne, under duress from the bride's father, Joan of France, the daughter King Louis XI of France and his wife Anne of France. There was no issue from this marriage.

When Louis ascended the throne he had the marriage to Joan annulled so he could marry the late King's widow Anne of Brittany. Joan, highly religious and a devotee of the Virgin Mary since childhood, founded the Order of Sisters of the Annunciation and was canonized by Pope Pius XII in 1950.

Louis married Anne of Brittany, former Queen Consort

to Louis VIII of France and they had nine children of which only two survived including Claude of France who married King Francis I of France.

His sister, **Joan of Valois (1409-1432)** married John II, Duke of Alençon, there was no issue from this marriage.

His sister, **Marie D'Orléans (1457-1493)** married Jean de Foix, Viscount of Nabonne. They had two children.

His sister, **Anne D'Orléans (1464-1491)** became a nun and later Abbess of Fontrevault.

House of Orléans-Angoulême

Francis I, King of France (1494-1547) reigned as King of France from 1515 until his death. Francis was a great and generous patron of the arts and kick-started the French Renaissance by inviting many Italian artists to his court in Paris including Leonard Da Vinci who brought the Mona Lisa with him and apparently Francis hung the now famous painting in his bathroom. He helped develop and advance a standardization of the French language and for this he was called the Father and Restorer of Letters. He also entertained King Henry VIII of England at the Field of the Cloth of Gold and bested him in wrestling[12], much to Henry's chagrin and annoyance.

He married twice, his first wife was his second cousin, Claude, Duchess of Brittany. They had seven children including Henry who succeeded his father and Madeleine who married King James V of Scotland. His second wife was Eleanor of Austria, there was no issue from this marriage.

His sister, **Marguerite d'Angoulême (1492-1549)** married twice, her first husband was Charles IV, Duke of Alençon. There was no issue from this marriage. Her second husband was Henry II, King of Navarre. They had two children.

---

[12] This is now thought to have been apocryphal.

Henry II, King of France (1519-1559) reigned as King of France from 1547 until his death. He introduced the idea of inventors protecting their inventions with a patent specification.

He married Catherine de'Medici and they had ten children including three sons who would become Kings of France. Henry, a great participant of jousting to celebrate the marriage of his daughter Elisabeth to King Philip II of Spain, received a mortal wound when a splinter of the lance of his opponent, Gilbert, Count of Montgomery, captain of the Kings Scottish Guards entered his visor. It was this accident and Henry's death that was a great factor in ending jousting as a sport.

His sister, **Madeleine of France (1520-1537)** married aged 16, King James V of Scotland. Her health deteriorated on the journey back to Scotland after the wedding. In June, her husband wrote to her father to tell him how much better she was feeling, but in July, just six months after her marriage and a month before her seventeenth birthday she died. There were no issue from this marriage. His brother, **Charles, Duke of Orléans (1522-1545)** died of the plague unmarried and without issue. His sister, **Margaret, Duchess of Berry (1523-1574)** was betrothed to Philip II of Spain but it came to nothing. At the age of 35 she married Emmanuel Philibert, Duke of Savoy. They had one son who succeeded his father to the Dukedom

Francis II, King of France and King Consort of Scots (1544-1560) reigned as King of France from 1559 until his death. He married Mary, Queen of Scots, there was no issue from this marriage.

His sister, **Elizabeth of France (1545-1568)** married **Philip II, King of Spain** at the age of fourteen. Philip was so captivated with her that he gave up his mistress and devoted himself to Elizabeth. They had two daughters. She died giving birth to an infant daughter, the child also died. Elizabeth was 23 years old. His sister, **Claude of France (1547-1575)** married

Charles III, Duke of Lorraine and had nine children of which only eight survived into adulthood. His brother, **Charles IX King of France (1550-1574)** reigned as King of France from 1560 until his death. He married Princess Elizabeth of Austria. They had one daughter. He had no legitimate male heirs and was succeeded by his brother Henry. His brother, **Henry III, King of France (1551-1589)** reigned as King of France from 1574 until his death. Despite many rumours of homosexuality with his courtiers, he married Louise of Lorraine. There was no issue from this marriage. Henry was assassinated by a monk named Jacques Clément who had gained access to him saying he had a secret message. He stabbed him in the stomach and was cut down on the spot. Henry nominated Henry of Navarre as his successor. His sister, **Margaret of France (1553-1615)** married King Henry IV of France. As the marriage was childless and because of his need for an heir, he had already sired illegitimate sons, they divorced and Henry married Marie de'Medici and had issue. His brother, **Hercules Francois de France, Duke of Anjou (1555-1584)** never married but was one of the only suitors of Queen Elizabeth I of England to court her in person. and had no issue.

House of Bourbon

Henry IV, King of France, Henry III King of Navarre, Good King Henry, the Green Gallant (1553-1610) was the grand-nephew of France I. He reigned as King of France from 1589 until his death. Henry de Bourbon was the son of Queen Jeanne of Navarre and King Antoine. He was baptized a Catholic but raised as a Protestant by his mother who had decided that Calvinism would be the state religion of Navarre. In his teens Henry fought with the Huguenot forces in the French Wars of Religion. Before she died his mother arranged for Henry to marry Margaret of Valois, the daughter of Henry II of France and his wife Catherine de'Medici. They married in a room over a porch in the Notre Dame Cathedral and just six days after the wedding, the St. Bartholomew's Day's Massacre began.

Several thousand Protestants were massacred by Roman Catholic hordes, many of the guests whom came for the wedding were also killed. Henry only escaped death because of his wife. It is believed that the massacre was instigated by his mother-in-law, Catherine de'Medici. His marriage to Margaret was not a very happy one and also childless. Henry in need of an heir finally annulled his marriage to Margaret and married Marie de'Medici. His reign was a time of great changes in France, changes to the state finances, agriculture and reclaiming of land by draining swamps. He had great feeling for his people and did his best to improve their lot. He is renowned for the saying 'a chicken in every pot'. Although he was well-liked he was the victim of at least two assassination attempts. Unfortunately the last attempt was successful and he was stabbed by François Ravaillac. They had six children including Louis who would succeed him.

His sister, **Catherine de Bourbon, Duchess of Albret and Countess of Armagnac (1559-1604)** married Henry II, Duke of Lorraine. There was no issue from this marriage.

Louis XIII, 'the Just' King of France (1601-1643) reigned as King of France from 1610 until his death. Louis was a reticent and suspicious person, and it may have been because it was reported that he had a speech impediment. He relied a lot on his Prime Minister, Cardinal Richelieu. He married Anne of Austria, daughter of Philip III of Spain and his with Margaret of Austria. They had six children of which only two survived into adulthood including Louis, who would succeeded his father. Here there is a link with the famous Man in the Iron Mask. A man was detained at Dunkirk in 1669 and conveyed to the fortress prison of Pignarol under the guardianship of Captain St Mars. He was not allowed to speak to anyone and St mars was ordered that if the masked man was to speak of anything other than his daily needs he was to be killed. Why was this man imprisoned for the rest of his life, what was his crime. There are many suggestions and the story by Alexandre Dumas that claims he was the brother of Louis XIV. Here's my opinion, Louis XIII was estranged for a long time from his wife and only met once in 15 years when Louis had to shelter at his wife house during a thunderstorm. It was after this brief encounter that it was announced that Anne was pregnant and eventually gave birth to the future Louis XIV.

The man arrested at Dunkirk was Eustache D'Auger de Cavoye, son of Louis de Cavoye a very close friend of Louis XIII. It was suggested that Louis XIV was actually Louis de Cavoye's child and that de Cavoye's natural son, Eustache was almost the exact image of Louis XIV that he was masked and locked away. He wore a black velvet mask actually, the iron mask was Dumas' invention

His sister, **Elisabeth of France (1602-1644)** married King Philip IV of Spain. They had issue including Infanta Marie Theresa who married Louis XIV of France. His sister, **Christine Marie of France (1606-1663)** married Victor Amadeus I, Duke of Savoy. They had eight children of which only four survived into adulthood. His brother, **Gaston, Duke of Orléans (1608-1660)** married twice, his first wife was Marie de Bourbon, Duchess of Montpensier. They had one daughter, but Marie died six days after giving birth. His second wife was Marguerite of Lorraine. They had issue. His sister, **Henrietta Maria of France (1609-1669)** married King Charles I of England, Scotland & Ireland. They had nine children of which only four survived into adulthood including Charles who eventually succeeded his father after the Interregnum and James who became James II.

Louis XIV 'the Sun King' King of France (1638-1715) he reigned as King of France from 1643 until his death. Louis came to the throne aged five and with his mother, Queen Anne as

Regent ably assisted by Cardinal Mazarin. He was a great patron of the arts and turned what was once a hunting lodge in the magnificent Palace of Versailles. Here Louis ruled as the Sun King. He married Maria Theresa of Spain and they had six children of which one survived to adulthood. This was Louis who would become the father of the next King of France. Louis XIV died of gangrene aged 76.

His brother, **Philippe I, Duke of Orléans (1640-1701)** married twice, his first wife was Princess Henrietta of England daughter of King Charles I and his wife Henrietta Marie. They had four children. His second wife was Elizabeth Charlotte of the Palatinate. They had three children.

Louis XV, 'the Well-beloved' King of France (1710-1774) reigned as King of France from 1715 until his death. Louis was the son of Louis, Dauphin of France and Marie Adélaïde of Savoy. He was the great-grandson of King Louis XIV, his father and grandfather, predeceased the King. He was betrothed to his first cousin, Infanta Maria Anna Victoria of Spain, the three year old daughter of King Philip V of Spain. It was decided that the Infanta was too young for the eleven year old Louis and that it would be a very long time before she could produce children.

Louis than married Marie Leszczyńska, daughter of the King of Poland. They had eleven children of which only seven survived until adulthood including Louis, the Dauphin of France. Louis XV's most famous mistress was Jeanne-Antoinette Poisson, later Marquise de Pompadour, known as Madame de Pompadour. Louis died in 1774 of smallpox and was succeeded by his grandson Louis XVI. He had no surviving siblings.

Louis XVI, King of France (1754-1792) reigned as King of France from 1774 until his death. He was the grandson of Louis XV as his father, the Dauphin, had predeceased his father. The story of Louis XVI is well-documented and I will not mention it here as we are interested in siblings. He married Marie Antoinette, the daughter of Francis I, Holy Roman Emperor and Maria Theresa. They had four children including Louis-Charles who would claim the title King Louis XVII but died at the age of ten. It is well-known that Louis and Marie Antoinette died on the guillotine during the French Revolution.

His brother, **Louis (1755-1824)** was born in 1755 and died in 1824. He was **Louis XVIII, King of France** for a short time following the First Republic and Napoleon's first rule as Emperor. He married Marie Josephine of Savoy. There was no issue from this marriage

His brother, **Charles (1759-1824)**. He was **Charles X, King of France** following Louis XVIII. He married Marie Theresa of Savoy. There was no issue from this marriage.

His sister, **Marie Clothilde of France (1764-1802)** married King Charles Emmanuel IV of Sardinia. There was no issue from this marriage.

His sister, **Princess Elisabeth of France (1764-1794)**. She died on the guillotine during the French Revolution. She died unmarried and without issue. Following the execution of Louis XVI and Marie Antoinette the First Republic was formed soon to be the First Empire when Napoleon created himself Emperor of France.

House of Bonaparte (First Empire)

Napoleon I, Emperor of France (1769-1821) reigned as Emperor of France from 1804 until 1814 (First Empire). He was the son of Carlos Buonaparte and Letizia Ramolino. Napoleon's rise to power is well-documented and I will not discuss it here. He was captured in 1814 and exiled to the island of Elba, he escaped and following the Battle of Waterloo he was exiled again on the island of St Helena where he died. He married twice, his first wife was Josephine de Beauharnais, there was no issue from this marriage. His second wife was Marie Louise of

Austria, they had one son named Napoleon.

His brother, **Joseph Bonaparte (1768-1844)** was created by his brother, King of Naples & Sicily, King of Spain & the Indies & Comte de Survilliers. He married Marie Julie Clary. They had two children.

His brother, **Lucian Bonaparte (1775-1840)** was created 1st Prince of Conino & Musignano. He married twice, his first wife was Christine Boyer, and had issue. His second wife was Alexandrine de Bleschamp. There was also issue from this marriage.

His sister, **Elise Bonaparte, Princesse Francaise (1777-1820)** was created Duchess of Lucca, Princess of Pionbina, Grand Duchess of Tuscany and Countess of Compignano. She married Felice Pasquale Baciocchi and had issue.

His brother, **Louis Bonaparte (1778-1846)** was created King of Holland. He married Hortense de Beauharnais, his step-niece and they had issue, including Charles Louis-Napoleon born in 1808 and died in 1873. He married Eugenie de Montijo. He became President of the Second Republic and after a coup d'etat, Emperor Napoleon III of France.

His sister, **Pauline Bonaparte, Sovereign Princess (1780-1825)** was created Duchess of Guastalla. She married twice, her first husband was Victor-Emmanuel Le Clerc and had one daughter, her second husband was Camillo Borghese, 6th Prince of Sulmona. There was no issue from this marriage.

His sister, **Caroline Bonaparte (1782-1839)** was created Grand Duchess of Berg and Cleves. She became Queen Consort of Naples when she married Joachim Murat,. They had four children.

His brother, **Jerome Bonaparte (1784-1860)** created King of Westphalia. He married three times, his first wife was Elizabeth Patterson. They had one son. His second wife was Catharina of Württemberg. They had three children. His third wife was Giustina Pecori-Suárez there was no issue from this marriage.

After Napoleon's exile to Elba. Louis XVIII returned to the throne but was soon ousted upon Napoleon's return after he escaped from exile.

Napoleon's reign lasted for a year and ended after the Battle of Waterloo and his exile to St .Helena where he died.

His son Napoleon reigned as Emperor as Napoleon II for just a month until King Louis XVIII returned.

House of Bourbon/Orléans

Louis XVIII, King of France (1815-1824) was succeeded by his brother **Charles X, King of France**. He died without issue. Charles was overthrown during the July Revolution and abdicated in favour of his 10 year old grandson, Henri of Bordeaux with Louis-Philippe of Orléans as Regent. The Chamber of Deputies not really wanting a minor on the throne and aware of Louis-Philippe's popularity offered him the throne.

Louis-Philippe I the Citizen King, styled King of the French (1773-1850) reigned as King of the French from 1830 until 1848. He was the son of Louis-Philippe, Duke of Orléans and his wife Louise Marie Adelaïde de Bourbon. He married Marie Amalia of Naples and Sicily and they had ten children. The early part of his reign was a quiet and pleasant time, he had the people's welfare on his mind, but as his reign continued, the people's working conditions worsened and the income gap widened so much that there was a Revolution in 1848 and he was forced to abdicate. His change of popularity was used by Victor Hugo in his novel Les Misérables.

His brother, **Antoine d'Orléans, Duke of Montpensier (1775-1807)**. He died of Tuberculosis in Salthill England. He died unmarried and without legitimate issue. His sister, **Princess Adelaide of Orléans (1777-1847)**. She died unmarried and without issue. His brother, **Louis Charles, Count of**

Beaujolais (1779-1808). He died of Tuberculosis unmarried and without issue.

In 1848 the title of King of France was abolished and the Second Republic was established. The President of the Second Republic of France was Louis-Napoleon Bonaparte, a nephew of Napoleon I. His machinations to restore the monarchy came to fruition when he after a 97% vote in favour he was created **Napoleon III of Emperor of the French (1808-1873)** He married Eugenie de Montijo and had one son. Louis-Napoleon, Prince Imperial. The Prince Imperial, died fighting for the British during the Zulu Wars in 1879. The title still exists today.

His brother, **Louis Bonaparte II, King of Holland (1804-1831)** married Charlotte Napoleon Bonaparte, his cousin. There was no issue from this marriage.

In 1870 the monarchy was finally abolished and the Third Republic established.

Kingdom of Greece (1833-1973)

The Kingdom of Greece was established in 1832 at the Convention of London where it was recognized, and secured independence from, the Ottoman Empire

House of Wittelsbach

Otto I King of Greece (1815-1867) reigned as king from 1833 until 1862. He was the first and only monarch to call himself King of *Greece,* all following monarchs took the title King of the *Hellenes.* Otto was a prince of Bavaria and the son of King Ludwig I. Ludwig was a great admirer of the Greeks and their culture, so this probably influenced Otto's acceptance of the throne. He married Amalia, daughter of Paul, Duke of Oldenburg and there was no legitimate issue from this marriage so he was succeeded by his brother George.

Whilst visiting the Peloponnese a coup occurred and Otto, who was advised not to fight against the coup, abdicated and left on a British warship and settled in Bavaria. For his other siblings see the *'Kingdom of Bavaria'.*

George I, King of the Hellenes (1845-1913) reigned from 1863 until his death. He was the son of Prince Christian of Schleswig-Holstein-Sonderburg-Glücksburg and his wife Louise of Hesse-Kassel. He was not the first choice of the Greek people but at the age of 17 he was elected King of the Hellenes. He married Olga Constantinovna of Russia and they had seven surviving children including Constantine who succeeded his father.

Constantine I, King of the Hellenes (1868-1923) reigned from 1913 until 1947 and then from 1920 until 1922. He was the first Greek born heir to the throne was warmly welcomed at his birth. He angered the Greek government by refusing to join the Allies against the Germans during World War I. Many thought him to be a German sympathizer and he and his wife were forced to leave Greece and the throne was given to his son Alexander.

He married Sophie, daughter of the German Emperor and they had six children including Alexander, George and Paul who would succeed him. He returned to the throne after Alexander's death as the Greek people still preferred a monarchy to a republic. He caused consternation once again for the Greek government and was forced to abdication in 1922 in favour of his son George. He left Greece and went into exile never to return and died in 1923.

His brother, **Prince George of Greece (1869-1957)**. His main claim to fame, apart from being brother to the Greek King, was that whilst on a tour of Japan, he saved his cousin, the future Tsar Nicholas II of Russia from an assassination attempt. He married Princess Marie Bonaparte, a great-grandniece of Napoleon Bonaparte and they had two children. His sister, **Princess Alexandra of Greece (1870-1891)** married Grand Duke Paul Alexandrovich, son of Emperor Alexander II of Russia. They had two children.

Whilst out walking, pregnant with her second son, she jumped into a moored boat and fell awkwardly. Although in her seventh month of pregnancy, she insisted on attending a ball the next day and collapsed on the dance floor with violent labour pains obviously brought on by her accident. She died six days after giving birth a her second son.

His brother, **Prince Nicholas of Greece (1872-1938)**. He was an accomplished painter and also assisted in organization of the first modern Summer Olympics in Athens in 1896. He married Grand Duchess Elena Vladimirovna of Russia and had three daughters including Princess Marina who was born in 1907 and died in 1968. She married Prince George, Duke of Kent, son of King George V of Great Britain and had three children including the present Duke of Kent. His sister, **Princess Marie of Greece (1876-1940)** married Grand Duke

George Mikhailovich of Russia and had two daughters. His brother, **Prince Andrew of Greece (1882-1944)** married Princess Alice of Battenburg and they had five children including Prince Philip later Duke of Edinburgh and consort of Queen Elizabeth II of Great Britain. His brother, **Prince Christopher of Greece (1888-1940)** married twice, his first wife was a wealthy American widow Nancy Stewart Worthington Leeds, their was no issue from this marriage. His second wife was Princess Françoise of Orléans and they had one son.

Alexander, King of the Hellenes (1893-1920) reigned from 1917 until his death. He was elected to the throne following his father's abdication and exile. He married Aspasia Manos, the daughter of an Athenian soldier. They had one daughter Alexandra who married the King of Yugoslavia. He died after being bitten by a Macaque monkey. He developed septicaemia and died aged 27. To keep the continuity of monarchy his father Constantine was invited back. Still causing controversy he abdicated again in in favour of his son George in 1922 and went into exile never to return to Greece.

His sister, **Princess Helen of Greece (1896-1982)** was born in 1896 and died in 1982. She married King Carol I of Romania and had one son Michael. His brother, **Prince Paul of Greece (1901-1964)** married Princess Frederica of Hanover and they had three children including Sophia who married King Juan Carlos of Spain and Constantine who succeeded his father. His sister, **Princess Irene of Greece (1904-1974)** married Prince Aimone of Savoy, 4th Duke of Aosta and they had one son. His sister, **Princess Katherine of Greece (1913-2007)** married major Richard Brandram and they had one son.

George II, King of the Hellenes (1890-1947) reigned in the first instance from 1922 until 1924 when a republic was formed. He was called back after a vote was taken to re-establish the monarchy he then reigned from 1935 until his death in 1947.

He married Princess Elizabeth, daughter of King Ferdinand of Romania. There was no issue from this marriage and he was succeeded by his brother Paul. His siblings are mentioned above.

Paul, King of the Hellenes (1901-1964) married Princess Frederica of Hanover and they had three children, Sophia who was born in 1938, Constantine, who was born on 1940 and succeeded his father and Irene who was born in 1942. His siblings are mentioned above.

Constantine II, King of the Hellenes (1940-) was born in 1940 and reigned from 1964 until 1973 when the monarchy was abolished and a republic formed. He married Princess Anne-Marie, daughter of King Frederick IX of Denmark and they have five children.

His **sister Princess Sophia of Greece (1938-)** the current King of Spain, Juan Carlos and they have three children. His **sister Princess Irene of Greece (1942-)** who was born in 1942 never married or had issue and is still close to her brother.

The Kingdom of Italy

Many families alluded to the title of King of Italy but I am beginning this list of Kings of Italy from the House of Savoy, when King Victor Emmanuel II conquered Rome and could effectively call himself King of Italy.

House of Savoy

Victor Emmanuel II, King of Italy (1820-1878) was born in 1820 and died in 1878. He reigned as King of Italy from 1861 until his death. He supported Giuseppe Garibaldi's usurpation of the King of the Two Sicilies and unified Italy under one King. He was the son of Charles Albert, Prince of Carignano and Marie Theresa of Austria. He married twice, his first wife was his first cousin, once removed, Adelaide of Austria. They had eight children including Umberto who would succeed his father.

His brother, **Ferdinand, Prince of Savoy, Duke of Genoa (1822-1855)** married Princess Elizabeth of Saxony and they had two children including Margherita who married King Umberto I of Italy. He had a sister, **Princess Maria Cristina of Savoy** who died in infancy.

Umberto I, King of Italy (1844-1900) reigned as King of Italy from 1878 until his death. He was the son of Victor Emmanuel II of Italy and his wife Adelaide of Austria. During Umberto's reign, Italy attempted colonial expansion in East Africa successfully gaining Eritrea and Somalia.

He had the soubriquet 'the Good' but was hated and detested by Leftist circles and anarchists because of his conservatism. He married his first cousin Margherita of Savoy and they had one son, Victor who would succeed his father. He was the victim of two assassination attempts, the first was at the beginning of his reign whilst he was touring the country. In Naples, he was attacked by Giovanni Passennante with a dagger, although an aide was seriously injured. Umberto held off the assailant with his sabre before the man was overpowered. Passennante was imprisoned and died in a psychiatric institution in later years. The second attempt was to prove successful. He was visiting Monza in 1900 and he was shot four times by anarchist Gaetano Bresci. Bresci was sentenced to penal servitude for life but committed suicide a year later. Many at the time thought that he had died at the hands of other prisoners or guards, but the official records state suicide.

His sister, **Princess Maria Clotilde of Savoy (1843-1911)** married Prince Napoleon Joseph Bonaparte and they had two children. His brother, **Amadeo, Prince of Savoy, Duke of Aosta and one-time King of Spain (1845-1890)** was King of Spain for three years from 1870 until 1873. He married twice, his first wife was Maria Vittoria dal Pozzo, they had three children. His second wife was Maria Letizia Bonaparte with whom he had one child. His brother, **Oddone Eugenia Maria, Prince of Savoy, Duke of Montferrat (1846-1866)** was always in delicate health and spent his short life collecting art and artefacts. He lived in Genoa because the mild climate was beneficial to his frail health. He died unmarried and without issue. His sister, **Maria Pia, Princess of Savoy, later Queen of Portugal (1847-1911)** married King Louis I of Portugal and had two children including Carlos who succeeded his father.

Victor Emmanuel III, King of Italy (1847-1947) reigned as King of Italy from 1900 until 1946. He also claimed the thrones of Ethiopia and Albania. He married Princess Elena of Montenegro and they had five children including Umberto who succeeded him. He abdicated his throne to his son in 1946. He was an only child and consequently had no siblings.

Umberto II, King of Italy (1904-1983) reigned as King of Italy for just over a month until the monarchy was abolished. He married Princess Marie José of Belgium and they had four children.

Kingdom of Poland - Grand Duchy of Lithuania

There were many rulers of Poland who were considered legendary or semi-legendary. As the intention of this book is to discuss actual siblings I have started with the first elected King of Poland-Lithuania.

House of Valois

Henry, King of Poland, Grand Duke of Lithuania (1551-1589) reigned as King of Poland-Lithuania from 1574 until 1575. He was elected to the throne by the Polish-Lithuanian Commonwealth cabal of Dukes and Nobles. He was the son of King Henry II of France and his wife Catherine de'Medici. While King in Poland he did not marry or have issue. He resigned the Polish throne upon the death of his father and went to France to become King Henry III of France. He was assassinated by a fanatical young Friar. For his siblings please see The Kingdom of France section.

House of Jagiellonian-Báthory

Anna I, Queen of Poland (sometimes referred to as King) (1523-1596) reigned, jointly with her husband, from 1575 until 1587. She was the daughter of King Sigismund I, known as 'the Old' a former King of Poland. She was elected to the throne by the Polish-Lithuanian Commonwealth with her husband Stephen I. She married Stephen Báthory in 1576. He died in 1586 and Anna gave up the throne in favour of her nephew Sigismund. They was no issue from this marriage.

Her sister, **Hedwig Jagiellon later Electress of Brandenburg (1513-1573)** married Joachim II Hector, Elector of Brandenburg and had four children Her sister, **Isabella Jagiellon, later Queen Consort of the Eastern Hungarian Kingdom (1519-1559)** married John Zápolya, Viovode of Transylvania and King of Hungary, they had one child. Her brother, **Sigismund II Augustus King of Poland-Lithuania (1520-1572)** reigned as King from 1548 until 1569. He married three time but had no issue from any marriage. Her sister, **Sophia Jagiellon, later Duchess of Brunswick-Lüneburg (1522-1575)** married Henry V, Duke of Brunswick-Lüneburg. There was no issue from this marriage. Her sister, **Catherine Jagiellon, later Queen Consort of Sweden (1526-1583)** married King John II of Sweden and they had two children.

House of Vasa

Sigismund III, King of Poland, Grand Duke of Lithuania, Ruthenia, Prussia, Masovia, Samogitia, Livonia and hereditary King of the Swedes, Goths & Vandals (1566-1633) reigned as King from 1587 until 1632. He was elected to the throne by the Polish-Lithuania Commonwealth. He was the son of King John III of Sweden and Catherine Jagiellon. (see above).

He married twice, his first wife was Anna of Austria the daughter of Archduke Charles II of Austria and his wife Maria Anne of Bavaria. They had five children including Vladislaus who succeeded his father. His second wife, Constance, sister of his first wife. They had seven children including John Casimir a future King of Poland.

His sister, **Anna Vasa of Sweden, Starosta**[13] **of Brodnica & Golub (1568-1625)** married or had issue. His brother, **John of Sweden, Duke of Finland, Duke of Ostrogothia (1589-1618)** married his cousin Princess Maria Elizabeth of Sweden. There was no issue from this marriage.

Vladislaus IV Vasa, King of Poland, Grand Duke of Lithuania, Tsar of All Russia (1595-1648) reigned as King of Poland and Grand Duke of Lithuania from 1632 until 1648 and Tsar of All Russia from 1610 until 1613. He was the son of Sigismund III and Anne of Austria. He married twice, his first

---

[13]Translates as 'Leader' or 'Elder'

wife was Archduchess Cecilia Renata of Austria, daughter of Ferdinand II Holy Roman Emperor and Maria Anna of Bavaria. Although she had three children, none of them survived childhood. He second wife was Maria Louise Gonzaga, daughter of Charles I, Duke of Mantua and Catherine of Guise. Vladislaus died two years into the marriage and there was no issue or legitimate heir. Maria Louise went on to marry her husband's brother John Casimir the next King of Poland.

His brother, **John Albert Vasa, Cardinal and Prince-Bishop of Warmia and Kraków (1612-1634)** died unmarried and without issue. His brother, **Charles Ferdinand Vasa, Prince-Bishop of Breslau-Wroclaw (1613-1655)** was an active patron of the arts and an avid supporter of the Society of Jesus (Jesuits). He died unmarried and without issue. His brother, **Alexander Charles Vasa Prince of Poland (1614-1634)** died of smallpox aged 20, unmarried and without issue. His sister, **Anna Catherine Constance Vasa, Princess of Poland (1619-1651)** married Philip William, Elector Palatine, there was no issue from this marriage.

John II Casimir Vasa, King of Poland and Grand Duke of Lithuania (1609-1672) was the brother and heir of King Vladislaus IV of Poland. He reigned as King from 1648 until 1668 when after the death of his wife, he abdicated the throne, became a Jesuit priest and eventually an Abbot. He married twice, his first wife was the widow of his brother King Vladislaus Maria Louise Gonzaga and had two children or which only one child, a daughter survived. His second marriage, just before his death, was morganatic of which there was no issue.

House of Wiśniowiecki

Michael I, King of Poland and Grand Duke of Lithuania (1640-1673) was elected to the throne after John Casimir's abdication by the Polish nobility. He reigned as King from 1669 until his death. He was the son of a Polish noble. He married Eleonora Maria of Austria, daughter of Ferdinand III, Holy Roman Emperor. They had no surviving children. He had no siblings.

House of Sobieski

John III Sobieski, King of Poland and Grand Duke of Lithuania (1629-1696) was elected to the throne by the Polish Nobility after the death of Michael I and reigned from 1674 until his death. He was the son of Jakub Sobieski a Polish-Lithuanian noble. He married Marie Casimere Louise de La Grange d'Arquien, daughter of a minor French nobleman. They had eight children.

His brother, **Marek Sobieski (1628-1652)**. He was killed fighting the Cossacks and was unmarried and without issue. His sister, **Katazyna Sobieska (1634-1694)** married twice, her first husband was Vladislaus Dominic Zaskawski, they had two children. Her second marriage was to Michael Kazimierz Radziwill. They also had two children.

House of Wettin

Augustus II, 'the Strong', King of Poland and Grand Duke of Lithuania (1670-1733) was the son of John George III, Elector of Saxony and his wife Princess Anna Sophia of Denmark.

He was elected by the Commonwealth of Polish Nobles after the death of John Sobieski. He reigned from 1694 until his death interrupted only by his deposition and the election of Stanislaw as King to keep a flexible man on the throne when dealing with the Russians. After the conflict, with Russia treating Poland as just a protectorate, the re-established Augustus as King, as Poland needed a strong king. His great physical strength earned him the soubriquets 'the Strong', the Saxon Hercules' and 'Iron Hand'. He married Christiane Eberhardine, daughter of the Margrave of Brandenburg-

Bayreuth. The had one son, Augustus who succeeded his father. He also had eight illegitimate children with five different mistresses.

His brother, **John George of Saxony, later Elector of Saxony (1668-1694)** married Eleonore Erdmuthe of Saxe-Eisenach, they left no legitimate issue.

Augustus III, King of Poland and Grand Duke of Lithuania (1696-1763) reigned as King from 1734 until his death. He was the only son and heir of Augustus II and his wife Christiane Eberhardine. He married Archduchess Maria Josepha of Austria, they had fifteen children of which only ten survived into adulthood. He had no legitimate siblings

House of Poniatowski

Stanislaw II August, King of Poland, Grand Duke of Lithuania (1732-1798) was elected King of Poland with the aid of his lover the future Catherine the Great of Russia. He reigned from 1764 until 1795 overseeing the end of the Polish-Lithuanian Commonwealth. He never married but had many illegitimate children. Russia soon acquired Finland and part of Poland and the throne passed to the Russian Royal Family.

House of Holstein-Goltorp-Romanov

Alexander I, Emperor of Russia, King of Poland and Grand Duke of Finland & Lithuania (1777-1825) was a grandson of Catherine the Great. He married Princess Louise of Baden and they had two daughters who both died young. He died of typhus. As he had no heir, he nominated his brother Nicholas to succeed him.

His brother, **Grand Duke Constantine Pavlovich of Russia** was born in 1779 and died in 1831. He married twice, his first wife was Princess Julianne of Saxe-Coburg-Saalfeld, his second wife was Joanna Grudzińska. There was no issue from either marriage. His sister, **Grand Duchess Alexandra Pavlovna of Russia (1783-1801)** married Joseph, Archduke of Austria, Count Palatine of Hungary and had one daughter but neither mother or child survived childbirth. His sister, **Grand Duchess Elena Pavlovna of Russia (1784-1803)** married Frederick Louis, Hereditary Grand Duke of Mecklenburg-Schwerin. They had two children. His sister, **Grand Duchess Maria Pavlovna of Russia (1786-1859)** married Karl Friedrich, Grand Duke of Saxe-Weimar-Eisenbach and had four children. His sister, **Grand Duchess Catherine Pavlovna of Russia (1788-1819)** married twice, her first husband was Georg, Duke of Oldenburg, they had two sons. Her second husband was Wilhelm I, King of Württemberg and had two daughters including Sophie Friederike Mathilde who was to become Queen of the Netherlands. His sister, **Grand Duchess Anna Pavlovna of Russia (1795-1865)** married William II, King of the Netherlands and had five children including William who would succeed his father.

Nicholas I, Emperor of Russia and King of Poland (1796-1856) succeeded his brother Alexander. He married Princess Charlotte of Prussia and had ten children including Alexander who would succeed his father.

His brother, **Grand Duke Michael Pavlovich of Russia (1798-1849)** married Charlotte, Princess of Württemberg and had five children.

The Kingdom of Poland was annexed into the Russian Empire and the last Tsar and King of Poland was **Nicholas II** who together with his wife, Heir and daughters were executed by the Bolsheviks during the Russia Revolution.

The Kingdom of Portugal

The Portuguese House of Burgundy

The Kingdom of Portugal was established in 1139 and the founder of this ruling house was **King Afonso I** of the Portuguese House of Burgundy. He was the eldest surviving son of Henry, Count of Portugal and his wife Theresa of Leon. He was born in 1109 and died in 1185. He reigned as King from 1139 until 1185. We begin here with Sancho I.

King Sancho I of Portugal (1154-1212) reigned from 1185-1212. He married Dulce of Aragon daughter of Raymond Berenguer IV and Petronilla of Aragon.

His sister, **Urraca of Portugal (1151-1222)** married Ferdinand III of Leon. There was one son from this marriage who became Alphonso IX of Leon. His sister, **Theresa of Portugal (1157-1218)** married twice, her first husband was Philip I, Count of Flanders and his second husband was Otto III, Duke of Burgundy. There was no issue from either marriages.

King Afonso II of Portugal (1185-1223) was the son of King Sancho I and his wife Petronilla of Aragon. He reigned from 1212 until 1223. He married Urraca of Castile and had four children of which two became Kings of Portugal.

His **sister, Theresa of Portugal (1178-1250)** married King Alfonso IX of Leon and had two children. The marriage was declared invalid as they were both first cousins. Theresa returned to Portugal and set up a Benedictine Monastery that eventually joined a large Cistercian convent with over 300 nuns. In 1705 she was beatified, along with her sister **Sancha**, by Pope Clement XI. His brother, **Peter of Portugal (1187-1258)** married Aurembiaix, Countess of Urgell. There was no legitimate issue from this marriage. His brother, **Infante Ferdinand of Portugal (1188-1233)** married Joan, Countess of

Flanders. Ferdinand was Count of Flanders in the right of his wife. Their marriage was spent keeping control of Joan's legacy of Flanders as various factions tried to rest it from her. They had one child from this marriage. His sister, **Branca of Portugal (1192-1240)** was the hereditary Lady of Guadalajara. She never married or had children. She became a co-founder of, and a nun at, a Dominican convent at Coimbra. His sister, **Berengaria of Portugal (1193?-1221)** married King Valdemar III of Denmark. They had four surviving children including three future kings of Denmark. His sister, **Infanta Malfalda of Portugal (1197-1256)** married the very young King Henry I of Castile. Henry was only 10 years old when he married so the marriage was not consummated. The marriage was eventually dissolved due to consanguinity. He died aged thirteen after being hit on the head by a roof tile.

King Sancho II of Portugal (1209-1248) reigned as King of Portugal from 1223 until 1247. He married Mecia Lopes de Haro. There was no issue from this marriage. He was deposed from the throne in 1247 Although a competent army commander, but as a ruling monarch he was less so. He was succeeded by his brother.

King Afonso III of Portugal (1210-1279) was the son of King Afonso II and his wife Urraca of Castile. He married twice. His first wife was Matilda, Countess of Boulogne. There was no surviving children. His second wife was Beatrice of Castile. Their son, Infante Denis, succeeded his father as King of Portugal.

His sister, **Leonor of Portugal (1211-1231)** was born in 1211 and died in 1231. She married Valdemar the Young, King of Denmark. There was no known issue of this marriage. His brother, **Infante Fernando, Lord of Serpa (1217-1246)** married Sancha Fernandez de Lara. There was issue from this marriage.

King Denis of Portugal (1261-1325) reigned as King of Portugal from 1279 until 1325. He married Saint Elizabeth of Aragon. They had two legitimate children, their son, Afonso succeeded him a King of Portugal. Because of her great faith and the miracles attributed to her, Elizabeth was canonized by Pope Urban VIII in 1625.

His sister, **Infanta Branca (Blanche) (1259-1321)** became a nun and was eventually Abbess of the Convent of Huelgas in Castile. His brother, **Infante Afonso, Lord of Portalegne (1263-1312)** married Violante Manuel of Castile. They had five children. His sister, **Infanta Sancha (1264-1302)**. Very little is known of her life. She died unmarried and without issue. His sister, **Infanta Maria (1264-1304)** spent most of her life as a nun in the convent of The Lady Canons of Saint John.

King Afonso IV of Portugal (1291-1357) reigned as King of Portugal from 1325 until 1357. He married Beatrice of Castile. They had three children. His son Peter succeeded him as King of Portugal.

His **sister, Constance of Portugal (1290-1313)** married King Ferdinand IV of Castile, they had three children.

King Peter I of Portugal (1320-1367) reigned as King of Portugal from 1357 until 1367. He married three times, his first wife was Blanche of Castile. There was no issue from this marriage. There was a lot of inter-marriage between Portugal and Castile. There was not a lot of open warfare but a lot of political sabre rattling. It seems dynastic marriages calmed things down for a while. Peter's second wife was Constance of Penafiel with whom he had three children. One of them was Ferdinand, who would succeed him as King of Portugal. He had many more children from mistresses. One of these lovers was Ines de Castro. After her death he succeeded to the throne and stated that he had married Ines in secret which made her Queen of Portugal. The only record of this marriage is Peter's insistence that it took place. Legend has it that he had her exhumed, crowned Queen and forced the clergy and nobility to kiss her bony hand. After a year or so in the ground not a thing to do lightly.

His sister, **Maria of Portugal (1313-1357)** married King Alfonso XI of Castile. They had one son, Peter, who succeeded his father as King of Castile. His sister, **Eleanor of Portugal (1328-1348)** married Peter IV King of Aragon. They was no issue from this marriage. After less than a year of marriage Eleanor died during the Black Death.

King Ferdinand I of Portugal (1345-1383) married Leonor Telles de Menezes. Apart from several illegitimate children Ferdinand and Leonor had one daughter, Beatrice who married King Juan I of Castile.

The Portuguese House of Aviz

King John I of Portugal (1358-1433) was the natural son of King Peter I of Portugal and a woman named Teresa. He was proclaimed King of Portugal by the Council of the Kingdom. They worried that as Peter's sole heir Beatrice had married the King of Castile, Portugal would end up as a satellite of Castile. He was the first King of Portugal from the House of Aviz. John married Philippa of Lancaster, daughter of John of Gaunt of England, 1st Duke of Lancaster and Blanche of Lancaster. They had six surviving issue, Their son Edward would succeed John as King of Portugal.

King Edward the Philosopher, King of Portugal (1391-1438) reigned as King of Portugal from 1433 until 1438. He was named after his great grandfather King Edward III of England. He married Eleanor of Aragon. They had five children including Afonso who succeeded Edward as King of Portugal.

His brother, **Infante Peter, Duke of Coimbra (1392-1449)** married Isabella of Urgell. They had six children.

His brother, **Infante Henry, Duke of Viseu (1394-1460)** is better known as Henry the Navigator. He explored the coast of Africa, an area unknown to most Europeans. His aim was to search for the source of the West African gold trade. He was also fighting against the pirate attacks on the Portuguese coast. His sister, **Infanta Isabella of Portugal (1397-1471)** was born in 1397 and died in 1471. She married Philip the Good, Duke of Burgundy. Their son became Charles the Bold of Burgundy. His brother, **Infante John, Lord of Reguengos de Monsaraz (1400-1442)** married Isabella of Braganza. They had three children.

His brother, **Infante Ferdinand the Holy Prince (1402-1443)** took part in the Siege of Tangier with his brother Henry the Navigator, but was captured and spent the rest of his life a prisoner. He died unmarried and without issue.

King Afonso V of Portugal was born in 1432 and died in 1481. He reigned as King of Portugal from 1438 until 1477. He married Isabella of Coimbra. They had two surviving children, their son John succeeded him as King of Portugal. He married his second wife Joanna of Castile in 1475 but there was no issue. Afonso passed his crown to his son John and spent the remainder of his life in a monastery.

His brother, **Infante Ferdinand of Portugal, Duke of Viseu** was born in 1433 and died in 1470. He married his cousin Beatrice of Portugal and they went on to have five children including the future **King Manuel I of Portugal**

His sister, **Infanta Eleanor of Portugal 1433-1470)** was the daughter of King Edward of Portugal and his wife Leonor of Aragon. She married Frederick III, Holy Roman Emperor and was the mother of the future Holy Roman Emperor, Maximilian I.

His sister, **Infanta Joan of Portugal (1439-1475)** married King Henry IV of Navarre. They shared the same maternal grandparents, Ferdinand I of Aragon and Eleanor of

Alberquerque, making them first cousins. They also shared the same paternal great grandfather, John of Gaunt 1st Duke of Lancaster, making them, in this instance, second cousins. Joan gave birth to a daughter, also named Joan. Rumour abounded that she was not the King's daughter as the King is said to have repudiated his first wife and that the marriage was never consummated due to his impotence. Joan had always been the subject of gossip. They said her clothes were scandalous and too revealing and that she had many lovers. She was banished from the court and King Henry eventually divorced her saying that the marriage had never been legal in the first place.

King John II of Portugal (1455-1495) was born in 1455 and died in 1495. reigned from 1481 until 1495. He married Eleanor of Viseu and had one son. During his reign he took a lot of power from the aristocracy and invested it in the crown. 'I am Lord of Lords, not server of servants' he is supposed to have said. Soon the nobles began to conspire and following this the King fought back with execution, murders, including the stabbing of his cousin and brother-in-law, the Duke of Viseu by his own hand. Many were imprisoned and others exiled. As the country was nearly bankrupt, he called together the best men of the kingdom to form a council to change this. New taxes and new discoveries, including the Congo River and the passage around the Cape of Good Hope soon filled the royal coffers.

His sister, **Infanta Joan of Portugal, Blessed Joan of Portugal (1452-1490)**. After refusing several offers of marriage, as she wished to pursue a religious life, she entered the Convent of Jesus in Aviero. Despite being brought back to court by her brother when another marriage proposal was tabled including offers from King Charles VIII of France and the recently widowed King Richard III of England, she remained at the convent and was buried there. Because of her devout and eager attitude to the church, she was beatified by Pope Innocent XII in 1693.

The Portuguese House of Aviz-Beja

King Manuel I of Portugal (1495-1521) He reigned as King of Portugal from 147-95 until 1521. He was the son of Infante Ferdinand of Portugal and Beatrice of Portugal and a grandson of King Edward of Portugal. He married three times, his first wife was Isabella, Princess of Asturias who died giving birth. His second wife was Maria of Aragon who had eight children including the future King John III of Portugal. His third wife was Eleanor of Austria, there were two children from this marriage.

His brother, **Infante John. Duke of Viseu (1448-1472)** died young, unmarried and without issue. Following his death his titles went to his younger brother (see below). His brother, **Infante Diogo of Portugal (1450-1484)** inherited all his brother John's titles. He was personally stabbed by King John II because of his treacherous actions towards the throne. His sister, **Infanta Eleanor of Portugal (1458-1525)** married King John II of Portugal, the killer of her brother Diogo. She and John had one son. His sister, **Isabella of Viseu (1459-1521)** married Fernando II, Duke of Braganza. They had two children, Jaime, Duke of Braganza and Dinis of Portugal who was an ancestor of King John III of Portugal.

King John III of Portugal (1502-1557) reigned as King of Portugal from 1521 until 1557. During his reign Brazil was colonized, China during the Ming Dynasty was contacted as well as Japan. He married Catherine of Austria, they had three children.

His sister, **Isabella of Portugal (1503-1539)** married Charles V, Holy Roman Emperor, They had three children including Philip, who would become King Philip II of Spain. His sister, **Beatrice of Portugal (1504-1538)** married Charles III, Duke of Savoy. They had nine children but only one, Emmanuel Philibert survived into adulthood to succeeded his father. His brother, **Infante Louis, Duke of Beja (1506-1555)** became the Prior of the Order of St. John of Jerusalem. He died unmarried and without legitimate issue. His brother, **Infante Ferdinand, Duke of Guarda and Trancoso (1507-1534)** married Guiomar Coutinho, Countess of Marialva and Loulé. There were no surviving issue. His brother, **Infante Afonso of Portugal (1509-1540)** became Cardinal-Infante of the Kingdom. He never married or had issue. His brother, **Henry, Cardinal King of Portugal (1512-1580)** reigned as King of Portugal from 1578 until his death. Not expecting to inherit the throne, Henry took holy orders becoming, in quick succession, Archbishop of Braga and Archbishop of Évora and a Grand Inquisitor and later a Cardinal. When the incumbent king died without issue he ascended the throne and requested the Pope to release him from his vows. The Pope refused to do this and although he could still reign as king, he could not marry or have issue.

Sebastian I, King of Portugal (1554-1578) reigned from 1557 until his death. He was a grandson of King John III. Although he was offered and undertook to make various proposals, he died unmarried and without issue aged 24. He had no siblings.

The Portuguese House of Hapsburg & Braganza

Philip I, King of Portugal and King Philip II of Spain (1527-1598) was of the House of Hapsburg. He ruled as King of Portugal from 1581 until his death. He made a promise that he would rule Portugal as a separate kingdom from Spain. Portugal was ruled as part of Spain until John IV became king.

John IV, King of Portugal of the House of Braganza (1604-1656) reigned as King of Portugal from 1640 until his death. He was the great, great grandson of King Emmanuel I of Portugal and the son of the Duke and Duchess of Braganza. He married Luisa de Guzmán and they had seven children including, Infante Afonso who succeeded his father and Infanta Catherine who married King Charles II of England. He was an only child and had no siblings.

Afonso VI, 'the Victorious' King of Portugal (1643-1683) reigned from 1656 until his death. He had suffered an illness at the age of three that left him paralyzed on the left hand side and mentally unstable. His mother Luisa acted as Regent. He married Marie Françoise of Nemours, daughter of the Duke of Savoy. She requested annulment of her marriage from Afonso from the Pope on the grounds of Impotency. This was granted and she married Afonso's brother Pedro, Duke of Beja, the future King Peter II. Through manipulation and pressure, Pedro became Prince Regent and exiled his brother to the Azores for seven years. Afonso returned to Portugal and died shortly after.

His brother, **Teodósio, Prince of Brazil (1643-1653)** was heir to the throne but died aged 19. His sister, **Joana, Princess of Beira (1635-1653)** unmarried and without issue aged 18. His sister, **Infanta Catherine of Braganza, Queen Consort of England (1638-1705)** married King Charles II of England. They had no issue. His brother, **Infante Pedro of Portugal, later Peter II, King of Portugal (1648-1706)** succeeded his brother Afonso as King of Portugal. He married twice, his first wife was, Marie Françoise of Nemours, his brothers ex-wife and had one daughter. His second wife was Maria Sophia of the Palatinate-Neuburg. They had eight children including John who succeeded him.

John V, King of Portugal (1689-1750) reigned as King of Portugal from 1683 until his death. His reign saw an increase in the wealth of Portugal helped by the gold and diamonds mined at the Portuguese colony of Brazil. The crown also became very wealthy as one-fifth of each ton mined was Crown Property. He married Maria Anna of Austria, daughter of Leopold I, Holy Roman Emperor and Eleonor Magdalene of Neuburg. They had six children of which four survived into adulthood including Joseph and Peter who succeeded their father.

His sister, **Infanta Isabel Luisa of Portugal, 2nd Princess of Beira (1669-1690)**. It was planned that she marry Victor Amadeus II of Savoy but this came to nothing as did several other proposals. It seems alliances with Portugal were not at the top of other European rulers lists. Her continual proposals and refusals she was given the sobriquet Sempre-noiva or 'Always Engaged'. She died of smallpox aged 21 years. His brother, **Infante Francisco of Portugal, Duke of Beja (1691-1742)** never married or had legitimate issue. His brother, **Infante Manuel of Portugal, Count of Ourém (1697-1736)** died unmarried and without issue. His sister, **Infanta Francesca Josefa of Portugal (1699-1736)** died unmarried and without issue aged 37.

Joseph I, King of Portugal (1714-1777) reigned as King of Portugal from 1750 until his death. He married Mariana Victoria of Spain and had four children including Maria who succeeded her father. During Joseph's reign the Great Earthquake of Lisbon occurred and approximately 100,000 perished. The earthquake caused Joseph to develop Claustrophobia and could not live in a walled building. He transferred the court to a tented complex in the hills.

His sister, **Barbara, Princess of Brazil (1711-1758)** married King Ferdinand VI of Spain. There was no issue from this marriage. His brother, **Pedro, Prince of Brazil (1717-1786)** was born in 1717 and died in 1786. He married his niece who became Queen Maria I of Portugal and he became King Peter III, King Consort of Portugal. They had seven children of which only three survived including John who succeeded his mother.

Maria I, Queen of Portugal (1734-1816) was the first de facto Queen Regnant of Portugal. During the Peninsular War during the battles with Napoleon, the whole court fled to the colony of

Brazil. It was during her reign that the colony of Brazil was upgraded to a Kingdom. She then held the title Queen of the United Kingdom of Portugal, Brazil and the Algarves. She married her uncle, Pedro, who became, in the right of his wife, King Peter III of Portugal. The had three surviving children of which, John, who succeed his mother. She suffered from religious mania and melancholia. When her husband died she went into a state of depression that she could not emerge from made worse by the death of her eldest son and heir José. In 1792 she was declared insane and was treated by Francis Willis, the same physician that treated King George III of Great Britain. She died in Brazil and when John was proclaimed King of Portugal he brought her body back to Portugal.

Her sister, **Infanta Mariana Francisca of Portugal (1736-1813)** fled with her family to Brazil when Napoleon Bonaparte invaded Portugal during the Peninsular War. She was viewed as a potential bride for Louis, Dauphin of France, but her mother refused it. She died unmarried and without issue in Rio de Janeiro. Her sister, **Infanta Maria Doroteia of Portugal (1739-1771)** was requested as a bridge for Philippe Égalité the son of the Duke of Orléans. She refused this and died unmarried and without issue. Her sister, **Infanta Benedita of Portugal 1746-1829)** married her cousin Infante Joseph, Prince of Beira but there was no issue from this marriage.

John VI, King of Portugal and the Algarves and titular Emperor of Brazil (1747-1826) married Carlota Joaquina of Spain, the daughter of King Charles IV of Spain and his wife Marie Luisa of Parma. Carlota was a devious plotting woman, mainly interested in directing her husband to favour things beneficial to her or her homeland. They had nine children including Pedro who became Emperor of Brazil and Miguel who became King of Portugal.

His brother, **José, Prince of Brazil (1761-1788)** was born in 1761 and died in 1788. He married his aunt Infanta Benedita of Portugal, daughter of King Joseph I of Portugal. There was no issue from this marriage and José died of smallpox aged 27. His sister, **Infanta Mariana Vitória of Portugal (1768-1788)**. She married Infante Gabriel of Spain and they had one son.

Peter IV, King of Portugal & Emperor of Brazil (1798-1834) married twice, his first wife was Maria Leopoldina of Austria. They had eight children of whom only four survived into adulthood including Maria who would succeed him as Queen of Portugal. His second wife was Amélie of Leuchtenburg, she was the daughter of General Eugène de Beauharnais, a stepson of Napoleon Bonaparte, they had one daughter. He was succeeded as Emperor of Brazil by his son Pedro.

His sister, **Maria Teresa, Princess of Beira (1793-1874)** married twice, her first husband was Infante Peter Charles of Spain and Portugal, they had one son. He second marriage was to Infante Carlos of Spain, the widower of her sister Maria Francesca (see below). There was no issue from this marriage. His sister, **Maria Isabel, Infanta of Portugal (1797-1818)** became Queen of Spain when she married King Ferdinand VII of Spain. There was no surviving issue. His sister, **Maria Francesca, Infanta of Portugal (1800-1876)** married Infante Carlos of Spain and Portugal and they had three children His sister**, Isobel Maria, Infanta of Portugal 1801-1866)** was Regent for Prince Pedro, the future Peter IV, from 1826 until 1828. She died unmarried and without issue. His brother, **Miguel, Infante of Portugal (1802-1866)** married Princess Adelaide of Löwenstein-Wertheim-Rosenburg. They had seven children. Miguel usurped throne from his niece Marie II but was forced to abdicate in her favour in 1834 and he went into exile for 32 years. His sister, **Maria da Assunção, Infanta de Portugal(1805-1834)** died unmarried and without issue in 1834. His sister, **Ana de Jesus Maria, Infanta of Portugal (1806-1857)** married Nuno José, Duke of Loulé, they had five children.

Maria II, Queen of Portugal (1819-1853) reigned twice, firstly from 1826 until she was usurped by her uncle in 1828 and then from 1834 when she forcibly regained the throne, until 1853. She married twice, her first husband was Auguste, 2nd Duke of Leuchtenberg a step grandson of Napoleon Bonaparte. There was no issue from this marriage. Her second husband was Prince Ferdinand of Saxe-Coburg and Gotha later **Fernando II King of Portugal** after the birth of their first child as was the custom with Kings Consort in Portugal. They had eleven children of which only six survived including Pedro and Luis, both future Kings of Portugal.

Her sister, **Princess Januária of Brazil, Infanta of Portugal (1822-1901)** married Prince Luigi, Count of Aquila, son of Don Francesco I, King of the Two Sicilies. They had four children. Her sister, **Princess Francisca of Brazil, Infanta of Portugal (1824-1898)** married Prince François, Prince of Joinville, son of Louis Philippe I, King of the French. They had three children. Her brother, **Prince Pedro of Brazil** later **Emperor of Brazil (1825-1891)** married Teresa Cristina of the Two Sicilies. They had four children. Her sister, **Princess Maria Amélia of Brazil (1831-1853)** died before she could marry her betrothed Archduke Maximiliano of Mexico, later Emperor of Mexico. Pedro also had five illegitimate children, of which four survived into adulthood. He recognised them all in his will and gave them shares of his estate.

The Portuguese House of Braganza-Saxe-Coburg-Gotha

Peter V, King of Portugal (1837-1861) reigned as King from 1853 until his death. He was the son of Queen Maria II and her de jure uxoris co-monarch Ferdinand II. He married Stephanie of Hohenzollern-Sigmaringen. She died a year into the marriage of Diphtheria and the marriage was without issue. He was succeeded by his brother Louis.

His brother, **Infante John, Duke of Beja (1842-1861)**

died aged 19 unmarried and without issue. His sister, **Maria Ana, Princess of Portugal (1843-1884)** married King George of Saxony. She became the mother of King Frederick August II of Saxony and grandmother of Charles I, last Emperor of Austria. His sister, **Infanta Antónia of Portugal (1845-1913)** married Leopold of Hohenzollern-Sigmaringen and was the mother of King Ferdinand I of Romania. His brother, **Infante Fernando of Portugal (1846-1861)** died of Cholera aged 15. His brother, **Infante Augusto, Duke of Coimbra (1847-1889)** died unmarried and without issue.

As Peter V had no surviving heirs he was succeeded by his brother Louis.

Louis I, King of Portugal (1838-1889) was King from 1861 until his death. He married Maria Pia of Savoy the daughter of Victor Emmanuel II, the first King of Italy. They had two sons including Carlos who succeeded his father. For his siblings, see above.

Charles (Carlos) I, King of Portugal (1863-1908) reigned as king from 1889 until his death. He married Amélie or Orléans the daughter of Prince Philippe, Count of Paris. They had two children Luis and Manuel. Charles was travelling in an open coach with his two sons in Lisbon in 1908 when two assassins opened fire, Charles died immediately and Luis was mortally wounded. Manuel was hit in the arm and survived to succeed his father.

His brother, **Infante Afonso of Portugal, Duke of Oporto (1865-1920)** married the American heiress Nevada Stood Hayes, there was no issue from this marriage.

Manual II, King of Portugal (1889-1932) reigned as king from 1908 until 1910 when the monarchy was abolished and the Portuguese Republic was established. He married Augusta

Victoria of Hohenzollern-Sigmaringen there was no issue from this marriage.

Kingdom of Prussia and the German Empire

The **Kingdom of Prussia** was formed in 1701 and lasted until the end of World War One when the monarchies of the German States was abolished and the German Republic was established.

House of Hohenzollern

Frederick I, King of Prussia (1657-1713) persuaded Leopold I Arch Duke of Austria and the Holy Roman Emperor to give him permission to upgrade his duchy to a kingdom. Because of the help he gave them against King Louis XIV of France during the War of the Spanish Succession this was granted. On the 18 January 1701 Frederick crowned himself King of Prussia. He married three times, his first wife was Elizabeth Henrietta of Hesse-Kassel, they had one child. His second wife was Sophia Charlotte of Hanover, a sister of the future King George I of England, she gave birth top Frederick William who would succeed his father. His third wife was Sophia Louise of Mecklenburg-Schwerin, there was no issue.

His brother, **Charles of Prussia, Electoral Prince of Brandenburg (1655-1674)** died unmarried and without issue during the Franco-Dutch War. His **sister Amalie and brother Henry** died as infants. His brother, **Philip William of Brandenburg (1669-1711)** married Princess Johanna Charlotte of Anhalt-Dessau. They had six children. His sister, **Marie Amalie of Brandenburg (1670-1739)** married twice, her first husband was Charles of Mecklenburg-Güstrow. There was no surviving issue. Her second husband was Maurice William, Duke of Saxe-Zeitz. They had five children. His brother, **Albert Frederick, Margrave of Brandenburg-Schwedt (1672-1732)** married Princess Maria Dorothea of Courland. They had seven children. His sister, **Elizabeth Sophie, Margravine of Brandenburg (1674-1748)** married her cousin, Duke Frederick Casimir Kettler of Courland. They had one son who succeeded her father. His brother, **Christian Ludwig, Margrave of**

Brandenburg-Schwedt (1677-1734) was an army officer all his adult life and died unmarried and without issue. He is also known as the recipient of Bach's Brandenburg Concertos.

Frederick William I, King of Prussia (1688-1740) reigned as King of Prussia from 1713 until his death. He did his best to improve the lot of his people, although he was quite an autocratic king. He married Sophia Dorothea of Hanover, the sister of King George II of Great Britain. They had fourteen children including Frederick who would succeed his father.

His sister, **Princess Luise Dorothea of Prussia (1680-1705)** was always in bad health and died in childbirth. There was no issue.

Frederick II 'the Great', King of Prussia (1712-1786) was a grandson of King George I and a nephew of King George II of Great Britain. He was a brilliant military campaigner but without an abiding interest in the art of war. He was primarily interested in music and philosophy and corresponded and met Voltaire on a regular basis. He brought Prussian bureaucracy up to date and was a great proponent of religious tolerance. He married Elizabeth Christine of Brunswick-Bevern, the daughter of Ferdinand II, Duke of Brunswick-Wolfenbüttel. Soon after the marriage, they parted and lived in separated residences only meeting up for state occasions. There was no issue from this marriage. As Frederick preferred male company and is not known to have taken mistresses, his sexuality was always a topic for ribald discussion at court.

His sister, **Luise Ulrike of Prussia (1720-1782)** married King Adolf Frederick of Sweden gaining the title, Queen Consort. She gave birth to five children including Gustav and Charles who both went on to become Kings of Sweden. His brother, **Augustus William, Prince of Prussia (1722-1758)** was always a military man, he fought in the Silesian Wars between Prussia and Austria. He married Luise of Brunswick-

Wolfenbüttel and had four children including Frederick William who succeeded his uncle as **King of Prussia**. His sister, **Anna Amalia, Princess of Prussia (1723-1787)** was put forward, with her sister Luise Ulrike, as a prospective bride for Crown Prince Adolf Frederick of Sweden, she lost out to her sister. She married, secretly, Baron Friedrich von der Trenck. A man whose exploits and adventures inspired Victor Hugo and Voltaire. When this was discovered that she had married and was pregnant, Frederick annulled the marriage and packed her off to Quedlinburg Abbey to have the child. He imprisoned von der Trenck for ten years. Anna eventually took holy orders and became Princess-Abbess of Quedlinburg Abbey. His brother, **Henry, Prince of Prussia (1726-1802)** served as a soldier and statesman and was once even considered as a President or King of the United States of America until this was vetoed by his brother. He married Princess Wilhelmina of Hesse-Kassel, there was no issue from this marriage. His brother, **August Ferdinand, Prince of Prussia (1730-1813)** was a General and Herrenmeister (Master of the Knights) of the Bailiwick[14] of Brandenburg of the Order of Saint John. He married his niece, Elizabeth of Brandenburg-Schwedt and they had seven children.

Frederick William II, King of Prussia (1744-1797) reigned as King of Prussia from 1786 until his death. A lover of the good life and self-indulgent, he caused Prussia to be weakened both inside the country and without. He married four times, his first wife was Elizabeth Christine of Brunswick-Lüneburg. They had one daughter who married Frederick, Duke of York and Albany, son of King George III of Great Britain. His second wife was Frederika Louisa of Hesse-Darmstadt, they had one son, Frederick William who succeeded his father. Frederick went on to have two further marriages but these were morganatic[15] and

---

[14] A territorial division of the Teutonic Order
[15] A morganatic marriage is where a person of higher rank marries one

had no issue. His brother, **Henry, Prince of Prussia (1747-1767)** caught smallpox and died unmarried and without issue.

His sister, **Wilhelmina, Princess of Prussia (1751-1720)** married William V, Prince of Orange and had three children including William who became the first King of the Netherlands.

Frederick William III, King of Prussia (1770-1840) reigned as King of Prussia from 1797 until his death. He ruled Prussia during a turbulent time in Europe. He was dealing with the Napoleonic Wars and the fragmentation of the old German Empire. He married twice, his first wife was Luise of Mecklenburg-Strelitz and was very much a love match. She endeared herself to the people of Prussia. She had ten children including Frederick who would succeed his father and Wilhelm who would succeed his brother and who would become the first German Emperor. As he was so happy with his first wife he didn't want another wife to be queen so he contracted a morganatic marriage to Auguste von Harrach. As she was not to be entitled Queen, Frederick gave her other titles such as, Princess of Liegnitz and Legnica and Countess of Hohenzollern. There was no issue from this marriage.

His sister, **Frederica Charlotte, Princess of Prussia, Duchess of York and Albany (1767-1820)** married His Royal Highness Frederick Duke of York and Albany, son of King George III of Great Britain. There was no issue from this marriage. His **brother, Louis Charles, Prince of Prussia (1773-1796)** married Duchess Frederica of Mecklenburg-Strelitz. They had three children. His **sister, Wilhelmine, Princess of Prussia (1774-1837)** married William of the Netherlands and they had six children of which only three survived into adulthood including William who succeeded his father. His sister, **Augusta, Princess of Prussia (1780-1841)** married William V,

---

of lower rank and it is agreed that the one of lower rank would not take or succeed to any titles.

Elector of Hesse. This was a politically arranged and unhappy marriage. They had six children including Frederick William who succeeded his father. His brother, **Wilhelm, Prince of Prussia (1783-1851)** married Landgravine Marie Anna of Hesse-Homburg. They had seven children.

Frederick William IV, King of Prussia (1795-1861) refused the title of German Emperor offered to him by the Frankfurt Parliament in 1849. He married Elizabeth, Landgravine of Bavaria. There was no issue. He was succeeded by his brother William.

William I King of Prussia, German Emperor (1797-1888). Under his leadership, with support from Otto von Bismarck, Germany was unified. William was proclaimed German Emperor in the Hall of Mirrors in the Palace of Versailles during the Franco-Prussian War. He married Augusta of Saxe-Weimar, daughter of Charles Frederick, Grand Duke of Saxe-Weimar. They had two children including Frederick who succeeded his father.

His sister, **Charlotte Princess of Prussia (1798-1860)** she married Nicholas I, Emperor of Russia, she became Empress Alexandra Feodorovna of Russia. They had seven children including Alexander who succeeded his father. His brother, **Charles, Prince of Prussia (1801-1883)** married Princess Marie of Saxe-Weimar-Eisenach. They had three children. His sister, **Alexandrine Princess of Prussia (1803-1892)** married Paul Frederick, Grand Duke of Mecklenburg-Schwerin. They had three children. His sister, **Louise, Princess of Prussia (1808-1870)** married Prince Frederick of the Netherlands. They had four children. His brother, **Albert, Prince of Prussia (1809-1872)** married twice, his first wife was Princess Marianne of the Netherlands and had six children. His second wife was Rosalie von Rauch, they had two children.

Frederick III, German Emperor and King of Prussia (1831-1888) reigned as Emperor and King of Prussia for only three months until his death. He married Princess Victoria, Princess Royal, daughter of Queen Victoria of Great Britain and Albert, Prince Consort. They had eight children including William, who succeeded his father. His sister, **Louise, Princess of Prussia (1838-1923)** married Frederick I, Grand Duke of Baden. They had three children.

William II, German Emperor and King of Prussia (1859-1941) reigned as German Emperor and King of Prussia from 1888 until 1918. He asked if he could retain his title of King of Prussia, but this was refused mush to his chagrin. His history is well-documented including his instigation of the First World War and his abdication and flight to exile in the Netherlands. He married twice, his first wife was Princess Viktoria of Schleswig-Holstein and they had seven children. His second wife was Hermione Reuss of Greiz whom he married when in exile. There was issue from this marriage.

His sister, **Charlotte, Princess of Prussia (1860-1919)** married Bernhard III, Duke of Saxe-Meiningen and had issue. His brother, **Henry, Prince of Prussia (1862-1929)** married Princess Irene of Hesse and by the Rhine and had three children. His brother, **Sigismund, Prince of Prussia (1864-1866)** died of Meningitis aged 21 months. His sister, **Victoria. Princess of Prussia (1866-1929)** married twice, her first husband was Prince Adolf of Schaumburg-Lippe, there was no issue from this marriage. Her second husband was Alexander Zoubkov, there was no issue. His brother, **Valdemar, Prince of Prussia (1868-1879)** died of diphtheria in aged eleven. His sister, **Sophie, Princess of Prussia (1870-1932)** married Constantine I, King of the Hellenes, they issue including two Kings of Greece. His sister, **Margaret, Princess of Prussia (1872-1954)** married Prince Frederick Charles of Hesse and had five children. The German Empire and Kingdom of Prussia were abolished and a German Republic was established. This was hijacked by Adolf Hitler who plunged his country into war.

Kingdom of the Romanians

The Kingdom of Romania, previously a principality, lasted from 1881 until 1947 when the last king was forcibly abdicated and a People's Republic declared.

House of Hohenzollern-Sigmaringen

Carol I, King of the Romanians, previously Ruling Prince of the Romanians (1839-1914) was the son of Charles Anthony, Prince of Hohenzollern and his wife Princess Josephine of Baden. Carol married Princess Elisabeth of Wied and they had one daughter, Princess Maria who died aged four. As there were no surviving heirs, King Carol was succeeded by his nephew Ferdinand.

His brother, **Leopold, Prince of Hohenzollern (1835-1905)** was suggested as a successor to the Spanish Crown after the overthrow of Queen Isabella II, but Emperor Napoleon III of France vehemently opposed it citing worries about Prussian expansionism. Leopold eventually married Infanta Antonia of Portugal, daughter of Queen Maria II of Portugal and had three children including Ferdinand who would succeed his uncle after Leopold and his eldest son William declined their rights to the throne. His sister, **Stephanie, Princess of Hohenzollern, later Queen-Consort of Portugal (1837-1900)** married King Peter V of Portugal and lived in, what she considered, the best luxury in the world until she died a year after the marriage of diphtheria. They never had any issue. His brother, **Anton, Prince of Hohenzollern (1841-1866)** died unmarried and without issue aged 24 years. His brother, **Friedrich, Prince of Hohenzollern (1843-1904)** married Princess Louise of Thurn und Taxis, there was no issue from this marriage. His sister, **Maria Luise, Princess of Hohenzollern, later Countess of Flanders (1845-1912)** was, at one time, considered as a bride for the future King Edward VII of Great Britain but her Roman Catholicism barred from the role of British Queen-Consort. She eventually married Prince Philippe, Count of Flanders, son of King Leopold I of the Belgians. They had five children including Albert who would become the Belgian King in time.

Ferdinand I, King of the Romanians (1865-1927) reigned as King from 1914 until his death. He became heir to his uncle Carol I, when his father Leopold and his older brother William renounced all rights to the throne. He married Princess Maria of Edinburgh, daughter of Prince Alfred, Duke of Edinburgh and his wife Grand Duchess Maria Alexandrovna of Russia and a granddaughter of Queen Victoria of Great Britain. Ferdinand and Maria had six children including Carol who would reign as King Carol II of the Romanians.

His brother, **William, Prince of Hohenzollern (1864-1927)** had given up his rights to the throne and married Princess Maria Teresa of Bourbon-Two Sicilies and they had three children including Auguste Victoria who would become Queen of Portugal after her first marriage to King Manuel II of Portugal. His brother, **Karl Anton, Prince of Hohenzollern (1868-1919)** married his first cousin Princess Josephine Caroline of Belgium, daughter of Prince Philippe, Count of Flanders and Princess Maria of Hohenzollern. They had four children.

Michael I, King of the Romanians (1921-) and at the time of writing is 91 years old. He is the great, great grandson of Queen Victoria and is a third cousin of Queen Elizabeth II. His reign was interrupted by his father who reigned from 1930 until 1940. Michael's first reign was from 1927 until 1930 when he was nine years old. He was forced to abdicate and went into a life of exile. His Father Carol II returned to Romania and reneged on the abdication and was proclaimed king in place of his son.

Carol II, King of the Romanians (1893-1953) was born in 1893 and died in 1953. He had previously renounced the throne in favour of his young son Michael but after Michael was exiled he returned to take the throne. He reigned as king from 1930 until 1940 when he abdicated again in favour of his son. He married three times, his first wife was Zizi Lambrino and they had one son, his second wife was Princess Helen of Greece and Denmark and they had their son Michael. His last wife was his former mistress Magda Lupescu whom he married after his abdication.

His sister, **Elisabeth of Romania, later Queen-Consort of Greece (1894-1956)** married the future King George II of Greece. The marriage was not happy or successful and there was no issue from the marriage.

Michael I, King of the Romanians returned to the throne in 1940 and reigned until his abdication in 1947. He married Anne of Bourbon-Parma and they had five children. He was again forced to abdicate and the country is now a republic.

Empire of Russia

House of Rurik

Russia has been known under various names including, Rus' Kievan Rus', the Grand Duchy of Moscow, the Tsardom of Muscovy and the Russian Empire. It was ruled by an assortment of princes and dukes until the last Grand Prince of Moscow assumed the title of Tsar of All the Russias.

Ivan IV Grand Prince of Moscow & Tsar of All the Russias (1530-1547) was the son of Vasili III, Grand Prince of Moscow and his second wife Elena Glinskaya. His soubriquet, 'the terrible' does not really mean mad or bad in this context, although he was both, he means fearless and formidable. He married eight times, but had children with only three of his wives. His first wife, Anastasia Romanovna gave birth to two surviving children, the **Tsarevich Ivan Ivanovich** who was born in 1554 and died in 1581. The Tsarevich was married three times, both of his first two wife were sent to convents by his father, his third wife, Yelena Sheremeteva was physically assaulted by the Tsar while heavily pregnant for wearing, what he considered, inappropriate clothing. The Tsarevich came running to his wife's aid and was struck down by his father using his iron sceptre, the Tsar was distraught and the Tsarevich died a few days later, his wife lost the baby through miscarriage. The Tsar's second son by Anastasia, Feodor, survived to succeed his father. The Tsar's other two wives had children but none survived into adulthood. The early part of his reign saw the Great Fire of Moscow that destroyed many areas as it was mostly made of wood. It also saw the building of St Basil's Cathedral. Legend has it that Ivan was so impressed with the building that he put out the eyes of the architect so he could not build anything as beautiful again. He also created a standing army, the Streltsy as well as his own personal bodyguard the Oprichnina which he used ruthlessly to put down the Boyars, the Russian aristocracy and persecuted everyone who caused Ivan to believe in real of imagined threats. He began to see threats everywhere and withdrew into himself and he died despite his believe in assassination attempts and poisoning, of a stroke whilst playing Chess.

His brother, **Yuri Vasilevich, Prince of Uglich (1532-1563)** was a deaf mute and while his brother read books and prepared to rule, Yuri enjoyed eating and games and was completely happy to be lodged in apartments in the servants quarters after Ivan's coronation. He married Princess Ulyana of Polekh but had no surviving children.

Feodor I, Tsar of All the Russias (1557-1584) reigned as Tsar from 1547 until his death. He was never intended for the throne until the death of his brother Ivan at the hands of his father. He was never really interested in politics and spent most of his time in meditation and prayer. He married Irina Godunova, the daughter of one of the Boyars who were Russia ancient aristocracy. They had one daughter who died aged 2 years. He had two other siblings apart from the slain Ivan, but they both died in infancy.

House of Godunov

Irina, wife and widow of Feodor, controlled Russia for a short while until it was taken over by her brother **Boris Godunov, Regent of Russia & Tsar of All the Russias (1551-1605)** a member of Ivan IV's court and then regent for Ivan's son Feodor who had married his sister. He took the throne from his sister. He married Maria Grigorievna Skuratova-Belskaya and they had two children including Feodor who succeeded his father. They are no recorded siblings.

Feodor II, Tsar of All the Russias (1589-1605) reigned for only a few months and died unmarried and without issue. Then there followed what was called False Tsars who reigned from 1605 until 1612. It was called 'The Time of the Troubles'. For continuity of rule we move onto the Emperors of Russia.

Emperors of Russia

Michael I first of the Romanov Tsar of All the Russias (1596-1645) reigned as Tsar from 1585 until his death. He married twice, his first wife was Maria Vladimirovna Dolgorukova who was a descendent of the ancient Grand Princes of Russia, They was no issue from this marriage. He second wife was Eudoxia Lukyanovna Streshnova. They had two children including Alexis who succeeded his father. No complete record of siblings extant.

Alexis I, Tsar of All the Russias (1629-1676) reigned as Tsar from 1645 until his death. He married twice, his first wife was Maria Ilyinichna Miloslavskaya and they had thirteen children including Feodor and Ivan both future Tsars. His second wife was Nataliya Kyrillovna Naryshkina and they had three children including Peter who would rule Russia as Peter the Great. He had no siblings.

Feodor III, Tsar of All the Russias (161-1682) was Tsar from 1676 until his death. He married twice, his first wife was Agraphia Simeonovna Gruszewska the daughter of a Ukrainian nobleman. She gave birth to a son and heir but both mother and child died soon after childbirth. His second wife was Marfa Matveievna Apraksina, there were no surviving issue.

His sister, **Tsarevna Sofia Alekseyevna of Russia (1657-1704)** ruled as regent for her two young brothers Peter and Ivan from 1682 until 1689. She received help and support from a courtier and politician, Prince Vasily Galitzine. She never married or had issue. His sister, **Tsarevna Natalya Alekseyevna of Russia (1673-1716)** was close to her brother

Peter and was very protective of him during the regency of her sister Sofia. She spent her days as a playwright with many successful plays produced. She never married or had issue. His brother, **Ivan V, Joint Tsar of All the Russias (1666-1696)** was co-ruler with his brother Peter but his rule was really just nominal as he had physical and mental problems. He chose his bride in the usual way, by choosing from a line of potential spouses who stood in front of him. This was the last time this procedure was used. He married Praskovia Saltykova and they had five children of which only three survived into adulthood, including Tsarevna Catherine Ivanovna, she married the Duke of Mecklenburg and had one daughter, Anna who married the Duke of Courland and was eventually Empress of Russia upon the death of Tsar Peter II. His brother, **Peter I. Emperor & Autocrat of All the Russias known as 'the Great' (1672-1725)**, firstly as co-ruler with his brother Ivan and then on his own, from 1682 until his death. His reign is well-documented regarding his expansion and modernization of Russia. But we are here to look at siblings. He married twice, his first wife was Eudoxia Lopukhina, the daughter of a minor nobleman. They had three children including his heir Alexis who was imprisoned by Peter for a revolt and he died in prison. His second wife was Martha Skavronskaya who gave birth to two daughters including Elizabeth a future Empress of Russia. Martha who had changed her name to Catherine upon her marriage reigned as **Empress Catherine I** as Peter had not nominated a successor.

Peter II, Emperor & Autocrat of All the Russias (1715-1730) was the son of the imprisoned Alexis, son of Peter the Great. He reigned for three years from 1727 until his death from smallpox in 1730. He died unmarried and without issue.

His sister, **Grand Duchess Natalya of Russia (1714-1728)** died unmarried and without issue in 1728. As he had no issue the Supreme Council in Moscow elevated the daughter of

Ivan V, **Anna** to the throne. She reigned from 1730 until her death in 1740.

Ivan VI. Emperor & Autocrat of All the Russias (1740-1764) was deposed by Elizabeth, daughter of Peter the Great one year later. He was imprisoned and was killed during an attempt to free him in 1764. He had no siblings.

Elizabeth, Empress of Russia (1709-1762) reigned as Empress from 1741 until her death. As mentioned above, she took the throne from the infant Ivan and imprisoned him. She married, morganatically, an ex-lover Alexey Razumovsky, there were no children from this marriage. As she did not have an heir she chose the son of her late sister Anna to succeed her. She found him a suitable bride and died after a decade of illness in 1762.

Peter III, Emperor & Autocrat of All the Russias (1728-1762) was the son of Charles Frederick, Duke of Holstein-Gottorp and Anna, a daughter of Peter the Great. He had married Princess Sophie of Anhalt-Zerbst who converted to the Russian Orthodox faith taking the name of Catherine and they had two children including Paul, a future Emperor of Russia. Peter ascended the throne after Elizabeth's death but reigned for only six months until he was overthrown by his wife, the future Catherine the Great. He was imprisoned and died, some say murdered, the same year. He had no siblings.

Catherine II 'the Great' Empress-Consort and later Empress of Russia (1729-1796) reigned as Empress-Consort in 1762 and as Empress in her own right from 1762 until her death. She took the throne from her husband and reigned for over 30 years. Stories of her lifestyle are well-known and too numerous to be mentioned here.

Her brother, **Frederick Augustus, Prince of Anhalt-Zerbst (1734-1793)** married twice, his first wife was Caroline, daughter of Prince Maximilian of Hesse-Kassel, the marriage was childless. His second wife was Fredericka Auguste Sophie, daughter of Victor Frederick, Prince of Anhalt-Bernburg. This marriage was also childless and the line of Anhalt-Zerbst ended with Prince Frederick.

Paul I, Emperor & Autocrat of All the Russias (1754-1801) reigned as Emperor from 1796 until his death. He married twice, his first wife was Wilhelmina Louise of Hesse-Kassel, there was no issue from this marriage. His second wife was Sophie Dorothea of Württemburg and they had nine surviving children including Alexander who succeeded his father. Paul, for many years, had dreams of assassination which actually in March 1801 when a group of disgruntled army officers broke into his bedroom and killed him.

Alexander I, Emperor & Autocrat of All the Russias & King of Poland (1777-1825) married Princess Louise of Baden and had no surviving legitimate issue. He caught a cold whilst travelling which turned into Typhus and died. He was succeeded by his younger brother Nicholas.

His brother, **Grand Duke Constantin Pavlovich of Russia (1779-1831)** married twice, his first wife was Juliane, Princess of Saxe-Coburg-Saalfeld, they had no legitimate issue. It was an unhappy marriage that caused Juliane to return to her native Germany and stay there despite Constantin's continual requests for her to return. After nearly 20 years separation the marriage was formally annulled and Constantin married, morganatically, Joanna Grudzińska, the daughter of a Russian nobleman. To be able to marry her, Constantin had to give up his right to the throne. There was no legitimate issue from this marriage. His sister, **Grand Duchess Alexandra Pavlovna of Russia (1783-1801)** married Archduke Joseph of Austria and died of puerperal fever following the still birth of their only child. His sister, **Grand Duchess Elena Pavlovna of Russia (1784-1803)** married Frederick Louis, Hereditary Grand Duke of Mecklenburg-Schwerin and they had two children including Paul who succeeded his father as Hereditary Grand Duke. His sister, **Grand Duchess Maria Pavlovna of Russia, later Grand Duchess of Saxe-Weimer-Eisenbach (1786-1859)** married Karl Friedrich, Grand Duke of Saxe-Weimer-Eisenbach and they had four children including Augusta who married Kaiser Wilhelm I of Germany. His sister, **Grand Duchess Catherine Pavlovna of Russia, later Duchess of Oldenburg and Queen Consort of Württemburg (1788-1819)** married twice, her first husband was Georg, Duke of Oldenburg and they had two sons. Her second husband was Wilhelm I, King of Württemburg, they had two daughters including Sophie Friederike Mathilde who became Queen of the Netherlands. His sister, **Grand Duchess Anna Pavlovna of Russia, later Queen Consort of the Netherlands (1795-1865)** married Wilhelm I, King of the Netherlands and they had five children including William who succeeded his father as King and married Sophie of Wurttemberg. His brother, **Grand Duke Michael Pavlovich of Russia (1798-1855)** married his first cousin Charlotte, Princess of Württemberg and had five daughters.

Nicholas I, Emperor & Autocrat of All the Russias (1796-1855) was the brother of Alexander I who had no legitimate children. His reign encompassed the Crimean War which was disastrous for Russia, although he was successful in creating an independent Greek state and defeating the Ottoman Empire. He married Princess Charlotte of Prussia and they had ten children of which only seven survived into adulthood including Alexander who succeeded his father. Nicholas died during the Crimean War of Pneumonia after refusing medication for a chill he had contracted. His sibling are mentioned above.

Alexander II, Emperor & Autocrat of All the Russias, King of Poland & Grand Duke of Finland (1818-1881) reigned as

Emperor from 1855 until his death. He is well-remembered for freeing the serfs of Russia and was called Alexander the Liberator for that. He married Maria of Hesse and by the Rhine and they had eight children including Alexander who would succeed his father. There were many unsuccessful attempts on his life, but one, in 1881 was to be fatal. Alexander stopped his carriage after a bomb exploded near it killing a Cossack officer, as he got out of the carriage another bomb was thrown at him which tore his legs and ripped open his stomach, he died a little later.

His sister, **Grand Duchess Maria Nikolaevna of Russia (1819-1876)** was an avid art collector and President of the Imperial Academy of Art in St Petersburg. She married twice, her first husband was Maximilian, Duke of Leuchtenburg, they had seven children. She then married, morganatically, Count Grigor Stroganov and they had two children. His sister, **Grand Duchess Olga Nikolaevna of Russia &Queen-Consort of Württemberg (1822-1892)** married Charles I, King of Württemberg. They had no children of their own and adopted their niece Grand Duchess Vera of Russia. His sister, **Grand Duchess Alexandra of Russia (1825-1844)** married Prince Frederick William of Hesse-Kassel and they had one son. His brother, **Grand Duke Konstantin Nikolayevich of Russia (1827-1892)** was held in high esteem but as his brother the Tsar refused reforms and Konstantin lost influence. He left his wife and had various affair and illegitimate children. He married Princess Alexandra of Saxe-Altenburg and they had six children including Olga who would become Queen of the Hellenes. His brother, **Grand Duke Nicholas Nikolayevich of Russia (1831-1891)** married Duchess Alexandra of Oldenburg and they had two children. His brother, **Grand Duke Mikhail Nikolayevich of Russia (1832-1909)** married Princess Cecily Auguste of Baden and they had seven children.

Alexander III, Emperor & Autocrat of All the Russias, King of Poland & Grand Duke of Finland (1845-1894) reigned from 1881 until his death. He married Princess Dagmar, the daughter of Christian Prince of Schleswig-Holstein-Sonderburg-Glücksburg. They had six children including Nicholas who succeeded his father. He fell ill with an inflammation of the kidneys and died a little later.

His brother, **Tsarevich Nicholas Alexandrovich of Russia (1843-1865)** was heir apparent to the throne and was engaged to marry Princess Dagmar of Sweden and when he fell ill and it was diagnosed as Meningitis he requested that Dagmar marry his brother Alexander. He died unmarried and without issue. His brother, **Grand Duke Vladimir Alexandrovich of Russia (1847-1909)**. Although very much a military minded man he was also a great patron of the arts and sponsor of the Imperial Ballet. He married Duchess Marie of Mecklenburg-Schwerin and they had five children. His brother, **Grand Duke Alexei Alexandrovich of Russia (1850-1908)** had a distinguished naval career and although he never married he is believed to have had several illegitimate children. His sister, **Grand Duchess Maria Alexandrovna of Russia (1853-1920)** married Alfred, Duke of Edinburgh, second son of Queen Victoria of the United Kingdom, later Duke of Saxe-Coburg-Gotha. They had five children including Maria who would become Queen of Romania. His brother, **Grand Duke Sergei Alexandrovich of Russia (1857-1905)** married Elizabeth of Hesse, they had no children of their own but adopted two children. He was assassinated by a bomb in 1905 thrown by a member of the Socialist Revolutionary Party. His brother, **Grand Duke Paul Alexandrovich of Russia (1860-1919)** was an army officer and rose to the rank of General. He married twice, his first wife was Princess Alexandra of Greece and Denmark and they had two children. His second wife was a commoner Olga Valerianovna Karnovich. His brother, the Tsar refused permission for this marriage so they married in Italy. They were exiled but eventually pardoned and returned to Court, their son and two daughters were given the titles of Prince and Princess. His brother, **Nicholas II, Emperor & Autocrat of All the Russias (1868-1918)**. His story is well told as are his final moments with his family and staff in the tiny cramped cellar in Yekaterinburg. There are many interesting stories including the power of Rasputin of the Tsarina, the escape from the cellar of his daughter Anastasia. The whole story is well worth the read and I recommend it. But we are dealing with siblings. His brother, **Grand Duke George Alexandrovich of Russia (1871-1899)**. He never married or had any issue. His death occurred after he went out for a motorcycle ride and was found much later by a search party lying on the side of the road. He was buried with honours and his brother the Tsar was devastated at his loss as they were very closed. His rest was disturbed many years later when his body was exhumed following the discovery of the supposed remains of Nicholas and his family in woodland. A sample of DNA was taken to help solve the identity of the bodies. He was re-interred with reverence and lies next to the remains of his brother the Tsar. His sister, **Grand Duchess Xenia Alexandrovna of Russia (1875-1960)** married her first cousin Grand Duke Alexander Mikhailovich of Russia and they had seven children.

His brother, **Grand Duke Michael Alexandrovich of Russia (1878-1918)** married Natalie Brasova the daughter of a Moscow lawyer and they had one son. During the Russian Revolution of 1917 he was named as successor to his brother but declined to accept until it was ratified by the elected Assembly. It was, of course, never ratified and Michael was imprisoned and eventually murdered. The monarchy was completely abolished and the Bolshevicks seized power.

Kings of Saxony

Saxony became a kingdom in 1806 after the end of the Holy Roman Empire

House of Wettin

Frederick Augustus I, King of Saxony (1750-1827) reigned as King of Saxony from 1806 until his death. He was the son of Frederick Christian, Elector[16] of Saxony and his wife Princess Maria Antonia of Bavaria. He married Amalie of Zweibrüken-Birkenfeld and they had one surviving daughter, Princess Maria Augusta, who died unmarried and without issue.

His brother, **Karl of Saxony (1752-1781)** unmarried and childless. His brother, **Anton of Saxony (1755-1836)** married twice, his first wife was Maria Carolina of Savoy. There was no issue from this marriage. His second wife was Maria Theresa of Austria. There was no surviving issue from this marriage. He would become **King of Saxony** after his brother as he left no surviving heir. His sister, **Maria Amalia of Saxony (1757-1831)** She married Karl II Augustus, Duke of Zweibrüken. There was no surviving issue from this marriage. His brother, **Maximilian of Saxony (1759-1838)** married twice, his first wife was Princess Caroline of Bourbon-Parma and had issue including Frederick Augustus who would become **King of Saxony**. His second wife was Princess Maria Luisa Carlota of Bourbon-Parma, his niece by marriage, There was no issue from this marriage.

Anton I of Saxony, King of Saxony (1755-1836) was the brother of King Frederick Augustus I. He reigned as King of Saxony from 1827 until his death. He married twice as mentioned above and had no surviving issue. His siblings were mentioned above.

---

[16] An Elector were members of the Electoral College who chose Holy Roman Emperors

Frederick Augustus II, King of Saxony (1797-1854) was born in 1797 and died in 1854. He reigned as King of Saxony from 1827 until his death. He was the son of Prince Maximilian of Saxony, brother of the two preceding Kings and Princess Caroline of Bourbon-Parma He married twice, his first wife was Archduchess Maria Caroline of Austria, daughter of Francis I, Holy Roman Emperor. There was no issue from this marriage. His second wife was Princess Maria of Bavaria, daughter of King Maximilian I of Bavaria. There was no issue from this marriage. He died accidentally when he fell in front of a horse that stepped on his head.

His sister, **Amalie of Saxony (1794-1870)** never married or had any issue. She was a composer of chamber music, opera and sacred music. She wrote comedies. She also played the harpsichord. She wrote her music and plays under two pseudonyms, Amalie Heiter and A Serena His sister, **Maria Ferdinada of Saxony (1796-1865)** was born in 1796 and died in 1865. She married Ferdinand III, Grand Duke of Tuscany. There was no issue from this marriage. His sister, **Maria Anna of Saxony (1799-1832)** was born in 1799 and died in 1832. She married Leopold II, Grand Duke of Tuscany. They had two children. His sister, **Maria Josepha Amalia of Saxony (1803-1829)** married Ferdinand VII of Spain. There was no issue from this marriage.

John I of Saxony, King of Saxony (1801-1873) was the brother of Frederick Augustus II. He promoted trade and extended the railway network. He married Amaile Auguste of Bavaria, daughter of Maximilian I Joseph of Bavaria and his second wife Karoline of Baden. They had six children including Albert and George, future Kings of Poland.

Albert I, King of Saxony (1828-1902) reigned as King of Saxony from 1873 until his death. He married Princess Carola, daughter of Gustav, Prince of Vara. There was no issue from this marriage and he was succeeded by his brother George.

George I, King of Saxony (1832-1904) reigned as King of Saxony from 1902 until his death. He married Maria Anna of Portugal. They had eight children including Frederick Augustus who succeeded him.

Frederick Augustus III, King of Saxony (1865-1932) reigned as King of Saxony from 1904 until 1918. He married Archduchess Luise, Princess of Tuscany. They had seven children. He was the last King of Saxony and abdicated in 1918 following the First World War when the German Republic was proclaimed.

Dukes and Kings of Württemberg

The Duchy of Württemberg was once of the German States. Surrounded by Bavaria and Baden it was only 225km from north to south and 160km from east to west. The Duchy came into existence in 1495 and was upgraded to a Kingdom in 1806 and was abolished with other German Kingdoms in 1918 following the end of the First World War.

Dukes of Württemberg 1495 - 1803

Eberhard I, 1st Duke of Württemberg (1445-1496) was the son of Count Ludwig I of Württemberg-Urach and his wife Mechthild of the Palatinate. Eberhard was the first Duke when the county was upgraded. He married Barbara, daughter of Ludovico II, Marquis of Mantua, they had no surviving children. He was succeeded by a cousin.

His sister, **Mechthild of Württemberg-Urach (1436-1495)** married Louis II, Landgrave of Hesse. They had four children of which only two survived into adulthood. His brother, **Ludwig II, Count of Württemberg-Urach (1439-1457)** died unmarried and with issue in 1457 aged 18. His sister, **Elisabeth of Württemberg-Urach (1447-1505)** was born in 1447 and died in 1505. She married twice, her first husband was Johann III, Count of Nassau-Weilburg and her second husband was Heinrich, Count of Stolberg. There is no known issue from either marriage.

Eberhard II, Duke of Württemberg (1447-1504) was the son of Ulrich V, Count of Württemberg-Urach and Elisabeth of Bavaria-Landshut. He married three times, his first wife was Elisabeth of Brandenburg but there was no issue from this marriage, A weak and ineffectual man he was soon deposed by the nobility and exiled.

His sister, **Katharina of Württemberg (1441-1497)**

became a nun in Laufen. His sister, **Margareta of Württemberg (1442-1479)** became a nun in Liebenau Monastery. His brother, **Henry, Count of Württemberg (1448-1519)** married twice, his first wife was Elisabeth of Zweibrüken-Bitsch. They had one child, Ulrich who succeeded his uncle. His second wife was Eva, Countess of Salm with whom he had two children. His sister, **Elizabeth of Württemberg** was born in 1450 and died in 1501. She married Count Frederick II of Henneberg, there was no known issue. His sister, **Margarete of Württemberg (?-1470)** married Count Philipp I of Eppstein-König. There is no record available of any issue from this marriage. His sister, **Philippine of Württemberg (?-1475)** married Count Jakob II of Horn. No issue recorded. His sister, **Helene of Württemberg (?-1506)** married Count Kraft VI of Hohenlohe-Neuestein. No children recorded.

Ulrich I, Duke of Württemberg (1487-1550) succeeded his uncle Eberhard II. He was the son of Eberhards's brother Henry and his wife Elisabeth. Following the death, after an altercation with Ulrich, of the husband that he had affection for, Ulrich was exiled in 1519 and Württemberg was annexed by Austria. Ulrich spent his exile in Germany, France and Switzerland. He was restored to the Dukedom of Württemberg in 1534 with help from Philip. Landgrave of Hesse who was anxious to have Ulrich's assistance on his fight against the Hapsburgs He married Sabina of Bavaria, a daughter of Albert IV, Duke of Bavaria. This was an unhappy marriage and they lived apart for most of the time. They must have met up sat least twice because of their two children that included Christoph who succeeded his father.

His sister, **Maria of Württemberg (1496-1541)** married Henry I, Duke of Brunswick-Wolfenbüttel and had issue. His brother, **George I of Württemberg (1498-1558)** Barbara of Hesse, daughter of Philip. Landgrave of Hesse, Ulrich's saviour. They had issue.

Christoph, Duke of Württemberg (1515-1568) reigned as Duke from 1550 until his death. He spent his reign reorganizing the church and the state as well as the educational system. He believed it was important to keep the Duchy in high profile so held many celebrations both religious and secular. He married Anna Maria of Brandenburg-Ansbach and they had twelve children including Ludwig who succeeded his father. He had no siblings.

Ludwig III, Duke of Württemburg (1554-1593) reigned as Duke from 1568 until his death. He married twice, his first wife was Dorothea Ursula of Baden-Durlach, daughter of Charles II, Margrave of Baden-Durlach and his second wife was Ursula of Veldenz, daughter of George John I, Count Palatine of Veldenz. There was no issue from either marriage.

His sister, **Hedwig, Princess of Württemberg (1547-1590)** married Louis IV, Landgrave of Hesse-Marburg, there was no issue from this marriage. His sister, **Elisabeth of Württemberg (1548-1590)** married twice, her first husband was Georg Ernst, Count von Henneberg-Schleusingen. He second husband was George Gustuv, Count Palatine of Veldenz-Lauterecken . There is no record of any issue from either marriage. His sister, **Sabine of Württemberg (1549-1582)** William IV, Landgrave of Hesse-Kassel, they has eleven children. His sister, **Emilie of Württemberg (1550-1589)** married Reichard, Count Palatine of Simmern-Sponheim. There is no record of any issue of this marriage. His sister, **Eleonore of Württemberg (1552-1618)** married twice her first husband was Joachim Ernest, Prince of Anhalt and they had ten children. Her second husband was George I, Landgrave of Hesse-Darmstadt, they had twelve children. His sister, **Dorothea Maria of Württemberg (1559-1639)** married Otto Heinrich, Count Palatine of Sulzbach. They had thirteen children. His sister, **Anna of Württemberg (1561-1616)** married twice, her first husband was John George, Duke of Ohlau and

Wohlan, they had two children. Her second husband was Frederick IV, Duke of Legnica and they had two children. His sister, **Sophie of Württemberg (1563-1590)** married Friedrich Wilhelm I, Duke of Saxe-Weimar. They had six children.

Johann Frederick, Duke of Württemberg (1557-1608). As his predecessor died with out issue and Johann was descended from the early line of Counts of Württemberg and a distant cousin. He married Sibylla of Anhalt, the daughter of the sister of Ludwig probably to maintain some sort of legitimacy. They had fifteen children of which ten survived into adulthood including Johann Frederick who succeeded his father.

His sister, **Sibylla Elisabeth of Württemberg (1584-1606)** married John George I, Elector of Saxony, there was no surviving issue. His brother, **Louis Frederick of Württemberg (1586-1631)**. He founded the later branch line of Württemberg-Mömpelgard. There is no record of marriage or issue. His brother, **Julius Frederick of Württemberg (1588-1635)**. There is no record of marriage or issue. He was the founder of the Württemberg-Weiltingen dynasty known as the Julian line. His sister, **Eva Christine of Württemberg (1590-1657)** married twice, her first husband was John George of Brandenburg and her second husband was Duke of Jägerndorf. There is no record of marriage or issue. His brother, **Frederick Achilles, Duke of Württemberg-Neuenstadt (1591-1631)** died unmarried and without issue. His sister, **Agnes of Württemberg (1592-1629)** married Francis Julius, Duke of Saxe-Lauenburg. They had seven children. His sister, **Barbara of Württemberg (1593-1622)** married Margrave Frederick V of Baden-Durlach and had seven children.

Eberhard III, Duke of Württemberg (1614-1674) reigned as Duke from 1628 until his death. He succeeded to the Duchy at the age of fourteen and was under the guardianship of two of his uncles, Louis Frederick and Julius Frederick. The Duchy was plundered frequently and after the disastrous battle of Nörlingen, Eberhard had to flee to Strasberg. After long negotiations with the Holy Roman Emperor, he was restored to the Duchy. Eberhard married twice, his first wife was Anna Katherina of Salm-Kyrburg, the daughter of Johann Kasimir of Salm-Kyrburg and Dorothea of Solm-Laubach, they had fourteen children including William Louis who succeeded his father. Eberhard's second wife was Countess Marie Dorothea Sofie of Oettingen, the daughter of Joachim Ernst, Count of Oettingen and Anna Sibylle, Countess of Solm-Sonnenwald, they had nine children.

His sister **Antonia, Princess of Württemberg-Stuttgart (1613-1679)** was a great literary force and a Christian Kabbalist. She spent her life rebuilding and refurbishing the churches and building that were plundered and damaged during The Thirty Years War. She died unmarried and without issue. His **brother, Frederick, Duke of Württemberg-Neuenstadt (1615-1682)**. He was the founder of a cadet branch of the Duchy. He married Clara Augusta, daughter of Augustus the Younger, Duke of Brunswick-Lüneburg. They had twelve children of which only four survived into adulthood including two sons who succeeded their father. His brother, **Ulrich, Prince of Württemberg-Neuenstadt (1617-1671)**. His sister, **Anna Johanna, Princess of Württemberg-Stuttgart (1619-1679)**. His sister, **Sibylle, Princess of Württemberg-Stuttgart (1620-1707)**. There are no extant records of their life.

Wilhelm Ludwig, Duke of Württemberg (1647-1677) reigned as Duke from 1674 until his death. He married Magdalena Sibylla of Hesse-Darmstadt and had four children including Eberhard Ludwig who succeeded his father. His sister, **Sofie Luise of Württemberg-Winnental (1642-1702)** married Christian Ernst, Margrave of Brandenburg-Bayreuth. They had six children. His sister **Christine Friederike of Württemberg-Winnental (1644-1674)** married Count Albert Ernest I of

Oettingen-Oettingen and had issue. His sister **Christine Charlotte of Württemberg-Winnental (1645-1699)** married Prince George Christian, Prince of East Frisia. They had one surviving son who succeeded his father. His brother **Frederick Charles, Duke of Württemberg-Winnental (1652-1697)** was a duke of the newly founded cadet branch of the family. He married Eleonore Juliane of Brandenburg-Ansbach. They had seven children including Charles Alexander who would become a future Duke of Württemberg.

Eberhard Ludwig, Duke of Württemberg (1676-1733) was duke from 1692 until his death. He married twice, his first wife was Joanna Elisabeth of Baden-Durlach from which he had no surviving issue, his second wife was Wilhelmine of Grävenitz. There was no issue from this marriage. His sister, **Magdalena Wilhelmine of Württemberg (1677-1742)** married Charles III William, Margrave of Baden-Durlach. They had three children of which only one survived into adulthood.

Charles Alexander, Duke of Württemberg (1684-1737) was Regent for the Kingdom of Serbia from 1720 until 1733 when he assumed the Duchy which he held until his death. He married Maria Augusta of Thurn und Taxis, they had six children including Karl Eugen who succeeded his father. His brother, **Henry Frederick of Württemberg (1687-1734)** was a Army General and died unmarried and without issue. His brother, **Maximilian Emmanuel of Württemberg (1689-1709)** was a volunteer in the army of, and devoted friend of, Charles XII, King of Sweden. He died unmarried and without issue. His brother, **Frederick Louis of Württemberg (1690-1734)** married Ursula von Alten-Brockun. There was no issue from this marriage. He was killed at the battle of Guastalla fought during the War of Polish Succession. His sister **Christiane Charlotte of Württemberg (1694-1729)**. She married William Frederick, Margrave of Brandenburg-Ansbach. They had three children.

Karl Eugen, Duke of Württemberg (1728-1793). He reigned as duke from 1737 until his death. He had a great enthusiasm for agriculture and travel. He inspired the building of Hohenheim University and his own botanical garden became the basis of the country's arboretum and the botanical gardens of Landesarboretum in Baden. He married twice, his first wife was Elisabeth Frederika Sophie of Brandenburg-Bayreuth. There was no surviving issue. His second wife was Franziska von Hohenheim, they had no issue. His brother **Louis Eugene** succeeded him, who in turn was succeeded by another brother, **Frederick II Eugene**. His sister **Auguste Elisabeth of Württemberg (1731-1787)**. She married Karl Anselm, 4th Prince of Thurn und Taxis. They had eight children.

Louis Eugene, Duke of Württemberg (1731-1795). He married Sophie Albertine of Beichlingen, a daughter of August Gottfried Dietrich, Count of Beichlingen and his wife Sophie Helene, Countess of Stoecken. They had three daughters, and with no male heir he was succeeded by his younger brother Frederick.

Frederick II Eugene, Duke of Württemberg (1732-1797). He married Friederike Dorothea of Brandenburg-Schwedt. They had twelve children including Frederick who succeeded his father.

Frederick I, Duke of Württemberg (1797-1803). He was elevated by the Holy Roman Emperor to **Elector of Württemberg** and finally after providing Napoleon Bonaparte with a large auxiliary force, he was recognized as **King of Württemberg** in 1806 and reigned until his death in 1816. He married twice, his first wife was Augusta of Brunswick-Wolfenbüttel, they had four children including William who succeeded his father. His second wife was Princess Charlotte,

Princess Royal. Daughter of King George III of Great Britain. There was no surviving issue from this marriage. His brother, **Louis Frederick Alexander, Duke of Württemberg (1756-1817)**. He married twice, his first wife was Maria Czartoryska, daughter of Prince Adam Kazimierz Czartoryski and his wife Isabella, Countess of Flemming. They had one son who succeeded his father. His second wife was Princess Henriette of Nassau-Weilburg. They had five children. His brother, **Eugene Frederick Henry, Duke of Württemberg (1758-1822)** married Princess Louise of Stolberg-Gedern and had five children. His sister **Sophia Maria Dorothea of Württemberg (1759-1828)**. She married Paul I, Emperor of Russia and had five children including Alexander who would succeed his father. His brother **William Frederick Philip, Duke of Württemberg (1761-1830)** was a soldier most of his life and married one of his mother's ladies-in-waiting, Wilhelmine, Freiin (Baroness) von Tunderfeld-Rhodis. They had six children. His brother, **Ferdinand Augustus Frederick of Württemberg (1763-1834)** married Princess Kunigunde of Metternich, daughter of Franz George Karl I, Count Metternich-Winneburg zu Beilstein His sister, **Friederike Elisabeth Amalie of Württemberg (1765-1785)** married Peter, Duke of Oldenburg and had two children. His sister, **Elisabeth Wilhelmine Luise of Württemberg (1767-1790)** married Francis I, Emperor of Austria. There were no surviving issue. His brother, **Alexander Frederick Charles, Duke of Württemberg (1771-1833)** was the founder of the fifth line and current holders of the Duchy. He married Antoinette of Saxe-Coburg-Saalfeld. They had five children including Marie who married Ernest I, Duke of Saxe-Coburg-Gotha and had two children including Albert who would become the husband and Prince Consort of Queen Victoria of Great Britain.

William I, King of Württemberg (1781-1864). He reigned as King from 1771 until his death. He married three times, his first wife was Caroline Augusta of Bavaria, daughter of King Maximilian I of Bavaria and his wife Princess Augusta

Wilhelmina of Hesse-Darmstadt, they divorced in 1814 without any issue. His second wife was his first cousin Grand Duchess Catherine Pavlovna of Russia, the daughter of Emperor Paul I of Russia and his wife Sophia Dorothea of Württemberg. They had two children including Sophie who married King William III of the Netherlands. His third wife was another first cousin, Pauline Therese, daughter of Duke Louis of Württemberg and his wife Princess Henriette of Nassau-Weilberg. They had three children including Charles who succeeded his father. His sister, **Catharina, Princess of Württemberg (1783-1835)** married Jérôme Bonaparte, King of Westphalia and brother of Napoleon Bonaparte. They had issue. His brother, **Paul, Prince of Württemberg (1785-1852)**. He married Princess Charlotte of Saxe-Hildburghausen. They had five children. Current Mayor of London, Boris Johnson, is descended from his illegitimate, but recognised daughter.

Charles I, King of Württemberg (1823-1891). He reigned as king from 1864 until 1891. He married Olga Nikolaevna, daughter of Tsar Nicholas I of Russia and his wife Charlotte. There was no issue from this marriage and he was succeeded by his nephew William. His sister, **Marie, Princess of Württemberg (1816-1887)**. She married Count Alfred von Neipperg, there is no known issue. His sister, **Sophie, Princess of Württemberg (1818-1877)**. She married King William III of the Netherlands, they had three children, including Wilhelmina who would become Queen of the Netherlands. His sister, **Augusta, Princess of Württemberg (1826-1898)** married Prince Herman of Saxe-Weimar-Eisenach and had issue.

William II, last King of Württemberg (1848-1921). He reigned as king from 1891 until 1918 when all German kingdoms were abolished in the aftermath of the First World War and a republic was formed. He married twice, his first wife was Princess Marie of Waldeck and Pyrmont, they had three children. His second marriage was to Charlotte of Schaumburg-Lippe, there was no issue from this marriage.

I hope you enjoyed this book of reference and found it as interesting to read as I found it interesting to write.

The End

Made in the USA
Charleston, SC
09 July 2014